How Much Is Enough?

How Much Is Enough?

money and the good life

_____

Robert Skidelsky
& Edward Skidelsky

OTHER PRESS
New York

First softcover printing 2013
ISBN 978-1-59051-634-8

Production Editor: Yvonne E. Cárdenas

Design revisions for this edition by Simon M. Sullivan

This book was typeset in 9.75 pt Sabon LT Std

An excerpt from the introduction appeared in the June 22, 2012 edition of the *Chronicle of Higher Education*. An excerpt from chapter 7 appeared in *Bloomberg View* on June 4 and 8, 2012.

10 9 8 7 6 5 4 3 2 1

LIBRARY OF CONGRESS CATALOGING-IN-PUBLICATION DATA

Skidelsky, Robert Jacob Alexander, 1939-
How much is enough? : money and the good life / Robert Skidelsky and Edward Skidelsky.
p. cm.
Includes bibliographical references and index.
ISBN 978-1-59051-507-5 (hbk.) — ISBN 978-1-59051-508-2 (ebook)
1. Wealth. 2. Economics—Sociological aspects. I. Skidelsky, Edward.
II. Title.
HB251.S64 2012
306.3—dc23
2012008052

To Hugo
That his possibilities may live up to the hopes
Keynes had for his "grandchildren"

Nothing is enough for the man to whom enough is too little.

Epicurus

Contents

Preface

As we were writing the book, friends of ours often asked us, half-jokingly, "Are you going to tell us how much you think is enough?" We found it sensible to riposte by asking, as if in the spirit of scholarly inquiry, "How much do *you* think is enough?" We often got the answer "Enough for what?" to which we replied, "Enough to live a good life." This sometimes did elicit a stab at a number, though, as was to be expected, the number varied markedly according to age, circumstances and nationality. The fact is, of course, that one can only hope to get a meaningful and perhaps binding answer to the question from people who accept that there is such a thing as a good life, independent of their own subjective desires. The purpose of this book is to persuade the reader that such a thing—the good life—does exist and can be known, and that we ought to strive to live it. How much money we need to live it comes at the end of the argument, not at the beginning.*

Many people have helped us. We are extraordinarily grateful to Armand Clesse, director of the Luxembourg Institute for European and International Studies, for organizing a symposium on the book in Luxembourg on May 27–28, 2011. Armand, who chaired in his usual vivacious style, had assembled an interdisciplinary galaxy: Michael Ambrosi, Christian Arnsperger, Tom Bauler, Mathias Binswinger, Ulrich Brand, Isabelle Cassiers, Aditya Chakrabortty, Andrew Hallam, Mario Hirsch, Sir Anthony Kenny, Charles Kenny, Guy Kirsch, Serge-Christophe Kolm, Axel Leijonhufvud, Felix

---

* In a previous book, Robert Skidelsky did venture to name a sum that the economist John Maynard Keynes would have considered "enough" to satisfy *average* needs: £40,000 or $66,000 or €46,000 a year (in today's money). See Robert Skidelsky, *Keynes: The Return of the Master*, 2nd edn. (London: Penguin, 2010), p. 142, which also reveals the basis of the calculation. But Keynes was assuming a more settled idea of what the good life was than is now true, and less pressure to lead a bad life than now exists.

Martin, Matt Matravers, John Milbank, Adrian Pabst, Guy Schuller, Larry Siedentop, Alfred Steinherr, Henryk Szlajfer and Paul Zahlen. They read an early draft of the manuscript, and some even braved the volcanic ash then hovering over Europe to come. We received much encouragement and stimulus from their suggestions.

Our UK agent Michael Sissons and our UK publisher Stuart Proffitt made notable contributions to the emergence of the proposal, and in nudging the book kindly but firmly towards publication, as did our enthusiastic American publisher Judith Gurewich, whose e-mails we will long remember. They all encouraged us to break academic cover and come out clearly with our own views.

Our warmest thanks go to the following for reading the whole or part of drafts of *How Much Is Enough?* and, by their comments and criticisms, helping to improve its arguments: Perry Anderson, Tony Bicat, Carmen Callil, Meghnad Desai, Robin Douglass, Pavel Erochkine, Richard Fynes, Peter Pagan, Pranay Sanklecha, Richard Seaford, Augusta Skidelsky, Will Skidelsky and Wu Junqing.

We thank Pete Mills and Christian Westerlind Wigstrom of Robert's Centre for Global Studies for their unstinting help with research and criticism. Pete in particular played a big part in assembling the data and shaping the argument of Chapter 1. Donald Poon provided welcome assistance as a summer intern on his way to the LSE. Our thanks go to the Librarian and staff of the House of Lords for meeting our insatiable demand for books and articles.

Above all, we enjoyed working together. The two months we spent in Languedoc in April/May 2011, writing and talking about the book, was an enormously happy time, a voyage of discovery, not least about each other: in its setting, a speck of the good life, for both of us.

Robert and Edward Skidelsky

List of Charts

How Much Is Enough?

Introduction

This book is an argument against insatiability, against that psychological disposition that prevents us, as individuals and as societies, from saying "enough is enough." It is directed at economic insatiability, the desire for more and more money. It is chiefly directed at the rich parts of the world, which may be reasonably thought to have enough wealth for a decent collective life. For the poor parts of the world, where the mass of the people still live in great poverty, insatiability is a problem for the future. But in rich and poor societies alike, insatiability can be seen wherever the opulence of the very rich runs wildly ahead of the means of existence of the many.

Marxists contend that economic insatiability is a creation of capitalism, which will disappear with its abolition. Christians argue that it is the product of original sin. Our own view is that it is rooted in human nature—in the disposition to compare our fortune with that of our fellows and find it wanting—but has been greatly intensified by capitalism, which has made it the psychological basis of an entire civilization. What was once an aberration of the rich is now a commonplace of everyday life.

Capitalism is a two-edged sword. On the one hand, it has made possible vast improvements in material conditions. On the other, it has exalted some of the most reviled human characteristics, such as greed, envy and avarice. Our call is to chain up the monster again by recalling what the greatest thinkers of all times and all civilizations have meant by the "good life" and suggesting changes in current policy to help us achieve it.

In doing this, we will be challenging the current obsession with the growth of Gross Domestic Product (GDP) as the chief goal of economic policy. We are not against economic growth as such, but we may reasonably ask not just growth *for* what, but growth *of* what. We want leisure to grow and pollution to decline. Both are part of any sane idea of human welfare. But both are excluded from GDP, which measures only that portion of domestic production that is traded in markets. There is no subtraction for pollution, and no addition for leisure. The extent to which further GDP growth will improve welfare is therefore moot. It surely does so for very poor countries, but it may be the case that rich societies already have *too much* GDP. Our view is that, for the wealthy nations of the world, GDP should be treated as a by-product of policies aimed at realizing the good life. Only experience will show whether the GDP outcome is positive, negative or stationary.

This book is not about the principles of justice, but about the constituents of the good life. Most modern political theory starts from the consideration of what is just, or fair, in the abstract, and proceeds to derive from this "just" social arrangements. Our approach is different. We start with the individual and his needs, from which we try to build up a picture of the common good. Questions of distribution, which lie at the center of modern discussions of justice, while vitally important, are only so to us in the context of the requirements of the good life.

Imagine a world in which most people worked only fifteen hours a week. They would be paid as much as, or even more than, they now are, because the fruits of their labor would be distributed more evenly across society. Leisure would occupy far more of their waking hours than work. It was exactly this prospect that the economist John Maynard Keynes conjured up in a little essay published in 1930 called "Economic Possibilities for our Grandchildren." Its thesis was very simple. As technological progress made possible an increase in the output of goods per hour worked, people would have to work less and less to satisfy their needs, until in the end they would have to work hardly at all. Then, Keynes wrote, "for the first time since his creation man will be faced with his real, his permanent problem— how to use his freedom from pressing economic cares, how to occupy the leisure, which science and compound interest will have won for him, to live wisely and agreeably and well." He thought this condition might be reached in about a hundred years' time—that is, by 2030.

Given when it was written, it is hardly surprising that Keynes's futuristic essay was ignored. The world had much more urgent problems to attend to, including getting out of the Great Depression. And Keynes himself never explicitly reverted to his vision, though the dream of a workless future was always there in the background of his thinking. Indeed, it was as a theorist of short-term unemployment, not of long-run economic progress, that Keynes achieved world fame, with his great book *The General Theory of Employment, Interest and Money.* Nevertheless, there are good reasons for returning to the questions Keynes raised, then dropped.

First, he asked something hardly discussed today: what is wealth for? How much money do we need to lead a good life? This might seem an impossible question. But it is not a trivial one. Making money cannot be an end in itself—at least for anyone not suffering from acute mental disorder. To say that my purpose in life is to make more and more money is like saying that my aim in eating is to get fatter and fatter. And what is true of individuals is also true of societies. Making money cannot be the permanent business of humanity, for the simple reason that there is nothing to do with money except spend it. And we cannot just go on spending. There will come a point when we will be satiated or disgusted or both. Or will we?

Second, we in the West are once more in the midst of a "Great Contraction," the worst since the Great Depression of 1929–1932. A great crisis is like an inspection: it exposes the faults of a social system, and prompts the search for alternatives. The system under inspection is capitalism, and Keynes's essay offers a vantage point from which to consider the future of capitalism. The crisis has brought to light two defects in the system, usually obscured by the near unanimous commitment to growth at almost any cost.

The first is its moral defects. The banking crisis has shown yet again that the present system relies on motives of greed and acquisitiveness, which are morally repugnant. It also divides societies into rich and poor, latterly very rich and very poor, justified by some version of the "trickle down" idea. The coexistence of great wealth and great poverty, especially in societies in which there is enough for everyone, offends our sense of justice. Second, the crisis has exposed capitalism's palpable economic defects. Our financial system is inherently unstable. When it goes wrong, as it did in 2008, we realize how inefficient, wasteful and painful it can be. Heavily indebted countries are told that the bond markets will not be satisfied till they have liquidated a large fraction of their national incomes. Such periodic collapses of the money-making machine are a great spur to thinking about better ways of life.

Finally, Keynes's essay challenges us to imagine what life after capitalism might look like (for an economic system in which capital no longer accumulates is not capitalism, whatever one might call it). Keynes thought that the motivational basis of capitalism was "an intense appeal to the money-making and money-loving instincts of individuals."[1] He thought that with the coming of plenty, this motivational drive would lose its social approbation; that is, that capitalism would abolish itself when its work was done. But so accustomed have we become to regard scarcity as the norm that few of us think about what motives and principles of conduct would, or should, prevail in a world of plenty.

So let us imagine that everyone has enough to lead a good life. What is the good life? What is it not? And what changes in our moral and economic system would be needed to realize it? Such questions are seldom asked, because they do not fall neatly into any of the disciplinary boxes that make up modern intellectual life. Philosophers construct systems of perfect justice, unmindful of the messiness of empirical reality. Economists ask how best to satisfy subjective wants, whatever these may be. Our book brings together the perspectives of philosophy and economics in the conviction that the two disciplines need each other, the one for the sake of its practical influence, the other for the sake of its ethical imagination. It aims to revive the old idea of economics as a *moral* science; a science of human beings in communities, not of interacting robots.

How Much Is Enough? opens by pondering the reasons for the failure of Keynes's prophecy. Why, despite the surprising accuracy of his growth forecasts, are most of us, almost a hundred years on, still working almost as hard as we were when he wrote his futuristic essay? The answer, we suggest, is that a free-market economy both gives employers the power to dictate hours and terms of work and inflames our innate tendency to competitive, status-driven consumption. Keynes was well aware of the evils of capitalism, but assumed that they would wither away once their work of wealth creation was done. He did not foresee that they might become permanently entrenched, obscuring the very ideal they were initially intended to serve.

Keynes, we add in Chapter 2, was not alone in thinking that motives bad in themselves might nonetheless be useful. John Stuart Mill, Karl Marx, Herbert Marcuse—even Adam Smith in bolder moments—all granted such motives a positive role as an agent of historical progress. In the language of myth, Western civilization has made its peace with the Devil, in return for which it has been granted hitherto unimaginable resources of knowledge, power and pleasure. This is, of course, the grand theme of the Faust legend, immortalized by Goethe. The irony is, however, that now that we have at last achieved abundance, the habits bred into us by capitalism have left us incapable of enjoying it properly. The Devil, it seems, has claimed his reward. Can we evade this fate? Perhaps, but only if we can retrieve from centuries of neglect and distortion the idea of a good life, a life sufficient unto itself. Here we must draw on the rich storehouse of pre-modern wisdom, occidental and oriental, which we outline in Chapter 3.

Opposition to the growth juggernaut has gathered pace in recent years. Growth, say critics, is not only failing to make us happier; it is also environmentally disastrous. Both claims may well be true, but they fail to capture our deeper objection to endless growth, which is that it is *senseless*. To found our case against growth on the fact that it is damaging to happiness or the environment is to invite our opponents to show that it is not in fact damaging in these ways—an invitation they have been quick to take up.* The whole argument then disappears down an academic cul-de-sac. The point to keep in

---

* Nigel Lawson and Bjørn Lomborg (among others) have argued that global warming is best dealt with by pressing ahead with technological progress so as to mitigate any adverse consequences. And some economists have argued that wealthier nations are indeed happier than poor ones. For details, see Chapters 4 and 5.

mind is that we know, prior to anything scientists or statisticians can tell us, that the unending pursuit of wealth is madness. This is the gist of our argument in Chapters 4 and 5.

We come finally, in Chapter 6, to the positive part of our proposal: the outline of the good life. Drawing on insights from all times and places, we identify seven "basic goods," possession of which constitutes living well. The first duty of government, we argue, is to realize, as much as lies within its power, these basic goods for all citizens. How this might in fact be achieved is the theme of Chapter 7, in which we suggest a number of policies for bringing the limitless desire for wealth under the control of an objective concept of the good. Unless that control is achieved we are a doomed civilization—on a hiding to nothing, or worse.

In discussing our ideas with friends and acquaintances, five objections have cropped up regularly. The first concerns timing. "Now of all moments," we are told, "is not the time to be talking about an end to growth. Wouldn't Keynes himself, were he alive, urge us to *resume* growth as rapidly as possible in order to bring down unemployment and pay off government debt?" We do not dispute this. But we need to distinguish between short-term policies for recovery after the worst depression since the 1930s and long-term policies for realizing the good life. In the two years after 2008, world output shrunk by 6 percent, and has only partly regained its previous level. We must at the very least retrieve the output we have lost because, as the economy is now organized, there is no other way to reduce unemployment and indebtedness, private and public. But we should not let the exigencies of the hour cloud our view of ultimate ends. Keynes's own utopia was penned at the bottom of the Great Depression. "My purpose in this essay," he wrote, "is not to examine the present . . . but to disembarrass myself of short views and take wings into the future." This is the spirit in which our book is offered.

The second query concerns the geographical scope of our proposals. Are we suggesting that nations in which millions remain ill-housed and ill-fed should be content with what they have? Of course not. Our arguments are addressed to that part of the world in which the material conditions of well-being have already been met. In places where they have not been met, growth remains, rightly, a priority. That said, if the developing world carries on developing, it will eventually face our predicament, so it may as well prepare for it in advance. It should not repeat our mistake of becoming so absorbed in the means that it forgets the end.

The next three objections cut deeper. "Your proposals," runs the first, "will have the effect of undermining all initiative, creativity, vision. They are a blueprint for universal idleness." It is sometimes added that our ideas reflect a decadent, "old-European" mind-set. This observation comes, unsurprisingly, mostly from Americans.

To lay these misapprehensions to rest, let us state firmly that our book is not an argument for idleness. What we wish to see more of is *leisure*, a category that, properly understood, is so far from coinciding with idleness that it is almost its polar opposite. Leisure, in the true, now almost forgotten sense of the word, is activity without extrinsic end, "purposiveness without purpose," as Kant put it. The sculptor engrossed in cutting marble, the teacher intent on imparting a difficult idea, the musician struggling with a score, a scientist exploring the mysteries of space and time—such people have no other aim than to do what they are doing well. They may receive an income for their efforts, but that income is not what motivates them. In our terms, they are engaged in leisure, not toil. This is an idealization, of course. In the real world, extrinsic rewards, including financial rewards, are never entirely out of mind. Still, insofar as action proceeds not from necessity but from inclination, insofar as it is spontaneous, not servile and mechanical, toil is at an end and leisure has begun. This—not idleness—is our ideal. It is only our culture's poverty of imagination that leads it to believe that all creativity and innovation—as opposed to that specific kind directed to improving economic processes—needs to be stimulated by money.

"That is all very splendid," our critic might retort, "but it is hardly likely that a reduction of externally motivated activity will lead to an increase of leisure, in your high-flown sense of the term. Slackers like us need the stimulus of money to move us to anything. Without it, our natural laziness comes to the fore, leading not to the good life but to boredom, neurosis and the bottle. Read a few Russian novels and you will see what I mean."

Such an objection can only be met with a declaration of faith. A universal reduction of work has never been attempted, so we do not know for sure what its consequences would be. But we cannot think them as dire as our critic suggests, or the central project of modern European civilization, to improve the well-being of the people, is empty and vain. If the ultimate end of industry is idleness, if we labor and create merely so that our descendants can snuggle down to an eternity of daytime television, then all progress is, as Orwell put it, "a frantic struggle towards an objective which [we] hope and pray will never be reached."[2] We are in the paradoxical situation of goading ourselves to ever new feats of enterprise, not because we think them worthwhile, but because any activity, however pointless, is better than none. We *must* believe in the possibility of genuine leisure—otherwise our state is desperate indeed.

Another reflection gives us hope. The image of man as a congenital idler, stirred to action only by the prospect of gain, is unique to the modern age. Economists, in particular, see human beings as beasts of burden who need the stimulus of a carrot or stick to do anything at all. "To satisfy our wants to the utmost with the least effort" is how William Stanley Jevons, a pioneer of modern economic theory, defined the human problem.[3] That was not the ancient view of things. Athens and Rome had citizens who, though economically unproductive, were active to the highest degree—in politics, war, philosophy and litera-ture. Why not take them, and not the donkey, as our guide? Of course, Athenian and Roman citizens were schooled from an early age in the wise use of leisure. Our project implies a similar educational effort. We cannot expect a society trained in the servile and mechanical uses of time to become one of free men overnight. But we should not doubt that the task is in principle possible. Bertrand Russell, in an essay written just two years after Keynes's effort—a further illustration of the stimulating effects of economic crisis—put the point with his usual clarity:

> It will be said that, while a little leisure is pleasant, men would not know how to fill their days if they had only four hours of work out of the twenty-four. In so far as this is true in the modern world, it is a condemnation of our civilization; it would not have been true at any

earlier period. There was formerly a capacity for light-heartedness and play which has been to some extent inhibited by the cult of efficiency . . . The pleasures of urban populations have become mainly passive: seeing cinemas, watching football matches, listening to the radio, and so on. This results from the fact that their active energies are fully taken up with work; if they had more leisure, they would again enjoy pleasures in which they took an active part.[4]

We might add that it is largely *because* leisure has lost its true meaning of spontaneous activity and degenerated into passive consumption that we throw ourselves, as the lesser of two evils, into work. "One must work," wrote Baudelaire in his *Intimate Journals*, "if not from taste then at least from despair. For to reduce everything to a single truth, work is less boring than pleasure."[5]

A fourth objection takes the form of a qualified defense of money-making: true, say our critics, it is not the noblest of human activities, but of the main goals of human striving it is the least harmful. Keynes put it well: "dangerous human proclivities can be canalized into comparatively harmless channels by the existence of opportunities for money-making and private wealth, which, if they cannot be satisfied in this way, may find their outlet in cruelty, the reckless pursuit of personal power and authority, and other forms of self-aggrandisement." But he added that "it is not necessary for the stimulation of these activities and the satisfaction of these proclivities that the game should be played for such high stakes as at present. Much lower stakes will serve the purpose equally well, as soon as the players are accustomed to them."[6] This perfectly captures our defense. We are not proposing that money-making should be banned, as it was in the Soviet Union, but that "the game" should be subject to rules and limitations that do not move society away from the good life.

The last, and deepest, objection to our project concerns its supposedly illiberal character. A liberal state, John Rawls and others have taught us to believe, embodies no positive vision but only such principles as are necessary for people of different tastes and ideals to live together in harmony. To promote, as a matter of public policy, a positive idea of the good life is by definition illiberal, perhaps even totalitarian. We return to this objection in due course; let us just say here that it rests on a thorough misconception of liberalism. Through most of its long history, the liberal tradition was imbued with classical and Christian ideals of dignity, civility and tolerance. ("Liberal," we should remember, originally designated what was appropriate to a free man, a usage surviving in phrases such as "liberal arts.") In the twentieth century, such prototypical liberals as Keynes, Isaiah Berlin and Lionel Trilling took it for granted that upholding civilization was among the functions of the state. It is a superficial conception of liberalism that sees it as implying neutrality between different visions of the good. In any case, neutrality is a fiction. A "neutral" state simply hands power to the guardians of capital to manipulate public taste in their own interests.

Perhaps the chief intellectual barrier to realizing the good life for all is the discipline of economics, or rather the deathly orthodoxy that sails under that name in most universities across the world. Economics, says a recent text, studies "how people choose to use *limited* or *scarce* resources in attempting to satisfy their unlimited wants."[7] The italicized adjectives are strictly redundant: if wants are unlimited, then resources are by definition limited relative to them, however rich we may be in the absolute sense. We are condemned to dearth, not through want of resources, but by the extravagance of our appetites. As the economist Harry Johnson put it in 1960, "we live in a rich society, which nevertheless in many respects insists on thinking and acting as if it were a poor society."[8] The perspective of poverty, and with it an emphasis on efficiency at all costs, is built into modern economics.

It was not ever thus. Adam Smith, the founder of modern economics, assumed that our inborn desire for improvement would eventually run up against natural and institutional limits, resulting in the achievement of a "stationary state." For Alfred Marshall, Keynes's teacher, economics was the study of the "material pre-requisites of wellbeing," a definition that preserved the Aristotelian and Christian concept of wealth as a means to an end. After Marshall, however, economics shifted gear. In a classic definition, Lionel Robbins wrote of economics as "the science that studies human behaviour as a relationship between ends and scarce means which have alternative uses."[9] Robbins's definition both puts scarcity at the center of economics and brackets out judgments of value. The domain of economics is the study of efficient means to ends, but the economist, qua economist, has nothing to say about those "ends." He assumes only that they will always outstrip the means at our disposal for attaining them, meaning that scarcity is a permanent feature of the human condition.

If scarcity is always with us, then efficiency, the optimal use of scarce resources, and economics, the science that teaches us efficiency, will always be necessary. Yet on any commonsensical view of the matter, scarcity waxes and wanes. We know that famines are periods of extreme scarcity and good harvests produce relative plenty. Thomas Malthus understood that when population grows faster than food supplies, scarcity grows; and in the reverse case, it declines. Moreover, scarcity, as most people understand it, has diminished greatly in most societies over the last two hundred years. People in rich and even medium-rich countries no longer starve to death. All this implies that the social importance of efficiency has declined; and with it the utility of economics.

The beginning of sanity in this matter is to think of scarcity in relation to needs, not wants. And this is how we do normally think of it. The man with three houses is not thought to be in dire straits, however urgent his desire for a fourth. "He has enough," we say, meaning "enough to meet his needs." Flagrant manifestations of insatiability—such as an uncontrollable desire to collect cats or dolls' houses—are widely viewed as pathological, not normal. (Economists, like psycho-analysts, tend to treat neurosis as the norm.) We are all, in principle, capable of limiting our wants to our needs; the problem is that a competitive, monetized economy puts us under continual pressure to want more and more. The "scarcity" discerned by economists is increasingly an artifact of this pressure. Considered in relation to our vital needs, our state is one not of scarcity but rather of extreme abundance.

The premise of what follows is that the material conditions of the good life already exist, at least in the affluent parts of the world, but that the blind pursuit of growth puts it continually out of reach. Under such circumstances, the aim of policy and other forms of collective action should be to secure an economic organization that places the good things of life—health, respect, friendship, leisure and so on—within reach of all. Economic growth should be accepted as a residual, not something to be aimed at.

Over time, such a shift is bound to affect our attitude to economics. To maximize the efficient use of our time will become less and less important; and therefore "scientific" economics, as it has developed since Robbins, will be demoted from its position as the queen of the social sciences. It can bring us to the threshold of plenty, but must then retire from its oversight of our lives. This is what Keynes had in mind when he looked forward to the day when economists would become as useful as *dentists*.[10] He always chose his words carefully: it was as dentists, not doctors, that humanity would come to need economists; at the margins of life, not as a continuous, much less controlling, presence.

1

Keynes's Mistake

No bounds to riches have been fixed for man.
—Solon

In 1928 Keynes addressed an audience of Cambridge undergraduates on the theme of "economic possibilities for our grandchildren." He knew they would be heavily disenchanted with capitalism and inclined to see the Soviet Union as a beacon of light. Keynes himself had recognized that progress was a "soiled creed, black with coal dust and gunpowder," and that communism beckoned so alluringly because, for all its barbarity, it might be seen as "the first stirrings of a great religion."[1] If Keynes was to entice his audience away from this false god, he needed to persuade it that capitalism, too, was a utopian project—a more effective utopian project than communism, because it was the only efficient means to the abundance which would make possible a good life for all. His speech at Cambridge was the first outing of his utopian fancy.

Two years later, when Keynes revised his talk for publication, the Great Depression had struck: capitalism seemed economically as well as morally bankrupt; communism even more alluring. But Keynes adroitly adapted his message to the new situation. "We are suffering," he wrote, "not from the rheumatics of old age, but from the growing pains of over-rapid changes, from the painfulness of readjustment between one economic period and another." The Depression was, at least in part, a symptom of "technological unemployment"—that is, "unemployment due to our discovery of means of economising the use of labour outrunning the pace at which we can find new uses for

15

labour." Technological unemployment pointed to a workless future, but one which was voluntary, not compelled.

Keynes deployed economic logic in the service of prophecy. Basing his idea on historical rates of capital accumulation and technical progress, Keynes proposed that if capital equipment continued to grow at 2 percent a year, and "technical efficiency" at 1 percent, "the standard of life in progressive countries one hundred years hence will be between four and eight times as high as it is today." This projection enabled Keynes to draw the "startling conclusion" that, "assuming no important wars and no important increase in population, the economic problem may be solved, or at least within sight of solution, within a hundred years."*

What Keynes meant by this was that humanity would be able to satisfy all its material needs at a fraction of existing work effort—at most three hours a day to "satisfy the old Adam in us." The abundance of time thus freed up might lead to a "nervous breakdown" of the kind already common among "wives of the well-to-do classes." But Keynes hoped not. Rather, he looked forward to a moment when the spontaneous, joyful attitude to life now confined to artists and free spirits was diffused throughout society as a whole. The essay culminates in a marvellous flight of rhetoric, interweaving Aristotle and the New Testament:

> I see us free to return to some of the most sure and certain principles of religion and traditional virtue—that avarice is a vice, that the exaction of usury is a misdemeanour, and the love of money is detestable, that those walk most truly in the paths of virtue and sane wisdom who take least thought for the morrow. We shall once more value ends above means and prefer the good to the useful. We shall honour those who

---

* Keynes anticipated Robert Solow's growth model, in which growth of GDP is explained by the growth of the factor inputs capital and population, and the rate of technical progress. Like most economists, Keynes assumed diminishing returns to capital—each additional piece of capital would produce less output than the last—with capital saturation setting in. Further growth of GDP would come to depend largely on improvements in the quality not quantity of capital, physical and human, that is, on technical progress. Growth of GDP per head would require technical progress to outstrip population growth.

can teach us how to pluck the hour and the day virtuously and well, the delightful people who are capable of taking direct enjoyment in things, the lilies of the field, who toil not neither do they spin.[2]

Keynes's friend, the philosopher Frank Ramsey, had a word for this paradisaical state. He called it "Bliss."

Capitalism, then, the life of economic striving and money-making, was a transitional stage, a means to an end, the end being the good life. What might such a life be like? Keynes was a disciple of the Cambridge philosopher G. E. Moore, who had written in *Principia Ethica* that "by far the most valuable things we know or can imagine are certain states of consciousness which may be roughly described as the pleasures of human intercourse and the enjoyment of beautiful objects." He went on to say: "It is only for the sake of these things—in order that as much of them as possible may at some time exist—that any one can be justified in performing any public or private duty ... It is they ... that form the rational ultimate end of human action and the sole criterion of social progress."[3]

This, Keynes later said, remained his "religion under the surface." As an economist and speculator Keynes lived most of his life in the nether regions of capitalist action, but he always had one eye on the heaven of art, love and the quest for knowledge, embodied for him by his Bloomsbury friends. His "Economic Possibilities" essay is his attempt to reconcile these two sides of his character—the purposive and the spontaneous—by projecting them onto the present and future respectively.

"Economic Possibilities" was virtually ignored at the time, considered too fanciful for serious discussion. Indeed, it was a *pièce d'occasion*, a *jeu d'esprit*. Its vision and argument were contained in barely twelve pages. There were lots of loose ends, objections raised only to be dropped. "Here was Keynes at his best and his worst," wrote one of his students. "His worst, because some of his social and political theory would not stand too close a scrutiny; because society is not likely to run out of new wants as long as consumption is conspicuous and competitive ... His best because of the roving, inquiring, intuitive, provocative mind of the man."[4]

But for all its futurism, "Economic Possibilities" links up directly with Keynes's main preoccupation: the problem of persistent mass unemployment. It provides the "ideal" motivation for the revolution in economic policy for which he is chiefly known: continuous full employment, uninterrupted by slumps, was the quickest route to the utopia towards which the essay beckoned. Keynes wanted to ensure that the capitalist system worked at full blast so as to hasten the day when it would come to an end.

More than eighty years have passed since he wrote his essay; we are his "grandchildren," even his great-grandchildren. So how well has Keynes's prophecy turned out?

The Fate of Keynes's Prophecy

Keynes's essay offered two predictions and one possibility. The predictions concerned growth and hours of work. Simplifying somewhat, Keynes thought that by now we in the West would be on the verge of having "enough" to satisfy all our needs without having to work more than three hours a day. The possibility—not a prediction, because Keynes moots the alternative "bored housewife" scenario—was that we would learn to use our extra leisure to live "wisely and agreeably and well." How have these speculations fared?

What Keynes expected to happen in the rich countries is illustrated diagrammatically in Chart 1. At the point of "Bliss," in 2030, growth of income would stop (because everyone would have enough) and necessary work would fall towards zero (because almost everything people needed would be produced by machines).

Now let us compare the two predictions with actual outcomes. What has happened to growth in the rich countries plotted against Keynes's prediction is shown in Chart 2, while what has happened to hours of work in rich countries, plotted against Keynes's prediction, shown in Chart 3. Growth of real income per capita has been much as Keynes expected. The coincidence is in fact a bit of a fluke. Keynes assumed no major wars and no population growth in the countries covered. In fact there was another world war, and population has grown by about one-third. But he underestimated productivity growth. The two mistakes cancelled each other out, with the result

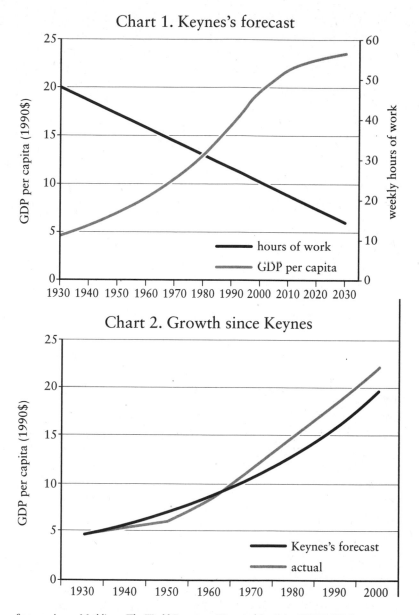

Chart 1. Keynes's forecast

hours of work
GDP per capita

Chart 2. Growth since Keynes

Keynes's forecast
actual

Sources: Angus Maddison, *The World Economy: Historical Statistics* (OECD, 2005); Measuring Worth (www.measuringworth.com); Eurostat; accessed 01/16/12

Chart 3. Weekly Hours since Keynes

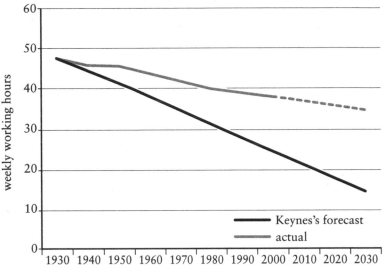

Source: Michael Huberman and Chris Minns, "The Times They are Not Changin': Days and Hours of Work in Old and New Worlds, 1870–2000," *Explorations in Economic History*, vol. 44 (2007), pp. 538–67

that per capita incomes indeed rose fourfold in the seventy years from 1930, up to Keynes's lower bound.

What, then, has happened to hours of work? Keynes's prediction that, under these conditions, hours of work would fall in line with productivity growth depended on the seemingly common-sense assumption that income had a diminishing marginal utility—that each extra bit of income yielded a little less extra satisfaction—so that as societies became richer they would increasingly prefer more leisure to more income. As a person's income rose, on account of his extra output per hour, his hours of work would fall until the utility of an extra hour of income was equal to that of an extra hour of leisure.

Things have not worked out like that. From 1870 to 1930 hours of work per person fell rapidly, and Keynes assumed that this fall would continue. "In our own lifetimes," he wrote, "we may be able to perform all the operations of agriculture, mining and manufacture with a quarter of the human effort to which we have been accustomed."[6] But though incomes and productivity have risen much in line with his expectations, hours of work per person are far from having fallen by three-quarters since 1930. In 1930 people in the industrial world worked roughly a fifty-hour week. Today they work a forty-hour week. On Keynes's reckoning, we should by now be well on our way to a fifteen-hour week, if not there already. If we project present trends forward to 2030, we might get to a thirty-five-hour week, but nowhere near a fifteen-hour week. The problem is to understand why hours of work have fallen so much less than the growth of output per hour worked led him to expect.

Keynes placed no geographical limit on his prediction. He probably thought that by 2030 the poor countries would be close to catching up with the rich ones. He was not wholly wrong. A small group of East Asian economies have achieved Western living standards, and there is a much larger band of middle-income countries which will get there before too long. But the sheer growth of population, which he did not foresee, has kept a quarter of the world's population desperately poor. In 1930 the world's population was 2.7 billion. Today it is 7 billion, more than two and a half times larger. Even in the rich world it is more than 30 percent greater. The awkward question Keynes did not face was how far the rich should go in postponing the arrival of their own "Bliss" to help the poor.

The Delusions of Averages

Before digging deeper into the question of why hours of work have failed to fall in line with the growth of the economy, we should be aware of what is concealed by our methods of measurement.

The average is simply the central tendency of a data set. Most people intuitively think of it as a "typical" number. For example, if we know that the average income of people in Britain in 2011 is £25,000 a year, we tend to assume that most of them earn £25,000 a year, with a few earning more and a few earning less. But this need not be so. Take a population of ten people (say a factory) in which the managing director earns £160,000 and the nine workers earn £10,000 each. The *mean* average of their incomes is £25,000, but what most of them earn is £10,000. This is a stylized representation of the situation in Britain and America today, in which most people earn less than the mean, and a small number earn vastly more. In 2011, the UK mean income was £27,000, but the median was £21,500. That means 50 percent of the population earned less than £21,500, and some much less.[7] The fallacy of deducing a "typical" situation from the study of mean averages is most relevant for income distribution. One cannot say whether the "welfare" of a country's citizens is going up or going down without knowing what has happened to income distribution. But the fallacy applies in many of the situations we are interested in.

First, the average number of hours worked hides sizeable (and growing) variations between countries, with industrious America at one end, "old Europe" at the other and Britain closer to the USA (see Chart 4). Although the flattening in the number of hours worked since the 1980s is common to all countries, we are left to explain why Americans and Italians work longer hours than the rest. "Americans today," reports one survey in 2011, "work an average of 122 more hours per year than the Brits, and 378 hours (nearly 10 weeks!) more than the Germans."[8] Some have suggested that in the United States hours of work have recently started to go up again. The Dutch have come closest to Keynes's state of "Bliss." In 2011, their 1,400 hours a year—or 34 hours a week—will gain them $42,000 per capita, whereas Britons' 1,650 hours get them only $36,000. (Americans get $48,000 per capita for 1,800 hours.)* It is tempting to trace these different attitudes to work, money and leisure to cultural divergences. In an immigrant society like America, money-making was seen as the royal road to success; in Europe, the legacy of a hierarchical culture that limited opportunities for money-making both at the top and the bottom led to the adoption of ways of life that downgraded money-making as a goal. Britain is an intermediate case, more open to wealth-creation than Continental Europe, less socially egalitarian than the United States. These cultural differences are embedded in, and reinforced by, the specific institutions of the tax system, welfare system and labor market. It may well be that the long Italian hours miss out those

---

* These figures are calculated according to purchasing power parity, which is a measure of what money can buy in different countries.

Chart 4. Hours of Work since 1983

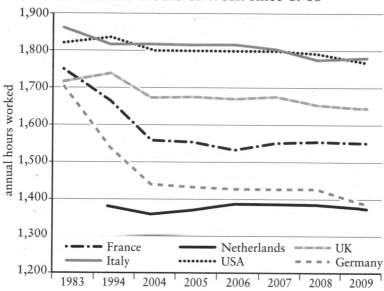

Source: OECD Employment Outlook 2011

who work only intermittent hours in the informal economy. (This seems to be a feature of all the Mediterranean countries.)

Second, the fall in average working hours conceals a divergence in hours worked by different groups within countries. While overall working hours have stalled, many lower paid workers are working less than they want to, while many of the rich are working more than they need to. It is a striking fact that working hours among the wealthy have risen, especially in the United States and Britain, reversing the negative relationship between work and income that, until recently, was widely supposed to hold.[9] In Keynes's day, the top of society worked shorter hours than the bottom. The aristocracy did no paid work at all; professionals spent remarkably few hours in the office. Today the "workaholic" rich have replaced the "idle" rich. Social status is no longer signified by immunity from labor. In our highly competitive society, people of talent but no fortune need to work ever harder to achieve the status effortlessly enjoyed in former times by people of fortune but no talent. This reversal of the traditional relationship between work and income is a good reason to believe that we are not heading for a workless future.

Third, average hours worked per year show a bigger fall than average hours worked per week, because they include vacation time. In Europe, statutory paid vacations have quadrupled since Keynes's day, from one to four weeks a year—a clear gain for leisure. However, offsetting this gain is the increase in time spent commuting and on household work. Household work in the UK, surprisingly, absorbs half an hour more each day than in 1961, despite all the new labor-saving gadgets.* But in addition many more women than in Keynes's day also go out to work, the high post-war demand for labor having pulled women into the labor market and forged careers for them. In the USA, the proportion of women who worked in 1930 was 25 percent; today it is 70 percent, a trend mirrored in other industrialized countries.[10] The modern version of Keynes's housewife is less likely to have a nervous breakdown from involuntary idleness than from the stress of combining paid work with the extra time she has to devote to shopping (including travelling to and from supermarkets, and queuing to pay) and to childcare (including the supervision of previously unsupervised play and conveyance to and from school).[11]

Further, because the statistics on working hours, whether weekly or yearly, include only people in work, they do not reflect the years spent in education or that ever-expanding gap between work and death known as retirement. Should one count the added years spent in education as an extension of work or leisure? It probably depends on the kind of education. If it is training for work, as most of it now seems to be, it should count as work; if it is a preparation for the good life, it should count as leisure.

Retirement is more naturally regarded as part of leisure; its extension may therefore be counted an addition to the possibility of the

---

* Households spend more time shopping, because of the increased distance and size of shops and the growth of self-service shopping. More time is also spent on childcare, which reflects changing attitudes towards child-rearing, exemplified by the phrase "quality time." In contrast, the time devoted to domestic chores such as cooking and cleaning has shrunk with the help of labor-saving devices. See Jonathan Gershuny and Kimberly Fisher, "Leisure in the UK across the 20th Century," in A. H. Halsey and Josephine Webb (eds.), *Twentieth Century British Social Trends* (London: Palgrave Macmillan, 1999), p. 634.

good life. In 1948, men in the UK worked on average till they were 65, and died two years later. Today they retire at 67 and live another eleven years. However, it must surely be wrong to concentrate so much leisure in the last years of a person's life. Not only will people have had little preparation in their working lives for the leisure to come, but their capacity for enjoying it may well have diminished. Nor can one conclude that leisure for society as a whole is bound to go on increasing simply as a consequence of increasing longevity. Because saving out of income has not kept pace with the growing cost of retirement,* both in terms of years and medical expenses, the years of work are inexorably rising, anti-ageism policies giving this trend legislative force. Thus the collapse of household saving during working life will inevitably curtail the years of retirement, unless the unhealthy lifestyles of rich societies produce the same result by reversing the increase in life expectancy.

However much we interrogate the averages, the central puzzle remains: we in the rich world are four or five times better off on average than we were in 1930, but our average hours of work have fallen by only a fifth since then.

Before considering why Keynes's prediction that hours of work would fall towards zero has failed, we may ask why he ever thought it was plausible. Why did Keynes think that the more income people had the less they would want to work? And why did he fix on a four- to eightfold increase as "enough"? Why not twice or three times or ten times as much?

The answer to the first question is that Keynes believed that people had a finite quantity of material needs that might one day be fully satisfied. He believed this because he failed to distinguish wants from needs; in fact, he used the two terms interchangeably throughout his essay. This, as we shall see, was a crucial error. Needs—the objective requirements of a good and comfortable life—are finite in quantity, but wants, being purely psychic, are infinitely expandable, as to both

---

* The interpretation of the data is not straightforward. The household saving rate has fallen dramatically in many Western countries, which suggests that people are working longer hours not to save for their old age but to spend. However, they may be "saving" by buying houses and financial instruments, which are treated in the national accounts as investments, not savings.

quantity and quality. This means that economic growth has no natural tendency to stop. If it comes to a halt, it will be because people *choose* not to want more than they need.

Why did Keynes think that four to eight times the average income of his day would constitute "enough"? The answer almost certainly is that he was thinking about a middle-class standard of life, the standard of those whom he considered to be "comfortably off." Professionals in the 1930s earned on average just over four times the average pay of manual workers, with doctors and lawyers earning 5.2 and 7.5 times as much respectively.[12] Keynes thought that when most people had incomes not much in excess of professional earnings they would have enough to lead a good life. Naturally enough, he would have made allowance for the general increase in standards of comfort. But he would have imagined that over time the poor would gain on the rich, as the rich, being closer to "Bliss," would reduce their hours of work faster than those less well off. He did not foresee the rich racing ahead of the poor by increasing their hours of work.*

Keynes's notion of enoughness did not require complete equality of incomes. It was based on an idea of what was fitting for a particular social role. This view of the matter, which goes all the way back to Aristotle, was common among Keynes's contemporaries. Thus the economist Alfred Marshall reckoned that £500 a year was "enough" for a thinking man. Virginia Woolf thought a writer needed £500 a year and a "room of one's own." These sums could be regarded as requirements of those particular occupations. The good life could be enjoyed at many different levels of income, provided the basic material needs, including standards of comfort, were satisfied for all.

Finally, what has happened to Keynes's "possibility"—that we would use our leisure to live "wisely and agreeably and well"? This is not a question we are yet in a position to answer, for leisure in today's rich societies is still an appendage to work, rather than its replacement. After grinding work, most people just want to "flop out."

---

* In fact, one might think of two effects. Either the rich would reduce their hours of work faster than the poor, because they had less need for additional income; or both rich and poor would reduce their hours in the same proportion, but the rich start from the position of already working less and therefore having fewer hours of work to shed.

Holidays are used to recharge the batteries for the next period of work. Much of how leisure is spent today, therefore, is not a fair test of how it would be spent if hours of work were really much reduced from what they are at present, or even if the character of most work were not so alienating. Moreover, for the higher echelons of the business world, work and leisure have merged into a generalized purposefulness. The executive who attends "off-site" meetings at exclusive golf clubs, hosts a party in order to "network" and is in constant electronic communication with his office even while on holiday is acting purposively in Keynes's sense; he is doing things not for their own sake but for the sake of other things. If anything, the culture of today's opulent societies has become more purposive, not less, more harried, not more leisurely. To explain this paradox will be one of the purposes of what follows.

Why Did Keynes's Prophecy Fail?

Explanations for the failure of average hours of work to fall in line with the growth of income fall into three broad camps. People are said to work the hours they do either because they *enjoy it*, or because they *are compelled to*, or because they *want more and more*.

The Joys of Work

"Who doesn't work, shall not eat," proclaimed Lenin, echoing St. Paul. Keynes followed the economics of his day in treating work as the cost of obtaining necessaries. As Adam Smith wrote, "The real price of everything ... is the toil and trouble of acquiring it." Or as Jeremy Bentham put it, "Insofar as labour is taken in its proper sense, love of labour is a contradiction in terms."[13] There was nothing novel in this treatment: the Bible tells us that man was condemned to work in painful expiation of his disobedience to God. But more recently, some have suggested that this age-old equation of work with "toil and trouble" does not hold, or holds to a decreasing degree. Work is no longer labor in the economist's sense, but a labor of love: a source of stimulation, identity, worth and sociability. In short, work is not just a means to an end: it provides intrinsic satisfactions. This is why people go on working longer than they "need."

Apostles of the joys of work concede that the economist's view of work as joyless labor that has to be compensated by an income may have fit the physically brutal, mechanical, stultifying work most people had to do in the past, but add that it is not true of work today. In the "post-modern" era, work has become less physically demanding, more interesting, challenging, innovative. This is particularly true of professional jobs, and explains why the higher paid often work longer hours than the lower paid. We have an ever expanding "creative" sector and much more choice of "necessary" work than formerly existed. People can discover their souls not just in their purchases but in their jobs. Keynes, critics add, had a Bloomsbury disdain for business, which led him to overlook the intrinsic satisfactions which even then many people found in work.[14]

The counterpart to love of work is said to be fear of leisure. It is often asked: what will people do if they don't have to work? Get drunk or drugged? Spend the day slumped before the television? Underlying this kind of question is the view that human beings are naturally lazy, so that work is necessary to make them productive, keep them "on the rails," stop them "going to the dogs." But there is something else. Work provides compulsory sociability; leisure can bring forced solitude. "Me? I dread weekends," remarks the workaholic journalist in Tom Rachman's novel, *The Imperfectionists*. "I wish I didn't have vacation time—I have no idea what to do with it. It's like a four-week reminder of what a loser I am."[15]

It would be foolish to deny that paid work has always had elements of intrinsic satisfaction: most people have not worked for bread alone. People may work long hours for companionship or to escape the troubles, or boredom, of family life. The question is whether the "joyful" element in work has been increasing over time. This is by no means clear. Some jobs have become more interesting; the number of vocational jobs—teaching, for example—has expanded. The Internet, it is often said, has made work more like play (even as it has made play more like work). It has also expanded opportunities for leisure at work; Facebook is only ever a click away. Work environments are increasingly designed to be "fun."* But the specialization that Adam Smith thought would take the skill out of work has also made much work less rewarding. What is called "skilling" is too often a euphemism for rendering mechanical what once demanded at least a degree of knowledge, alertness and involvement. The skills of the craftsman, the mechanic, the builder, the butcher, the baker have decayed; a great deal of work, reduced to the purely routine, remains literally stupefying. The work routines of modern supermarkets and call centers have been dubbed "digital Taylorism," in homage to the inventor of the conveyor belt.[16] Drastic cost reductions have reduced "face time," as sociability is now called. The "creativity" of many jobs is just branding: "hard-working passionate chefs creating every day" runs an advertisement for a well-known fast-food chain. Even for top financial professionals, the "joys of work" come a distant second to salaries and bonuses.[17] The willingness of top earners to work longer hours than they did in the past may testify, not to the increasing interest of their jobs, but to the increasing insecurity of their incomes. A small proportion of jobs, and parts of jobs, may have become lovable; most continue to be unloved.

Despite the so-called joys of work and fear of idleness, more workers in most developed countries, including the United States, would prefer to work less rather than more. A recent survey on future employment options shows a widespread desire for shorter working hours, even knowing that this might mean lower pay—51 percent wanted shorter hours, with only 12 percent choosing longer hours.[18] Similar results were found for Japan. In the United States, the figures were more evenly balanced, but the preference was still for shorter

---

* The new Royal Bank of Scotland headquarters in Edinburgh, a splendid contemporary structure, was built round a mock high street with all modern conveniences—coffee shops, pharmacies, florists, a hair stylist, etc. The Bank went bust in 2009. See Alastair Darling, *Back from the Brink* (London: Atlantic Books, 2011), p. 60. Douglas Edwards writes that Google's headquarters, the Googleplex, "was so much more fun than home," packed with video games, bouncy balls, air hockey, bins of M&Ms, a juice bar and a piano. But the consequence of the lack of structure was crippling insecurity: "At Google, I was in worker's paradise, but I felt I didn't deserve it." (*I'm Feeling Lucky: The Confessions of Google Employee Number 59* [London: Penguin, 2011], p. 126.)

rather than longer hours (37 percent as against 21 percent).[19] What people say they would do in hypothetical circumstances is not, of course, what they would necessarily do if faced with those circumstances. Nevertheless, there remains at least a bias in favor of shorter hours.

The increasing pleasures of work, or fear of leisure, may be part of the explanation why hours of work have stopped falling, but it cannot be the main explanation. The curse of Adam may have lightened, but it has not entirely lifted.

The Pressure to Work

Marxists have traditionally argued that workers under capitalism are forced to work longer than they need to, or would choose to, because they are "exploited"—that is, paid less than their work is worth to their employers, whose control of the labor market makes this possible. That means that they are deprived of the full gains of increased productivity. In the "social democratic" years of the mid-twentieth century, powerful trade unions were able to push up workers' real wages, and the state used the taxation system to redistribute non-wage income from the wealthy to the poor. But these equalizing trends encroached on profits and left the wealthy relatively worse off.

They were reversed in the 1980s, at about the same time as hours of work stopped falling. The explanation of the flat hours of work line seems obvious: workers have not reduced their work time because they have not in fact achieved those gains in real income that might have induced them to work less. Workers may determine their own trade-offs between work and leisure, but in a system in which the capitalist class calls the shots.

The data shows that inequality of wealth and income in the United States and Britain has grown hugely since 1980, with the rich gaining most from the increase in productivity (see Chart 5).

The headline figures are well known: in 1970 the pay of a top American CEO was under 30 times that of the average worker; today it is 263 times.[20] In Britain, the basic pay of CEOs in FTSE top companies was 47 times the average worker's pay in 2000; by 2010, it was 81 times. Since the late 1970s, the income of the richest fifth

Chart 5. Income Share of the Richest 1%

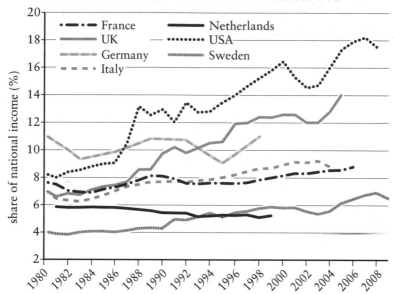

Source: World Top Incomes Database (http://g-mond.parisschoolofeconomics.eu/topincomes/)

has increased nine times as fast as the poorest fifth in the USA, and four times as fast in the UK.[21] Chart 5 confirms that the rich have been capturing an ever-increasing share of national income. This explains why, although average income has gone up in most countries, median income—that is, the income of the person in the middle of the distribution—has not risen as much, and in America has remained flat for more than forty years. According to a recent census, 46 million Americans live in poverty. "In the UK," writes Larry Elliott of the *Guardian*,

> the professional middle classes, particularly in the south east, are doing fine, but below them in the income scale are people who have become more dependent on debt as their real incomes have stagnated. Next are the people on minimum wage jobs, which have to be topped up by tax credits so they can make ends meet. At the very bottom of the pile are those who are without work, many of them second and third generation unemployed.[22]

The dominant recent influence on income distribution has been the growth of the service economy and the failure to use the tax system to offset the natural tendency of inequality to grow with the relative growth of services. Both have set a limit to the fall in hours worked. In Keynes's day, manufacturing in developed countries accounted for 80 percent of output, services for 20 percent. Today this ratio is reversed. Service jobs on average are less well paid than the manufacturing jobs they replaced, partly because they cannot be automated to the same extent—think of schoolteachers, nurses, hairdressers, taxi drivers—and partly because they cannot be unionized as effectively. The failure to redistribute income in the United States and Britain has meant that many of those employed in the lower ranks of the service sector of these two countries, especially in retail, hospitality and personal services, have had to increase their hours of work in order to escape poverty.*

The sociologist Juliet Schor has drawn attention to a specific feature of capitalist domination of the labor market. In *The Overworked American*, she argues that competitive pressures, combined with poor protection of workers' rights, has led to employers working their existing workforces longer rather than spreading the workload thinner over a larger number of workers, since the latter would involve the employer in additional costs of training and managing, not to mention statutory paid vacations, health insurance and the like. As Schor puts it, "It becomes far more profitable for a company to hire a smaller number of people for long hours than to extend those hours over more workers (who would also be paid benefits)."[23] The consequence is that the labor force is becoming segmented into a shrinking core of full-time permanent employees, who probably work more than they want, and an expanded periphery of unemployed and partly employed who work less than they want, and whose wages need to be topped up with tax credits to keep them in employment at all.

In this type of account, consumerism figures as a sop to workers deprived of the leisure they crave. To relieve their frustration (and

---

* In the USA, working hours for the lowest-paid quintile increased by 26 percent between 1986 and 2004. However, this pattern was not present in all rich countries; the equivalent OECD average was a 5–10 percent drop in working hours for the lowest paid. See OECD, *Divided We Stand: Why Inequality Keeps Rising* (Paris: OECD, 2011).

keep them docile), they are offered a stream of useless, mind-numbing consumer goods. Shopping is wittily, but accurately, called "retail therapy"—a compensation for unpleasant or depressing experiences. The creation of artificial needs ensures workers' loyalty to the work ethic. As Schor puts it in her essay "Towards a New Politics of Consumption," "there may well be a path for the economy that involves less work and less stuff, and is preferred by people to the high-work/ high-consumption track. But if that option is blocked, then the fact that we buy a lot can no longer be taken ipso facto as proof of our inherent consumer desires. We may merely be doing what is on offer."[24] In other words, we adapt our preferences, ending up wanting what we get, not getting what we want.

The left-wing account of the income/leisure trade-off is not wholly persuasive. There is no denying that since the 1980s median incomes have not kept pace with average incomes, and this fact alone would explain a large part of the failure of hours of work to fall since then. But the Marxist account of consumer behavior is less plausible. Even if consumer preferences can diverge from real needs, they cannot be entirely independent of those needs; they cannot be simply "instilled" in us by the "productive apparatus" or some other such monster. To assert this is to deny individuals all agency, to reduce them to ants or drones. The Marxist sociologist André Gorz seems to do this when he writes of the individual under capitalism: "It is not 'I' who acts, but the automated logic of social systems that work through me as Other."[25] Advertising can shape desires, but it cannot create desires out of nothing. (It cannot, for instance, persuade us to buy dog turd, except possibly by associating it with some already existing object of longing.) There must be some prior tendency in human nature for advertising to latch on to; otherwise, its empire over us would be mysterious.

Structural explanations for failure of hours of work to fall must be supplemented, then, with an exploration of the intrinsic nature of human wants and satisfactions.

Insatiability

Keynes assumed that material wants could be sated, that we could "have enough." But suppose they are insatiable? By insatiability we mean what the dictionary says: a continuous, unsatisfied craving for more than one has. "These 'romantic' Jaipur tents [cost, £3,800] create excellent additional entertaining space in the garden," runs one advertisement targeted at "those who have everything."[26] The question is: why do people who "have everything" always seem to want more?

There are two approaches to answering this question, the first of which starts with the nature of human wants in isolation, and the second which considers them in relation to those of others. The opposition between the two is admittedly largely artificial. Wants are individual; but the way they get expressed, the way they are encouraged or suppressed, is social. Which explanatory variable the investigator chooses to emphasize depends largely on whether he is interested in establishing the facts of individual psychology or whether, taking these facts as given, he tries to work out their consequences for social behavior.

A good example of the individualist approach is Tibor Scitovsky's influential 1976 book, *The Joyless Economy*. Scitovsky's explanation for insatiability was quite simply *restlessness*. We become bored with what we have. The satisfaction of all needs, the elimination of all discomforts, produces a state, not of contented tranquillity, but of dissatisfaction, which has to be relieved by novelty, as an itch needs to be relieved by scratching. As affluence increases, boredom grows, provoking an ever more frantic search for stimulating experiences. Our nature is such that we are never satisfied with what we have. So we keep on working to stimulate our jaded appetites.

A second individualist explanation for insatiability focuses on the inherent scarcity of certain goods. Holidays in top resorts, beautifully landscaped gardens and many other such rarities cannot be enjoyed by everyone in a society, however wealthy they are. Escalating demand presses on a fixed supply. The result is a continuous rise in the cost of such goods relative to average prices, which puts them permanently beyond the reach of ordinary incomes. But instead of accepting this unfortunate fact, people go on wanting the best, which, in the nature of things, they cannot all have. This, then, is another important source of insatiability.

Keynes's disciple Roy Harrod called such inherently scarce goods "oligarchic," in an essay that implicitly punctured the rosy vision of his master.[27] A classic example is Old Masters. All the fine old paintings that exist have already been produced: their supply cannot be increased. Admittedly, everyone can get a glimpse of them in a museum, and this is the "democratic" solution to this particular problem. But in terms of individual satisfaction, rationing by queue is much inferior to rationing by price, to having the best that has been created available for appreciation in the privacy of one's own home.

Oligarchic goods do not have to be physically scarce. They may also be "socially scarce," meaning that their multiplication destroys the characteristics that made them desirable in the first place. "Unspoilt" holiday resorts remain unspoilt only so long as access to them is limited. Harrod wrote:

> A young man may have the ambition that, when he grows rich, he will live in the choicest part of New York, have good seats at all the best plays and operas, go to the most select night clubs ... patronise the best living artists. And he may get all these things, if he grows rich oligarchically, but democratic wealth can never achieve them. If an unequal distribution prevails, the richer people will price these rare things beyond the pockets of the average man.

Harrod drew a further implication. Only the minority of the rich are able to afford servants and therefore the upkeep of "great mansions to live in, private parks and gardens, stables ... yachts," all of which require the existence of a servant class. But the more equal wealth becomes, the fewer servants will be available and affordable. No labor-saving inventions can compensate for the disappearance of the personal service needed for gracious living.

The economist Fred Hirsch relabelled Harrod's "oligarchic" goods "positional," because access to them depends not on our absolute level of wealth but on our *position* relative to others. Like top prizes in a tournament, positional goods cannot be won by everyone.[28] They will always be scooped up by the richest in society, whatever the overall level of affluence. Competition to acquire them will therefore never cease. In fact, it will intensify with growth, as a progressively larger proportion of household income is liberated for positional spending. The existence of positional goods dims Keynes's vision of a society in which everyone has "enough." For even if everyone earned the requisite £500 a year, or its modern equivalent, they would not all (logically) be able to live in the best houses or buy the best seats at the opera.

A third individualist explanation of insatiability draws heavily on the economist's picture of the human being as a rational utility maximizer. The pioneer work here is that of the American economist Gary Becker.[29] Keynes looked on leisure as a benefit universally desired, but another way of looking at it is as a cost—the cost of not working. Becker pointed out that the cost of an evening at the theatre is not simply the price of the ticket but the cost of not earning in those hours. Leisure is a subtraction from hypothetical income, and Becker pictured the individual balancing at the margin the advantages of earning income and of spending it. Stated this way, the choice between work and leisure is essentially a time-allocation problem. Leisure is not free time, it is costly time. And the higher your income, the costlier the time. If Becker is right, there is no a priori reason to believe that hours of work will fall as wealth grows. It is just as plausible to believe that they will rise, as the cost of not working increases.

The Swedish economist Staffan Linder wrote a book, *The Harried Leisure Class*, expanding on Becker's analysis. Linder's main point was that the return on leisure must become as high as the return on work if people are to give up working. The main way of increasing the "yield" of leisure is to pack it with equipment. "Just as workers become more productive by working with more tools and capital equipment, consumers get more out of their leisure time when more gadgets are used per time unit."[30] A trip to the seaside or holiday resort becomes incomplete without barbecue, windbreaks, wetsuits, surfboards, tennis rackets, footballs, beach balls and golf clubs.

Linder is mainly concerned to explain the consequence for the nature of leisure of gadget-filled consumption, but his argument can be used to explain the failure of working hours to fall in line with Keynes's prediction. The more consumer durables—cars, boats, trailers, televisions, DVD players and so on—are used to augment leisure, the larger the incomes needed to afford them. The increasing array of goods required for productive consumption keeps us tethered to work.

None of these individualist explanations of insatiability—innate restlessness, positional competition, utility maximization—involves a comparison between what one wants and what others have. To that extent they are unrealistic, since the expression of wants always has a social character. The main sociological explanation of insatiability hinges, therefore, on the relative character of wants. At no level of material wealth will I feel satisfied with what I have, because someone will always have more than I do. Once competition for wealth—or the consumption by which it is normally signified—turns into competition for status, it becomes a zero-sum game, because everyone, by definition, cannot have high status. As I spend more on prestige goods, I gain status but cause others to lose it. As they spend more to regain status they reduce my own. There is no reason why the escalation of income to maintain and acquire status should ever end.

Oddly enough, Keynes was well aware of status spending. Human needs, he wrote in an important aside in his essay, fall into two classes:

> those needs which are absolute in the sense that we feel them whatever the situation of our fellow human beings may be, and those which are relative in the sense that we feel them only if their satisfaction lifts us above, makes us feel superior to, our fellows. Needs of the second class, those which satisfy the desire for superiority, may indeed be insatiable; for the higher the general level, the higher still are they. But this is not so true of the absolute needs—a point may soon be reached, much sooner perhaps than we are all of us aware of, when these needs are satisfied in the sense that we prefer to devote our further energies to non-economic purposes.[31]

Keynes raises the spectre of socially generated insatiability only to ignore it; the rest of his essay proceeds on the assumption that all needs are absolute. Why this oversight? Probably he thought "relative needs" too insignificant to dwell on. Keynes lived in an era when the vast bulk of household expenditure was on bread, shelter, clothing, heating and other such utilities. Money devoted to competitive consumption was a small fraction of the total. Today, that situation is reversed: the bulk of household expenditure, even by the poor, is on items that are not necessary in any strictly material sense, but which serve to confer status. The very notion of a "material good" has broadened to include anything that can be bought or sold, including ideas, scraps of melody, even identities.

Economists and sociologists have identified three types of spending designed to enhance status.[32] The details are technical, but the mechanisms are familiar. First, there are "bandwagon goods": goods that are desired because others already have them. This is partly a matter of envy, but also of wanting to be like everyone else. Both longings are particularly strong in children, causing parents to work harder than they otherwise might to satisfy them. Then there are "snob goods," goods that are desired because others do not have them. Snob goods cater to the desire to be different, exclusive, to stand apart from "the crowd." They are not necessarily the most expensive, but mark their possessors as having superior taste. Contemporary examples might include obscure underground bands, cult films and exotic restaurants. Snob and bandwagon goods are not of course mutually exclusive: many snob goods mutate into bandwagon goods, leading to their abandonment by true snobs. This perpetual circle is familiar from the worlds of art and fashion.

Overlapping with both snob and bandwagon goods are "Veblen goods," so called in honor of the great American theorist of conspicuous consumption, Thorstein Veblen. Veblen goods are desired insofar as they are expensive and known to be expensive; they function, in effect, as advertisements of wealth. In the still hierarchical world of business, whether one travels first, business or economy class signals one's rank in the company. Another Veblenesque phenomenon is the "bling effect." The brand labels favored by celebrities are widely known to be expensive, and that is a large part (perhaps the whole part) of their appeal: the higher the price, the more exclusive the brand. Were they to fall in price, demand for them might fall too. A Russian joke sums it up. Two newly rich Russians meet. "How much did your tie cost?" asks one of them. "A thousand dollars," replies the other. "Bad luck," says the first, "Mine cost two thousand." Conspicuous consumption is a well-known characteristic of the nouveaux riches of all countries and ages.

Success in competition is usually signalled by more lavish consumption, but it need not be, nor need this be the motive for competition. Possession of money may be a sufficient index of success, without the need to display this possession in costly objects. In the past, spending money was the main means of signalling to the world that one had money, but, with the spread of public knowledge of people's incomes and fortunes through such league tables as the *Sunday Times* Rich List, competition for money has become detached from competition for goods. In the upper echelons of the business world, money is sought after not only as a means to consumption but as an index of superior achievement. As the late H. L. Hunt, then one of the richest men in the world, put it, money is "just a way of keeping score."

There is no denying that some forms of relational consumption have had beneficial effects. A good deal of philanthropy stems from conspicuous consumption. The desire to impress others with one's wealth, power or taste has adorned our cities with great buildings and commissioned most of the works of art now displayed in our museums. Today the same impulse is seen in the competition among American billionaires to give away their money. However, as Keynes's friend the art critic Roger Fry pointed out, it is only in periods of high civilization that snobbery has produced a critical mass of objects desirable for their own sake.[33] Most of today's benefactions have to be justified by utilitarian purposes.

Evidently, the individual and social sources of insatiability intertwine. Many goods described as "socially scarce" are scarce mainly because of their snob appeal or because they provide opportunities for conspicuous consumption: a degree from a "top" university has a snob value quite apart from the access it provides to "top jobs." Persons of refined taste may love the "best things of life" for their own sake; but by their acquisition they are also signalling that they are persons of superior taste—and wealth. Linder's gadget-packed leisure does not simply reflect an individualist hunger for a "yield" equivalent to work, but also a comparison with other people's gadgets. The failure to identify the overlap between the individual and social sources of insatiability is largely a creation of the way we divide up our disciplines, setting aggressive limits to their understanding of human behavior.

But it is not necessary for us to choose between the various explanations of insatiability, or even weight them in order of importance. It is enough to realize that, if carried beyond a certain point, insatiability leads us away from the good life.

Is there any escape from this logic? A tendency to insatiability has long been recognized and condemned by philosophers and moralists, as we shall see in Chapter 3. It is rooted in human nature and the social character of man, not (as Marxists would have it) in the dynamics of a particular economic system, capitalism. But the Marxists are right to this extent: capitalism has inflamed our innate tendency to insatiability by releasing it from the bounds of custom and religion within which it was formerly confined. This inflammation takes four distinct though related forms.

First, capitalism's competitive logic drives firms to carve out new markets by (among other things) manipulating wants. Advertising may not create insatiability, but it exploits it without scruple, whispering in our ear that our lives are drab and second-rate unless we consume "more." Advertising is the "organized creation of dissatisfaction," as a former director of General Motors Research Lab once nicely put it.[34]

Second, capitalism greatly broadens the scope of status competition. In his nineteenth-century classic, *Democracy in America*, Alexis de Tocqueville noticed that America's "general equality of condition" was the most fertile soil for the growth of the work ethic and acquisitive instinct.[35] In Europe, Tocqueville claimed, no one cared about making money, because the lower classes had no hope of it, and the upper classes thought it vulgar to think about it. Only in the United States could workers believe that through hard work they might achieve the fortunes necessary to enjoy the luxuries of the rich. The American combination of social equality and income inequality has since become the capitalist norm, leading to a situation in which every member of society is in a sense competing against every other. And the greater the inequality, the greater the competitive pressure. "If pay varies greatly," writes economist Richard B. Freeman, "there is a sizeable incentive to do what it takes to climb up the earnings distribution, including putting in long hours." Countries with higher inequality tend to have longer working hours; workers in occupations with bigger wage variations tend to work harder than those in other occupations.[36] This plausibly explains why Americans and Britons work longer hours than continental Europeans.

Third, the ideology of free-market capitalism has been consistently hostile to the idea that a certain sum of money could represent "enough." Such an idea is seen as effete and patronizing, as thwarting our natural desire to better our condition. "There is scarce perhaps a single instant," wrote Adam Smith, setting the tone, "in which any man is so perfectly and completely satisfied with his situation as to be without any wish of alteration or improvement."[37] Smith's go-getter was for a long time held back by customary standards of gracious living (always stronger in Europe than the United States), but he has finally triumphed over all obstacles. In former times a banker bought an estate as soon as he could and retired from the business; now he may buy an estate but makes sure he stays in constant touch with the stock market so he can accumulate further. It would be preposterous today, as it would not have been eighty years ago, to explain why one did not work by saying "I have enough to live as a gentleman."

Finally, capitalism enlarges insatiability by increasingly "monetizing" the economy. This has two aspects. First, because of its tendency to marketize more and more goods and services—that is, make them exchangeable for money—capitalism constantly enlarges the sphere of monetary measurement and thus the ease of direct comparison. Before land was valued in monetary terms two estates could not readily be assessed against each other. Today the comparison is easy and automatic. More and more things we value are "priced" and thus enter the sphere of relational competition. Education, for instance, is increasingly seen not as a preparation for the good life but as a means to increase the value of "human capital."

More insidiously, by increasing the sphere of money measurement, capitalism inflames the love of money for its own sake. As Marx reminds us, quoting Goethe, money comes to have "love in its body."[38] Traders in futures, derivatives and other rarefied financial products need know nothing at all of the actual goods that lie at the end of their transactions. Living in a world of pure money, they lose feeling for the value of things. If cynicism is knowing the price of everything and the value of nothing, then the centers of world finance are breeding grounds of cynicism.

Keynes's mistake was to believe that the love of gain released by capitalism could be sated with abundance, leaving people free to enjoy its fruits in civilized living. This is because he thought of people as possessing a fixed stock of natural wants. He did not understand that capitalism would set up a new dynamic of want creation that would overwhelm traditional restraints of custom and good sense. This means that, despite our much greater affluence, our starting position for the realization of the good life is worse than it was in the more traditional society of his day. Capitalism has achieved incomparable progress in the creation of wealth, but has left us incapable of putting that wealth to civilized use.

How did we come to set up a system in which the love of gain was released from its moral constraints, and why has it become almost impossible to get it back under control? This is the subject of the next chapter.

2

The Faustian Bargain

Are you an angel of salvation? Or will you drag me to
damnation?

—Tatyana, in *Eugene Onegin*

Keynes was deeply ambivalent about capitalist civilization. It was a civilization that unleashed bad motives for the sake of good results. Morality had to be put in cold storage till abundance was achieved, for abundance would make possible a good life for all. "For at least another hundred years," Keynes wrote, "we must pretend to ourselves and to every one that fair is foul and foul is fair; for foul is useful and fair is not. Avarice and usury and precaution must be our gods for a little longer still. For only they can lead us out of the tunnel of economic necessity into daylight."[1] Keynes understood that capitalist civilization had, at some level of consciousness, undertaken to license motives previously condemned as "foul" for the sake of future reward. It had struck a bargain with the forces of darkness, in return for which it would secure what earlier ages could only dream of—a world beyond the toil and trouble, violence and injustice of life as it actually is. We have called this bargain "Faustian," in honor of the famous doctor who sold his soul to the Devil in return for knowledge, pleasure and power.

The story starts with the ancient dream of utopia, and then mutates into the historical project of creating a paradise on earth, which has gripped the Western imagination for the last three hundred years and on which the human race is still fitfully engaged. On the way, the idea of moral limits to human ambition, which underpinned all pre-modern conceptions of the good life, was lost, and dormant energies of creativity and destructiveness were set free in the hope that they would carry humanity to a pinnacle of achievement and mastery of the natural world. At various stages on this journey, the greatest thinkers of the age tried to envisage an end state, a point at which humanity could say "enough," only to find that the machine it had created was out of control, a Frankenstein's monster that now programmed the game of progress according to its own insane logic. This is the story of how it happened—how we came to be ensnared by the dream of progress without purpose, riches without end.

The Idea of Utopia:
From Dream to History

Men and women have always dreamt of a world without suffering, injustice and above all, without *work*. Adam and Eve are placed in a garden planted with "every tree that is pleasant to the sight, and good for food." It is only later, after the Fall, that God condemns them to eat their bread in sweat and sorrow. The Greek poets speak of a "golden age" when the "fruitful earth yielded its abundant harvest of its own accord" (Hesiod) and "every torrent flowed with wine ... and fishes would come to the house and bake themselves, then serve themselves on the tables" (Telecleides).[2] The outlines of this ancient fantasy have hardly changed over the centuries. The medieval land of Cockaigne was populated by roast pigs wandering around with carving knives in their backs, and "Big Rock Candy Mountain," a popular song of the 1920s, depicts a world where hens lay soft-boiled eggs, alcohol trickles down the rocks and they "hung the jerk who invented work."

These folk utopias, gaudy and naive, voice the perennial human longing for idleness and comfort. Less endearing are the civic utopias of the philosophers, in which appetites are subjected to rational government rather than simply gratified. The prototype is Plato's *Republic*, an ideal city ruled over by an enlightened elite of guardians who share everything in common, including women, with whom they breed periodically on the order of the state. Thomas More's *Utopia* of 1516, the work that gave the genre its name, is equally grim. Here not just the rulers, but all classes hold property in common. Short working hours—Utopians work only six hours a day—are made possible not by technological advance but by the strict rationing of appetite. The result is "heavy casualties in the minor pleasures of life."[3] Alcohol is forbidden, and everyone wears the same drab clothes. Leisure time is spent, not in consumption (there is nothing much to consume), but in "learning joyously, in debating, in reading, in reciting, in writing, in walking, in exercising the mind and body, and with play."[4] (The same consumer deprivation inspired the promotion of chess as a leisure pursuit in the Soviet Union.) There is also more than a hint of Big Brother. "Everyone has his eye on you, so you're practically forced to get on with your job, and make some proper use of your spare time." Women are subordinate to men, and repeated adultery is punishable by death.[5]

All these pre-modern utopias share one characteristic: they are outside history. Either they belong to some mythic, never-to-be-recaptured past (Eden, the golden age) or they have no temporal location at all. Plato's Republic is a pure idea, floating above the empirical world; More's Utopia is, as its Greek name implies, an *ou-topia*, a "no-place." Neither Plato nor More had any idea how his ideal might be realized, except perhaps by dint of its own persuasive power. (Plato talked hopefully about philosophers becoming kings, but it is not clear how seriously he meant it.) The trouble is that history, as then conceived, offered no point of entry for utopia. It embodied no progressive momentum, only a cyclical oscillation of birth, flowering and decay, analogous to the seasons. Periods of vigor and expansion would be followed by periods of luxury and decadence, and so on in endless alternation. Niccolò Machiavelli neatly summarized the classical view: "valour begets tranquillity, tranquillity ease, ease disorder, and disorder ruin. And conversely out of ruin springs order, from order valour, and thence glory and good fortune."[6] This tradition survived. As late as 1891 Pope Leo XIII was claiming that "the events of one century are wonderfully like those of another."[7] And in the twentieth century we had the grand cyclical visions of Spengler, Toynbee, Sorokin.

It was the Jewish prophets, Isaiah in particular, who first offered an alternative vision of history as the story of the struggle of good against evil, culminating in the victory of good. Prophetic history is directional, not cyclical, ethical, not tragic. In place of Machiavelli's endless see-saw, it looks forwards to a point of completion, when "the wolf shall dwell with the lamb, and the leopard shall lie down with the kid." This directional understanding of history was inherited by the early Christians, with the climactic moment now identified as Christ's Second Coming. The Book of Revelation, source of so much poetry and madness, prophesies a "new heaven and a new earth," in which "there shall be no more death, neither sorrow, nor crying, neither shall there be any more pain: for the former things are passed away."

The millenarian seed lies deep in the Christian consciousness, ready to sprout forth lusciously in times of hardship or turmoil. But mainstream Christianity has kept a wary distance from it. St. Augustine, a former Platonist, positioned his "city of God" not at the end of history but outside time altogether, abandoning the "city of man" to its old cyclical fate. Sacred history was thus sharply distinguished from mundane, secular history. However, the potential for intermingling was always there. Joachim of Flora, a twelfth-century mystic, developed an ingenious theory of human history based on the three persons of the Trinity. The age of the Father had ended with the birth of Christ; the age of the Son was coming to a close; the age of the Holy Spirit, in which all Christians would be united in a new spiritual kingdom, free from the letter of the law, was at hand. Sure enough, the appointed year came and went, nothing happened, and Joachim's teachings were declared heretical.[8] But they cast a long subterranean shadow, stretching all the way to Hegel and Marx.

Particularly relevant to our Faustian theme is the idea, lurking just under the surface of many Christian theories of history, that evil is part and parcel of the scheme of salvation. As many Church Fathers observed, had Adam not fallen, Christ would not have come into the world. Adam's sin was, then, a "happy" sin, a *felix culpa*. But the precedent was a dangerous one. "Shall we continue in sin, that grace may abound?" asks St. Paul rhetorically. His answer is swift and decisive: "God forbid!" Christian orthodoxy has never given any other answer. To permit evil for the sake of future good belongs exclusively to God's providence. We humans must take our bearing not from God's providence, but from his law, which forbids evil absolutely.

However, as the grip of doctrinal orthodoxy loosened in post-Reformation Europe, St. Paul's question was raised again, this time in earnest. Jacob Boehme, the sixteenth-century Lutheran mystic, discerned a dark, dynamic quality in God himself, which he termed the *Ungrund* or abyss. John Milton's Satan is a noble, eloquent figure, a far cry from the hideous man-goat of medieval imagery. (Milton, said William Blake famously, was "of the Devil's party without knowing it.") Blake himself, more radical than either Boehme or Milton, saw evil as a vibrant, creative force, a necessary complement to the static and somewhat prissy good. "Without Contraries is no progression," he wrote in *The Marriage of Heaven and Hell*. "Attraction and Repulsion, Reason and Energy, Love and Hate, are necessary to Human existence. From these contraries spring what the religious call Good & Evil. Good is the passive that obeys Reason. Evil is the active springing from Energy."[9]

Elements of this mystical tradition were possibly whirling around in Keynes's mind when he wrote "Economic Possibilities." (He was, incidentally, fascinated by alchemy, and even invested some money in a scheme to transmute base metal into gold.) But the more immediate source of Keynes's endorsement of the Faustian theme lies in the purely secular tradition of economics.

The Economists: From Avarice to Self-Interest

The Renaissance invented—or rediscovered—the idea of *using* human desires to govern societies rather than castigating them as wicked. The wise prince, wrote Machiavelli, treats people as they are, not as they should be: he exploits their fickleness, hypocrisy and greed to attain his ends. The test of virtue in politics is success, not goodness. Machiavelli's doctrine was so shocking to Christian moralists that "old Nick" became an English byword for the Devil. But it was heeded all the same. Thomas Hobbes and John Locke both followed Machiavelli in depicting government as a contrivance for satisfying human desires peacefully, not proscribing them. The laudable ambition behind these "realistic" doctrines of state was to minimize violence in human life—religious violence in particular. Then in the eighteenth century, a more peaceable age, the idea of diverting human passions to useful ends migrated to economics.

In pre-scientific thinking about the economy, love of money was regarded as both morally opprobrious and historically destructive. Augustine had denounced it as the worst of man's sins, worse than love of power or sex. Political moralists tended to agree. Experience showed that avarice and luxury sapped the valor of civilized nations, leaving them prey to warlike barbarians, still uncontaminated by wealth. This age-old pattern underlay the cyclical view of history of Sallust and other Romans, and was still vivid in the minds of Machiavelli, Montesquieu and Gibbon.

The idea that too much wealth led to decadence came naturally to warrior aristocracies or republics with citizen militias. But in the states of early modern Europe, where soldiering was a special profession, it made much less sense. Here, monarchs had every reason to encourage wealth-creation, for it provided a source of revenue with which they could hire mercenaries or pay for standing armies. In this perspective, the accumulation of wealth could be seen as the means to power, not the vice that brought about its decline. And if wealth and power went hand in hand, then the old cycle of rise and fall might finally be broken. Permanent economic progress became a possibility.

By the early eighteenth century, this new system of ideas had become the effective basis of government in Europe's leading merchant powers, England and Holland. Yet both nations were still officially wedded to a morality in which avarice and luxury were vices. Hypocrisy was the inevitable result. It took an Anglo-Dutch scribbler, Bernard Mandeville (1670–1733), to apply the needle of satire to it.

Mandeville is the Machiavelli of economics—one of those irritating people who try to see human nature as it is, rather than as moralists say it should be. He attacked the hypocrisy of those who enjoyed the benefits of avarice and usury while preaching against it. "The moral virtues," he famously wrote, "are the political offspring which flattery begot upon pride."[10] There was something devilish about Mandeville. A doctor of medicine, he specialized in the treatment of "hypochondriack and hysterick passions." In his spare time he wrote satires and political pamphlets. Critics were shocked by his cynicism. Among the learned his writings were judged to have Satanic inspiration.[11]

Mandeville's best-known work, *The Fable of the Bees, or Private Vices, Publick Benefits*, is a curious performance. A long piece of doggerel verse accompanied by a philosophical commentary, it recounts the fortunes of a fractious beehive that is unmistakably eighteenth-century England. Mandeville's bees are addicted to "Fraud, Luxury, and Pride," yet succeed, through "State's Craft," in transforming these "private vices" into the "public benefits" of commerce and industry:

> The Root of Evil, Avarice,
> That damn'd ill-natur'd baneful Vice,
> Was Slave to Prodigality,
> That Noble Sin; whilst Luxury
> Employ'd a Million of the Poor,
> And odious Pride a Million more:
> Envy it self, and Vanity,
> Were Ministers of Industry.[12]

Enter Virtue: prosperity dwindles, and the hive is ruined. This depiction of a slump in fortune brought on by an onset of frugality delighted Keynes, who quoted several passages from *The Fable* in his *General Theory*. Mandeville's moral is plain: you can have riches and vice, or poverty and virtue, but not riches and virtue. Which do you want?

Mandeville's cavalier treatment of the vices fitted the mood of post-Restoration England, but half a century later a kind of secular puritanism had taken hold. It would now have seemed impious to make vice the foundation of a new science of improvement, even ironically. But the more progressive thinkers of the day soon found a way to rob Mandeville's paradox of its sting. The trick was to *redefine* the virtues and vices so as to bring them into line with economic utility and disutility. "It seems upon any system of morality," wrote David Hume, a pioneer of the new approach, "little less than a contradiction in terms, to talk of a vice, which is in general beneficial to society."[13] The old term "avarice" was gradually sidelined in favor of the colorless "self-interest." It was retained, if at all, only for pathological or criminal forms of acquisition such as hoarding or swindling.

Meanwhile, ordinary commercial activity was described in language suggestive of a benign if unheroic pastime. "There are few ways in which a man can be more innocently employed than in getting money," was how Dr. Johnson famously put it. His French contemporary Montesquieu talked of the *douceur* of commerce.[14]

Once money-making had been stripped of its ethical opprobrium, it became open to treatment in terms of cause and effect. Hume's friend, the Scottish philosopher Adam Smith, took the lead. *The Wealth of Nations*, his masterpiece of 1776, presents humans as driven by a natural desire for self-improvement, which under conditions of free competition leads them "as if by an invisible hand" to promote the public well-being. Newton's mechanical science of nature was thereby extended to economic relations, with self-interest in the role of gravity. This was a revolutionary invention. Traditional morality had conceived of society as an enterprise devoted to the common good. For Smith, by contrast, it is a purely causal nexus of self-regarding individuals. God, whom Smith quaintly calls "The Great Director of the Universe," has merely set the machinery in motion, leaving it to self-love to work its benefits. As the poet Alexander Pope put it: "Thus God and Nature formed the general frame / And bade self-love and social be the same."[15]

Smith's doctrine of self-interest did more than just turn avarice into a virtue; it turned classical virtue into a vice. Extravagant display was shunned in favor of "frugality" or "saving." In Smith's political economy, asceticism becomes the virtuous form of self-interest, the efficient cause of capital accumulation.* Alms-giving was discouraged because it promoted idleness. Lust alone retained its deadly status, as a distraction from money-making and the building up of stable fortunes. Whether in the form of extravagance, generosity or sexual pleasure, the wanton scattering of one's seed acquired all the connotations of sinfulness. The progress of wealth required, as Freud would later put it, the repression of the instincts.

Smith's economics was a triumph of intellectual *economizing*—an ingenious application of Occam's razor to man's social behavior. The

---

* The economic significance of Protestantism has been famously explored in such classic texts as Max Weber's *The Protestant Ethic and the Spirit of Capitalism*, tr. Talcott Parsons (London: Routledge, 1992; first pub. 1905); and Richard Tawney's *Religion and the Rise of Capitalism* (London: J. Murray, 1926).

turbulent passions were reduced to the single motive of self-interest. This gave economics its unique analytic power. It would not have to worry, as did the political science bequeathed by Machiavelli, about understanding and managing the varied and contradictory passions. One master motive, the self-interested pursuit of wealth, subsumed all others. Smith himself was less parsimonious than his followers; he acknowledged, alongside self-interest, an independent motive of "sympathy," which he developed at length in his *Theory of Moral Sentiments*. But as economics took shape, these complexities were ironed out. The study of man as he "really is" rather than as he "ought to be" turned into an unassailable fortress of mathematics, bewitching its acolytes and reducing everyone else to futile protest.

Smith's defense of self-interest did not convince everyone. It gave economics the reputation of robbing virtue of its splendor and vice of its sting. An early critic, Thomas Reid, saw Smith's ethical theory as a device for wrapping up selfishness in impartiality. Edmund Burke sounded the classic conservative lament: "But the age of chivalry is gone; that of sophisters, economists, and calculators has succeeded, and the glory of Europe is extinguished forever."[16] Resistance to commercialism also came from the American and French revolutionaries who harked back to the agrarian "Republican virtues" of pre-Caesarist Rome.

Smith took himself to have refuted "the selfish system" of Mandeville, but he had not in fact left it all that far behind.[17] Mandeville's central mechanism—the utilization of vice for public benefit—lives on in his invisible hand, purged of its demonic flavor by the simple expedient of redefining "vice" as an innocuous natural quality. With a few exceptions, this has been the strategy of economics ever since. The value-neutral language of "utility" and "preferences" renders capitalism's Faustian bargain necessarily invisible.

Only in a few places does Smith reveal the extent of his debt to Mandeville. One is the famous passage in *The Theory of Moral Sentiments* describing how the vices of the wealthy redound to the benefit of society as a whole. (This, incidentally, is the first time Smith uses the metaphor of the "invisible hand.") Though the rich, he writes,

> mean only their own conveniency, though the sole end which they propose . . . be the gratification of their own vain and insatiable desires,

they divide with the poor the produce of all their improvements. They are led by an invisible hand to make nearly the same distribution of the necessaries of life, which would have been made, had the earth been divided into equal portions among all its inhabitants, and thus without intending it, without knowing it, advance the interest of the society."[18]

Here Smith reverts openly to the old moral language of rapacity, vanity and insatiability. The mask has temporarily slipped.

Nor could Smith ignore, despite his best efforts to gloss it, the bad effects of the commercial system on the lives and characters of workers. His description of the warping effects of the division of labor anticipates Marx:

> The man whose whole life is spent in performing a few simple operations, of which the effects are perhaps always the same, or very nearly the same, has no occasion to exert his understanding or to exercise his invention in finding out expedients for removing difficulties which never occur. He naturally loses, therefore, the habit of such exertion, and generally becomes as stupid and ignorant as it is possible for a human creature to become. The torpor of his mind renders him not only incapable of relishing or bearing a part in any rational conversation, but of conceiving any generous, noble, or tender sentiment, and consequently of forming any just judgment concerning many even of the ordinary duties of private life.[19]

Smith concludes, somewhat lamely, with the hope that education will counteract these stultifying tendencies. Then he drops the theme. He clearly considered the mind-numbing labor of the pin factory a necessary cost for the sake of future benefits.

It is worth pausing for a moment to consider what was gained and lost by Smith's overthrow of the classical scheme of virtues and vices. The gain was the release of motives that promoted economic growth. Acquisitiveness was licensed on condition it served the social good. What was lost was the idea of the social good as a collective achievement. It became a result of individuals pursuing their self-interest in markets. The logic of contract was sundered from the logic of reciprocity, which in most human cultures and societies has been an integral part of the economy. As economics developed, it became increasingly difficult to distinguish wants from needs. In this respect, Keynes was heir to the neoclassical tradition, which is why his idea of "satiety" seems quaint.

Writing before the industrial age, Smith did not think of economic progress as growth without end, but as much growth as the institutions, habits and policy of a people allowed. In fact he and his contemporaries did not talk about growth at all but about "improvement," a term encompassing moral as well as material conditions. At the end of this road lay the "stationary state"—a state in which the possibilities of improvement were exhausted. All the classical economists had this end point in mind, at varying degrees of affluence.

Smith's two famous successors, Thomas Malthus and David Ricardo, were much less optimistic than Smith himself. Malthus's *Essay on the Principle of Population* (1798, 1826) was written to challenge William Godwin's utopian claim that property redistribution would make possible abundance for all. Its logic was straightforwardly cyclical. Without strenuous moral "checks," population would inevitably outstrip the land available to support it: variations in population pressure would determine cycles of rising and falling incomes. When Ricardo's *Principles of Political Economy* (1817) added diminishing returns from land to the Malthusian picture, the best that economists could offer was a modest improvement on the past, attainable by hitherto unachieved feats of moral and practical efficiency. Economics acquired its reputation as the "dismal science."

A more utopian prospect was opened up by John Stuart Mill in the middle of the nineteenth century, after industrialization had started to do its work. Mill thought that with the level of affluence already achieved, it would be possible, supposing population increase were controlled, for Britain even then to afford a good life for all its inhabitants. He recognized the relational character of wants, but saw no reason why competition should not be restrained by a more equal distribution of incomes:

> I confess I am not charmed with the ideal of life held out by those who think that the normal state of human beings is that of struggling to get on; that the trampling, crushing, elbowing, and treading on each other's

heels, which form the existing type of social life, are the most desirable lot of human kind, or anything but the disagreeable symptoms of one of the phases of industrial progress. It may be a necessary stage in the progress of civilization, and those European nations which have hitherto been so fortunate as to be preserved from it, may have it yet to undergo ... But the best state for human nature is that in which, while no one is poor, no one desires to be richer, nor has any reason to fear from being thrust back, by the efforts of others to push themselves forward.[20]

After Mill, the idea of the "stationary state," whether dismal or utopian, dropped out of economics till Keynes revived it. Technology had started to hold out the prospect of wealth-accumulation without limit.

Faust as Literary Metaphor

Truths obscured by the rational language of secular science emerge with startling and disconcerting clarity in poetry. The bargain with evil for the sake of progress, which economists could not openly avow, or could treat only in the anaesthetized form of a "cost," finds its perfect symbol in the Faust legend. Faust is the uniquely modern myth, the greatest myth not to have come down to us from pagan antiquity or the Bible. It embodies the thought, alien to classical and mainstream Christian culture, that evil is not just a negative to be resisted but a positive, creative force in human affairs.

The Faust legend is based on the real figure of a German scholar, Johann Faust (c. 1480–1540), whose exploits were attributed by the credulous to a pact with the Devil. In the earliest versions of the story, Faust is a purely medieval figure, an alchemist and magician, who uses his demonic powers for the low purposes of seduction and trickery. But as the legend develops, he sheds his alchemical past and becomes a distinctly modern figure, a scientist who strives to master nature and suffers a horrible fate for his presumption.

The Elizabethan dramatist Christopher Marlowe produced the first great literary Faust. In his play *Doctor Faustus*, the sin of the Doctor is the quest for unbounded knowledge and power. Faustus dreams not only of sexual conquests, but of the power to accomplish great deeds—to wall Germany with brass, to cause the Rhine to encircle Wittenberg, to clothe its students in silk, and to drive out Spain from the Netherlands. In fact, he fritters away his Devil-fuelled power in trivialities, and, like the original Faust, comes to a grisly end when the Devil claims his bond. But his ambitions were not entirely to be despised. "In 50 years Faust had developed from a historical and then legendary trickster . . . to a power-crazed Renaissance tragic hero."[21]

When Marlowe conceived his Faustus, he may have been thinking of his contemporary, the philosopher and statesman Francis Bacon. Bacon was the prophet of modern technology, the first man to think of mastering nature to fashion a history of human improvement. In place of the speculative methods of ancient and medieval science, he called for an "enquiry into the true causes of things," with a view to exploiting them for human ends. "Human knowledge and human power meet in one," he wrote famously, "for where the cause is not known the effect cannot be produced." Marlowe discerned something demonic about this enterprise. He cast a Faustian pall over the Baconian project that, in Europe at least, has never left it.

By the early nineteenth century, in Goethe's classic retelling (1808 and 1832), Faust has become a symbol of endlessly striving modern man, fallible but ultimately worthy of love. Goethe's *Faust* can be seen as the literary expression of the *felix culpa* of the political economists. God sends humanity (Faust) the Devil (Mephistopheles) to rouse it from its slumber. With the help of Mephistopheles, Faust does all kinds of terrible things, but at the end his soul goes to heaven because he has "striven greatly." Faust's elevation from wicked prankster to world-historic hero reflects the weakening of Christian orthodoxy and its absolute prohibition on evil. It insinuates the heretical thought that in our dealings with the Devil it is *we* who can come off winners.

Goethe's first innovation is to open his play with a "Prologue in Heaven," in which God explains his problem to the demon Mephistopheles. Humanity—made in God's image—has the potential for progress, but is naturally lazy and incurious; "It's so easy for men to slump and before long they want to do nothing at all." So God offers Mephistopheles a deal: he can stay in this world, as opposed to being banished forthwith to the "dust" to which the God of Genesis has consigned the serpent, as long as he continues to keep man active. Mephistopheles sees his chance to capture humanity for a life of sinful pleasure. "I'm not afraid of losing my bet," he tells God, confident that he can lead God's servant Faust astray. Goethe's next innovation is to turn Faust's traditional pact with Mephistopheles into a wager. Instead of the traditional time limit of twenty-four years, Mephistopheles offers Faust his services indefinitely with the right to claim him if they afford Faust full satisfaction. Faust accepts the bet, knowing that the life of pleasure, luxury and power that Mephistopheles offers will never content him. He tells Mephistopheles that if ever he declares himself satisfied with things as they are, he will accept eternal damnation: "If ever the passing moment is such that I wish it not to pass and say to it 'You are so beautiful, stay awhile,' then let that be the finish. The clock can stop. You can put me in chains and ring the death-bell. I shall welcome it and you will be quit of your service." Mephistopheles accepts the terms of the wager, and Faust embarks on his new life: "A whirl of dissipation is what I seek, this and nothing more."[22]

The rest of *Faust* is the working out of the consequences of the double bargain. The theme of the *felix culpa* dominates the action, with each of Faust's crimes a precondition for an improvement in his character. In Part I, Faust is tempted by his love for a simple peasant girl, Gretchen, to "stop the clock." But Mephistopheles, who wants to prolong his stay on earth, sabotages the love affair by offering Faust any woman he wants. When a series of Devil-inspired mishaps causes Gretchen's death, Faust vows he will prove worthy of her love: sin is necessary for redemption.

The idea of the *felix culpa* recurs throughout Part II, where Goethe reworks the magical and fantastical material of Marlowe's play into a developmental narrative. Several years after Gretchen's death, Faust arrives at the court of Charles V. But instead of summoning up the spirit of Alexander the Great for the Emperor's amusement, as in Marlowe, Faust uses sorcery to flood the kingdom with money, allowing the court to finance lavish masques. Goethe's moral is clear: money is only a means to culture. The play ends with the aged Faust installed as the improving landlord of an imperial fiefdom, building dykes and canals to push back the sea. But the progress of his project requires the eviction (which Mephistopheles turns into the murder) of an obstinate old peasant couple, Philemon and Baucis, who refuse to budge from their tiny plot—a clear reference to the eighteenth-century enclosure movement that expelled peasants from their common land. Imagining the completion of his project without the further help of sorcery, Faust exclaims: "Now I could almost say to the passing moment: Stay, oh stay awhile, you are beautiful. The mark of my endeavours will not fade. No, not in ages, not in any time. Dreaming of this incomparable happiness, I now taste and enjoy the supreme moment."[23]

On uttering the fatal words, "I now taste and enjoy the supreme moment," Faust falls dead, as he swore he would if he ever succumbed to satisfaction. This should have been the "end state," the achievement of the earthly paradise to which Faust had latterly aspired. But Goethe evades the conclusion by the trick of putting Faust's expression of satisfaction into the conditional: the Devil can only lead humanity so far; perfection is for heaven. So he divides the spoils between God and Mephistopheles: the Devil gets Faust's body but God gets his soul, because he has striven so mightily.

Goethe himself called Faust "mad stuff"[24] and never tried to explain "what it meant." Like all great poetry, it is both precise and elusive. In philosophical terms, its most important legacy is the dialectic—the idea that progress depends on a continuous "negation" or overturning of traditional morality. This notion, which was to pass from Goethe to Hegel and thence to Marx, has been a fateful legacy to modern thought.

Today we are less disposed to sanction wickedness for the sake of progress. Goethe's Mephistophelean flirtations strike us as hopelessly innocent, the indulgence of an age that had forgotten the reality of evil. "We encountered situations," wrote the German philosopher Karl Jaspers in 1948, "in which we had no inclination to read Goethe, but turned instead to Shakespeare, Aeschylus or the Bible, if indeed we could still read at all."[25] Goethe did not believe in the perfectibility of man, but he did not believe in original sin either. Moreover, he thought that Europe had permanently progressed beyond the age of savagery. He could not otherwise have made Mephistopheles such an amiable demon. To our age, Goethe just does not seem morally serious. This was the implication of Thomas Mann's novel *Doktor Faustus* (1947), which, significantly, reverts to Marlowe's original title and has the Faust figure go insane—the secular equivalent of damnation.

The Failed Apocalypse of Karl Marx

Karl Marx loved Goethe and throughout his work he used the figure of Mephistopheles to strip away the veil that economists since Adam Smith had wrapped round capitalism's Faustian bargain. He revealed capitalism in its true Mandevillean colors, voracious and insatiable. But he also added something not found in Mandeville: the conviction that capitalism's costs are not voluntarily incurred by individuals for their own benefit or that of their families, but forced on them by the power of the capitalist class. Violence was necessary to shatter this power, to establish on earth the kingdom of righteousness. Here, Marx revealed himself heir to the wilder strains of Judeo-Christian apocalyptic, with their visions of "cleansing bloodshed." This gave his Faustian bargain a terror lacking in Goethe and the more peaceable English versions.[26]

Marx's critique of capitalism was fundamentally moral. It was, he thought, too hateful and unjust to survive. It forcibly alienated the worker from his tools of production and hence his specifically human substance, leaving him vulnerable to exploitation. It sacrificed the "productive life of man" to the "money system," use-value to exchange-value. Here Marx was successor to Aristotle and his medieval followers; he was "the last of the schoolmen," as R. H. Tawney called him.

But if capitalism was unjust, it was at the same time the instrument of the people's liberation from poverty. In short, it was another *felix culpa*, a happy sin, part of the working of providence. In a newspaper article of 1853, Marx praised British rule in India for stirring up a stagnant society: "Whatever may have been the crimes of England she was the unconscious tool of history . . ."[27] Moral ambivalence towards capitalism has troubled Marxists ever since. On the one hand, it is an evil to be overthrown; on the other, it is the indispensable instrument of progress.

Hegel's dialectic was the perfect intellectual instrument for resolving Marx's ambivalence towards capitalism. In Hegel's philosophy—really a secularization of Joachim of Flora's—history is the story of the growth of reason. Each partial, incomplete stage of human consciousness, or understanding, produces its negation, or denial, which is absorbed into a more complete, higher level consciousness till the attainment of absolute reason, in which the whole of reality is determined by Mind. Thus the historical mission is "fulfilled unconsciously, despite their crimes and passions, by particular nations or classes."[28]

Marx took up this idea, but, influenced by early political experiences that made him doubt Hegel's claim that the Prussian state was the embodiment of Reason, he turned Hegel's clash of ideas into a clash of classes. History was the story of class conflict: existence determines consciousness, not the other way round. Hegel's successive, antagonistic stages of reason were simply antagonistic systems of property relations. As Marx came to see it, religion, the great enemy for the thinkers of the Enlightenment, was the spiritual veil used by the propertied to blind the propertyless to their true situation.

Marx only worked out one phase of his "dialectical materialism," the transition from feudalism to capitalism.[29] In this story, the increasingly wealthy but politically subordinate "burghers" of the towns become the class of "bourgeoisie," which overturns the land-based manorial system. The bourgeoisie is the first class to exploit labor systematically and use the extracted surplus for capital development rather than luxuries, wars, cathedrals and so forth. But capitalism, in turn, becomes a fetter on the further development of the productive forces, so it must be overthrown by the proletariat it has created, inaugurating the classless reign of communism.

At the technical level, Marx had a problem explaining why capitalism ever *had* to end. It deserved to end; the expropriators deserved to be expropriated. Justice would be denied if this did not happen. But why and how would it end? This was a problem to which Marx devoted most of his life, and he never solved it. There was no way he could prove the coming of the capitalist apocalypse that his biblical sense of justice demanded.

The most coherent expression of Marx's dialectical approach before he became an economist is in the compressed, explosive prose of the *Communist Manifesto* of 1848. No one has portrayed the Faustian character of capitalism more vividly than Marx.* The bourgeoisie has created "more massive and more colossal productive forces than have all preceding generations together."[30] It has drawn "even the most barbarous nations into civilization ... create[d] a world after its own image."[31] But the cost has been horrendous: "All fixed, fast-frozen relations, with their train of ancient and venerable prejudices and opinions, are swept away, all new-formed ones become antiquated before they can ossify. All that is solid melts into air, all that is holy is profaned ..."[32]

Marx was the first economist to give capitalism's destructiveness its proper moral weight. Like Adam Smith and Goethe, he thought of it as the necessary "price" of progress. But because he wrote seventy years after the start of the Industrial Revolution, he understood that both the price and the progress would be much greater than they had imagined. Nonetheless, from Marx's dialectical standpoint, capitalism's unsettling of "fixed, fast-frozen relations" is historically justified, because, by its brutality in unleashing human potential, it is bringing into existence the weapons and the class that will destroy it.

But at this point in the *Communist Manifesto* the thread of argument snaps, and rhetoric takes its place. Echoing Mary Shelley's novel *Frankenstein*, Marx likens capitalism to "the sorcerer, who is no longer able to control the powers of the nether world whom he has called up by his spells."[33] It has created its own "grave-diggers."[34] Belief in the apocalyptic moment never left Marx, despite the repeated failure of history to live up to his expectations. "The knell of capitalist private property sounds," he was to prophesy ringingly in *Das Kapital* twenty years after the *Communist Manifesto*. "The expropriators are expropriated."[35]

The conviction that capitalism was bound to collapse had come to Marx before Marx came to economics. After the *Communist Manifesto* he spent twenty years in the British Museum trying to prove it,

---

* Marx never talked about "capitalism." He used the word "bourgeoisie" to emphasize the class-based character of the capitalist system. But "capitalism" can be substituted without loss of meaning. To be pedantic, capitalism is a system in which the ownership of capital is concentrated in the hands of a single class—the bourgeoisie—which puts it to use for profit.

and never did. In fact, he was not an intuitive economist at all. No one who starts economics at the age of 40 ever is. There is too much other stuff in one's head. Economists have to start innocent of all distracting ideas. They have to have minds sufficiently empty to construct or accept those axiomatic models of human behavior that are their bread and butter. Late adolescence is the ideal time to start such a training.

Marx produced two possible scenarios for the collapse of capitalism, the "crisis of profitability" and the "crisis of realization." The first, and best developed, rests on the exploitation theory that stemmed from his mid-life confrontation with Ricardo. Marx argued that, by robbing workers of everything but their labor power, capitalists were able to extract more value from them than they paid for. This difference represented "surplus value," the source of profits. It seemed to follow that, as machines (which could not be paid less than it cost to install them) increasingly replaced labor in making things, the rate of profit would fall. Attempts to maintain surplus value by increasing the "rate of exploitation" would finally produce that wrathful explosion of the proletariat that would destroy the system. In the later nineteenth century Marxists were nonplussed by the observed tendency of workers' real wages to rise. Something had gone wrong with the theory. What Marx failed to allow for was the possibility of increasing the productivity of labor by investing in labor-saving technology. This would allow an increase in real wages without a decline in the profit rate. There was no need for the rate of profit to fall over time.

The *Communist Manifesto* hints at another source of crisis: the crisis of realization. "In commercial crises a great part of not just products but also of productive capacity is periodically destroyed ... because there is too much civilization, too much industry, too much commerce ... The conditions of bourgeois society are too narrow to comprise the wealth created by them."[36] These inexact phrases, to which Marx never subsequently attached much importance, point to a theory of under-consumption, later developed by the English liberal J. A. Hobson and the German Marxist Rosa Luxemburg. Rosa Luxemburg asked how, given the stagnation of real wages, the manual working class could provide an adequate market for the ever increasing volume of goods being turned out by the new machines. "After all," she reasoned, "the only purpose of investment was to produce things which could be sold at a profit. And if things cannot be sold, why should capitalists keep investing?"[37] Keynes asked the same question in the 1930s, and it remains pertinent in the light of what happened in the first decade of this century, when real wages in Western countries have fallen relative to the returns to capital.

The theory of imperialism was invented to explain the unexpected survival power of the capitalist system. Whereas Lenin saw poor countries as a reservoir for the further exploitation of labor, Luxemburg saw them—together with armaments production—as a vent for extra markets to absorb the surplus of capitalist production over consumption. Whatever one might think about the validity of either explanation, neither points to the collapse of capitalism, rather to its ability to rescue itself from internal crises, notably through globalization. As Marx's modern commentator Meghnad Desai writes, "Marx fails to come up with a single story about the dynamics of capitalism that in any way predicts—even with various conditions attached—its eventual downfall."[38] Realization that his economics failed to establish the apocalyptic moment is probably why Marx never finished the last two volumes of *Das Kapital*.

Given the huge uncertainties surrounding the "fall" of capitalism, it is hardly surprising that Marx failed to give much attention to life after capitalism. His friend and collaborator Friedrich Engels talked about a "kingdom of freedom" that lay beyond the "kingdom of necessity." But Marx refused to bother himself with what he called the "cookshops of the future." In a famous passage from the preface to the *Contribution to the Critique of Political Economy*, he wrote: "No social order ever disappears before all the productive forces for which there is room in it have been developed; and new higher relations of production never appear before the material conditions of their existence have matured in the womb of the old society itself. Therefore, humanity only sets itself such tasks as it can solve."[39] That was his way of dismissing the utopian experiments of his day. His ideas about the coming utopia were equally vague. Human beings, he thought, might "hunt in the morning, fish in the afternoon, rear cattle in the evening, criticize after dinner ... without ever becoming hunter, fisherman, shepherd or critic."[40] Hardly more sensible was Leon Trotsky's prediction that under communism the average human type "will rise to the heights of an Aristotle, a Goethe, or a Marx. And above this ridge new peaks will rise."[41]

Marx presented a compelling case for why capitalism *should* come to an end, not why it *would*. He failed to reckon on the continuing dynamism of the capitalist system, its ability to overcome obstacles. More seriously, Marx was blind to the temptations of dialectical reasoning. It would be a travesty to say that he would have welcomed Stalinism, but his method offered no principled ground for resistance to it, or for that matter to Maoism. Mao is said to have shrugged off the millions of deaths caused by his Great Leap Forward with the callous remark, "Death is indeed to be rejoiced over ... We believe in dialectics, and so we can't not be in favor of death."[42]

The Failed Payoff:
From Marx to Marcuse

In the hundred years following the publication of *Das Kapital* in 1867, revolutionary socialism was vanquished in countries supposedly ripe for it, and victorious in countries that Marx did not think ready for it. By the late 1950s it was capitalism, not socialism, that seemed to have cracked the economic problem in the West: not, to be sure, the capitalism red in tooth and claw analyzed by Marx, but a capitalism so modified by state management, social security and trade-union organization that some doubted whether it was the same animal at all. If this was capitalism, there was no need for socialism.[43] In 1956, John Kenneth Galbraith switched attention to the diseases of wealth. His best-selling work, *The Affluent Society*, argued that the citizens of Western countries were now so well off that the economic problem was no longer pressing. In short, Keynes's era of plenty had arrived (ahead of schedule!). It was time to ease off growth, and turn attention to the good life. Galbraith's idea of this was rather austere: more of the new wealth should be channelled into public services. But his message was absorbed by the young radicals of the 1960s and turned to a more exciting project: that of sexual liberation. Their God was not Marx but Freud.

There was something particularly heady about the 1960s that permanently marked those who *consciously* experienced it at the right age. Although there had been utopian writings and utopian communities in the past, this was the first time in history that utopia moved, briefly, out of the shadows into the light, as both theory and practice. The utopian dream of a life free from toil and trouble, conflict and war, came close to capturing the minds and hearts of a generation of young people. Free love and plenty were features of all folk utopias, and this one was no exception. The hippies were plausible lilies of the field, with flowers in their hair. They rejected the work ethic demanded by scarcity, because the world no longer seemed to need them to work for a living. Sex, drugs, music, mysticism, anti-war protest, revolutionary romanticism got mixed up in an orgiastic moment of liberation. Marijuana was a "truth serum"; "from every erection flew the Red Flag."[44]

The material basis for the sexual utopia was "an uninterrupted stream of comfortably high earnings."[45] This freed the baby-boom generation born in the 1940s from the job insecurity that had plagued their parents. In the twenty-five years after the Second World War not only had the developed world grown at a faster rate than ever before, but growth was much steadier. And even the developing countries seemed to be catching up. The fear of capitalist crisis disappeared.[46] The problem was no longer one of obstacles to the achievement of abundance, but obstacles to the enjoyment of the abundance achieved.

For the philosophers of sexual utopia, the serpent in the Garden was not capitalism as such but technology. Theodore Roszak talked of "technocratic totalitarianism."[47] The specific indulgence of its insanity was the nuclear arms race, which threatened to kill off the world just as it was on the point of regaining paradise. *Dr. Strangelove* is this nightmare's classic filmic encapsulation. Technology, though, was Janus-faced, for it had also liberated man—or at least North American man—from poverty. As Charles Reich put it:

> The crucial point is that technology has made possible that "change in human nature" which has been sought so long but could not come into existence while scarcity stood in the way. It is just this simple: when there is enough food and shelter for all, man no longer needs to base his

society on the assumption that all men are antagonistic to one another. That which we called "human nature" was the work of necessity—the necessity of scarcity and the market system. The new human nature— love and respect—also obeys the laws of necessity. It is necessary because only together can we reap the fruits of the technological age.[48]

Although student protest spread by contagion through all the educational centres of the Western world in the late 1960s, its heartland was the United States.* There were several reasons for this: the American tradition of utopian experiment, the greater prosperity of Americans as compared to Europeans, and the Vietnam War. Perhaps the most important factor was the much higher proportion of young Americans in universities and colleges of higher education. The world of work was further away for many young Americans—five or six years further away—than it was for most young Europeans. This created a psychic discordance between adolescence and work that was enough, in the opinion of some Hegelian philosophers of revolution, to achieve the status of a contradiction. The new Freudian Marxists saw the universities as educational factories breeding a new revolutionary class. The radicalism of the 1960s was a campus phenomenon, theorized and promoted by the professors.

Of these, none was more influential than the émigré philosopher Herbert Marcuse, who proclaimed the new doctrine of erotic liberation with heavy Germanic learning. Marcuse's books *Eros and Civilization* (1955) and *One-Dimensional Man* (1964) became the bibles of student protest. His phrase "repressive tolerance" defined for radicals the particular quality of American civilization. Like Marx, Marcuse was in the tradition of Jewish messianism in which "all discussion of real and authentic human values is reduced to eschatology" and that "opens the door to an impenitent and optimistic utopia, which cannot be described in terms of concepts based on an unredeemed world."[49]

Despite his often impenetrable prose, Herbert Marcuse was a playful devil. The only truly progressive attitude, he said, was one of denial.

---

* The revolt of the young against their parents' values was not confined to students, but the political radicalism of the 1960s was.

"That which is cannot be true" was one of his *mots*. Since the given facts that appear to common sense as the truth are in fact the negation of the truth, the truth can only be discovered by the "negation of the negation." "Critical theory" was his tool of emancipation from conventional wisdom. One student who attended his classes at the University of San Diego in California wrote that "Marcuse has the unique talent of making Kant, Hegel, and Marx relevant to a student body that looks like the cast of one of Hollywood's teen-age beach movies."[50]

Eros and Civilization offered a Freudian interpretation of Western civilization, but without Freud's pessimism. What Freud had called the "death instinct" was not inherent in human nature, but in its repression, and particularly its "surplus repression" by Western capitalism. This repression had now been rendered redundant by the automation of work, though it was still perpetuated by the powerful, whose interests it served. Resexualization was thus the key to the revolution. Humanity needed to return to the infant state of "polymorphous perversity," in which the entire body is the source of erotic pleasure, so as to destroy the psychology of repression on which capitalism rests.

By the time he wrote *One-Dimensional Man*, Marcuse's hope of revolution had faded. "The containment of social change is perhaps the most singular achievement of advanced industrial society," he wrote. "Consumerism, advertising, mass culture, and ideology" had integrated individuals into the capitalist order and effectively destroyed any prospect of "critical philosophy."[51] Modern society no longer needed terror, it had technology.

One-Dimensional Man portrays a nightmare world of "happy consciousness" that rivals dystopias like *Brave New World* except it is set in contemporary America. Technology gives each instinct a limited, administered expression. Oppositional thought no longer needs to be suppressed: it does not happen. Culture is assimilated to shopping. Deviations are consigned to psychiatrists. The point is that this is a happy world, one of what Marcuse calls "repressive de-sublimation," repressive "precisely to the degree to which it promotes the satisfaction of needs which require continuing the rat race of catching up with one's peers and with planned obsolescence ..."[52] Liberation is no longer sought, because it has been delivered in beautiful gift wrappings. War goes on but only "outside"—in underdeveloped countries.

In the world of happy consciousness, the social basis for change has disappeared. The working class has become a prop of the established order; absolute refusal is "politically impotent." Automation might free people from work, but technology still controls their minds. In *Eros and Civilization*, Marcuse had celebrated the "critical" function of "sexual perversions" like homosexuality. "Sexual deviance represents . . . a protest against genital tyranny."[53] But the later volume dropped this theme: "perversions" had become part of the new normal. There was no escape.

Or was there? "Underneath the conservative popular base is the substratum of the outcasts and outsiders, the exploited and persecuted of other races and other colors, the unemployed and unemployables."[54] This is the new spectre of revolution. But it is a much feebler one than Marx conjured up to alarm his bourgeois readers. Marcuse ends: "It is nothing but a chance."

We know of course that no sexual utopia was established. This is not surprising. Utopias are perfected societies: they will never come to being in this world. It is more interesting to consider why more progress was not made towards realizing the dreams of the sexual utopians.

The most obvious reason was the failure of Western economies to sustain the promise of general abundance. In practice, the protest movements of the 1960s were rapidly followed by the collapse of the Keynesian state on which the expectations of imminent abundance had been built. This killed off utopianism. Marcuse became a museum piece in the West (though not in Latin America) even before his death. The world of insecure work returned; the trend to more equal income distribution was reversed; creative destruction was back. Under Reagan and Thatcher capitalism recovered much of its old piratical, buccaneering spirit, and the dream of instinctual liberation from a springboard of managed affluence receded.

But even if growth had continued at the old pace, the utopianism of the 1960s was bound to fail. Marcuse himself came to recognize capitalism's capacity to "contain" social change. The sex, drugs and rock and roll culture of the young proved entirely compatible with the continuation of existing relations of dominance, albeit in a modified way. Capitalism, as it turned out, was very successful at commercializing the sexual revolution, absorbing it and turning it into reliably sellable products. Violence, whether criminal or revolutionary, has become a standard part of the entertainment industry. The capitalist system has displayed enormous capacity to absorb punishment without being toppled. It is like a great punching bag that, however much it is hammered, always comes back at you, not necessarily in the same shape but recognizably of the same substance.

Nevertheless, Marcuse's choice of the word "containment" prejudges the case. Containment also involves pluralism. Liberal democratic societies give shelter to many actors opposed to the love of gain. To Marcuse (as to Marxist intransigents), social democratic governments and trade unions were all part of the same repressive system, which had to be negated *in toto*. Similarly, Marcuse failed to give anything like proper weight to the qualitative differences between fascism and democracy and the scale of their respective horrors. His overemphasis on the "death wish" was, of course, heavily influenced by the actual Nazi Holocaust and the threat of a nuclear holocaust. His most ironic passages on the "happy consciousness" are about nuclear shelters equipped with fitted carpets and the clutter of a consumerist society.

Marcuse's fundamental error was that of all utopians: he closed his eyes to the obvious fact of "original sin." It was this that allowed him to view all the evils attendant on sex—jealousy, pornography, sadism and so forth—as products of its repression by capitalism. Remove that repression, and sex would revert automatically to the condition of childlike innocence. This was a facile philosophy, which Freud himself never embraced. Sexual desire is bound up at its source with power and vulnerability, meaning that its regulation is not a transitory phenomenon but a basic condition of any civilized existence.

Marcuse overlooked the depth not only of lust but of greed. Like other Marxists, he thought that the multiplication of wants was forced upon us by an evil productive apparatus. We had only to free ourselves from this apparatus, and our wants would shrink back to their "natural" level. He failed to see that wants will multiply of their own accord, unless held in check by moral discipline. The hedonism of the 1960s led naturally to the consumerism of the 1980s.

Capitalism, we have argued, was founded on a Faustian pact. The devils of avarice and usury were given free rein, on the understanding that, having lifted humanity out of poverty, they would quit the scene for good. A paradise of plenty would ensue, with all men free to live as only the happy few had lived. Versions of the myth can be found in Marx, Mill, Marcuse and others. Timetables and mechanisms varied, but all agreed that, sooner or later, in one way or another, the happy hour would come. To what end, otherwise, was the toil, squalor and deformation of feeling? Capitalism needed its radiant vision; without it, its humiliations were intolerable.

However, as fairy tales tell us, the Devil honors his promise in letter only, not in spirit. True, we are richer now than ever, and, true, working hours have declined, if not to the level foreseen by Keynes. But the paradise of plenty has not come. Relentless pursuit of material advantage—Mill's "trampling, crushing, elbowing, and treading on each other's heels"—remains our lot for the foreseeable future. The tunnel of economic necessity, which was to lead out into the daylight of economic bliss, looms without end.

Keynes's error, we suggested in Chapter 1, was to assume that material wants are naturally finite. It was for this reason, and this reason only, that he could tolerate the spectacle of their unbridled indulgence: he believed that they would one day be fully satisfied, leaving us free for "higher things." We now know better. Experience has taught us that material wants know no natural bounds, that they will expand without end unless we consciously restrain them. Capitalism rests precisely on this endless expansion of wants. That is why, for all its success, it remains so unloved. It has given us wealth beyond measure, but has taken away the chief benefit of wealth: the consciousness of having enough.

The thinkers of the pre-modern world were free from such illusions. Like Keynes, they saw acquisition as having an inherent end or goal, but, unlike Keynes, they did not envisage it grinding obligingly to a halt once that goal was reached. They knew that the accumulative impulse tends always to excess, that keeping it in bounds is a work of will. They had no thought of releasing it from moral restraints, for they saw no "dialectic" to turn it to good effect. Ancient wisdom was unanimous on this point. Even Epicurus, the arch-hedonist, thought that pleasure was best achieved by suppressing all unnecessary desires, including the desire for wealth. His advice is overlooked by most modern hedonists, inheritors of the romantic cult of excess.

Pre-Enlightenment economic thought is often dismissed as a hotchpotch of bigotry and ignorance. But the failure of the modern age to make good its utopian promise casts it in a kindlier light. Capitalism, it is now clear, has no spontaneous tendency to evolve into something nobler. Left to itself, the machinery of want-generation will carry on churning, endlessly and pointlessly. Let us revisit, then, those half-forgotten pre-modern figures, for it may be they who hold the key to our contemporary predicament.

3

The Uses of Wealth

Who is rich? He who desires nothing. Who is poor?
The miser.

—Ausonius

Before the Faustian project took wing, thinking about wealth was governed by the idea of limits. The exact location of these limits was disputed, but their existence was never in doubt. Virgil, Machiavelli and St. Francis could all agree on this point, whatever else their differences. Writers from as far afield as India and China could also agree on it, as we shall see.

Aristotle is the classic source of pre-modern economic thought, for two reasons. First, unlike his more radical predecessor Plato, he did not try to conjure a social ideal out of pure reason. His goal was simply to organize the opinions of his educated contemporaries, to forge them into a system. Joseph Schumpeter's description of his economic writings as "decorous, pedestrian, slightly mediocre, and more than slightly pompous common sense" is a caricature, but not a complete distortion.[1] Second, and related to this, Aristotle was the dominant influence on all economic theorizing from the twelfth to the seventeenth century. He created a framework of ideas that was to survive, with various modifications, until its replacement by the equally imposing edifice of Adam Smith.

"Aristotle's economic writings" is of course an anachronism. Aristotle knew of no such thing as economics. He knew of *oikonomikē*, the word from which "economics" is derived, but that was the art of household management and included such things as viniculture and the punishment of slaves. What we now know as Aristotle's economics is culled from two sections of his *Politics* and *Nicomachean Ethics*, dealing with acquisition and exchange respectively. The focus of these discussions is overridingly ethical and political; commerce is presented as an aspect of our life in common, subject like all other aspects to justice and its sister virtues. There was no economics for Aristotle because there was no *economy*—no distinct social sphere with its autonomous laws of motion.

Aristotle's innocence of the "the economic" as a category is hardly surprising. Athens in the fourth century BC was still an overwhelmingly agricultural society. The basic unit of production was the household, consisting of a head, his family and dependants, slaves and the occasional hired hand. Most households were self-sufficient. Production for exchange was small-scale and limited to certain kinds of goods. Money was widespread, but there was very little capital or credit. Owners of coin simply buried it in the ground. In a society of this type, acts of trading and lending were naturally understood in personal terms, as cases of friendly or unfriendly conduct. The specifically commercial motive was not unknown, but was regarded as a sinister anomaly, not as a normal part of social functioning. The ethical perspective was all-encompassing.*

The first principle of Aristotle's ethical thought is that man, like all species, has a *telos*, a state of fulfilment or completion. Aristotle identifies this *telos* with the good life, the *euzēn*, for this is the only thing of which it makes no sense to ask, "What is it for?" Life has no goal beyond its own perfection; to sacrifice this perfection to some distant object—to revolution, say, or the success of the corporate brand—is foolish or worse. But this is not a licence for self-indulgence. The hobo in the song who dreams of a world where hens lay soft-boiled eggs and alcohol streams from the rocks is not aspiring to a good life in Aristotle's sense. The good life is not simply one of satisfied desire; it indicates the proper *goal* of desire. Desire is to be cultivated, directed

---

* This interpretation is controversial. We are here following the so-called primitivist school, which sees a radical gulf between the ancient economy and modern capitalism. See Scott Meikle, *Aristotle's Economic Thought* (Oxford: Clarendon Press, 1995), a work to which we are greatly indebted.

to the truly desirable. Moral education is an education of the sentiments.

Today, with ethical debate dominated by the champions of duty on one side and subjective self-expression on the other, Aristotle's idea of the good life has few defenders. To the party of duty, it appears self-centered and preening. "My obligation is not to lead a good life," an environmental activist might say, "but to save the planet." And to the party of self-expression, it appears horribly paternalistic, if not meaningless. Surely "the good life" is something to be worked out by each individual for himself, according to his own tastes and convictions. "I did it my way," sings Frank Sinatra, and we applaud. These two principles, duty and self-expression, between them carve up the modern moral life, the one governing our dealings with fellow citizens, the other our private explorations. No space remains for the good life.

In the ancient world, by contrast, the question of how best to live was at the very center of ethical debate. Answers to it ranged from the political activism of Pericles through to the philosophical quietism of Epicurus and his followers. Aristotle's contribution to this debate is typically conciliatory. He is as generous as he can be to the ethic of civic and military honor, but comes down finally on the side of philosophy—a way of life full of pleasures "amazing in purity and stability."[2] (Aristotle clearly had no inkling of modern academic philosophy.) What matters here, though, is not so much the details of this debate as two assumptions shared by all its participants. These are (a) that some one way of life *is* better than others, independent of taste or conviction, and (b) that this best way of life is one of leisure. Work for the ancient Greeks was strictly a means to an end, so not even a contender for the title of good life. Only activities without extrinsic purpose—above all philosophy and politics, both conceived non-instrumentally—could make it onto the short list. These attitudes were to leave a long legacy, as we shall see.

The good life, argues Aristotle, requires not only the various excellences of character and intellect (courage, moderation, generosity, wisdom and others) but also the "external goods" necessary to realize these excellences. "No man can live well, or indeed live at all, unless he be provided with necessaries."[3] Aristotle is thinking of such things as land for farming, slaves to work it, housing, clothes, furniture and so forth—"use-values," as Marxists say. The precise nature and number of these use-values depends on the type of life they are called on to support. A political life needs somewhat more, a philosophical life somewhat less. But no version of the good life can dispense with them entirely, as Socrates' more austere followers claimed; and any version of it, austere or splendid, implies a proper limit to their pursuit. One only needs so many coats, beds, houses, etc.; to continue hoarding after this point, like Imelda Marcos and her 2,700 pairs of shoes, is simply crazed. The just and temperate person accumulates just those things he needs for a good life, and then stops.

Alongside use-value, however, possessions have another kind of value, which lies in their capacity to be exchanged. The relation of use-value to "exchange-value"—as we can call it, again following Marx—causes Aristotle much headache.* Use-values are heterogeneous and incommensurable. A bed and a pig contribute to the good life in very different ways: the one is for sleeping in, the other for eating. A bed can be better than another bed, but it makes no obvious sense to say that a bed is better than a pig, still less that it is five times better. Yet whenever we exchange a bed for a pig, or value them both in monetary terms, we presuppose just such a common measure. This transformation of the "unequal" into the "equal" is a mystery Aristotle never finally resolves, nor indeed can resolve, given his premises. Exchange remains a metaphysical scandal, a violation of the qualitative uniqueness of things. Many subsequent thinkers have felt a similar disquiet. The German sociologist Georg Simmel lamented "the reduction of the concrete values of life to the mediating value of money."[4] Keynes too was a true Aristotelian in his preference for "shops which are really shops and not merely a branch of the multiplication table."[5]

Aristotle is not so radical as to condemn exchange outright, for all its metaphysical impropriety. He accepts what he calls the "natural art of wealth-getting"—the art of supplying households and states with the good things of life. Problems arise, however, when this natural kind of wealth-getting runs over into another, unnatural kind. Money is the

---

* It is not an accident that Marx's terminology fits Aristotle's account so well. Marx was deeply influenced by Aristotle.

serpent in the Garden, for it suggests the possibility, unknown to barter, of buying things, not in order to use them but to sell them on for *more*. Originally and properly a means of exchange, money soon becomes an end in itself, with use-values degraded to means. Houses, farms and utensils are stripped of their true purpose and converted into so many indifferent repositories of monetary value. This perversion of means into ends and ends into means reaches its climax with usury, "which makes a gain out of money itself, and not from the natural object of it."[6]

Two aspects of this process particularly trouble Aristotle. The first is its power to subordinate the proper end of every human activity to the ancillary end of money-making. "Some men turn every quality or art into a means of getting wealth."[7] The results of this corruption are evident across the board: doctors think only of their fee; soldiers fight only for pay; sophists trade wisdom for gain. Craftsmanship also suffers. Aristotle singles out the "Delphian knife," a shoddy article designed for both cutting and hammering and no good at either. (The sofa-bed might be a modern equivalent.) Aristotle's point is that things done primarily for profit and not for their own sake are liable to be done badly, or as badly as possible consistent with retaining custom. If the business of General Motors is making money, not cars, as its CEO Thomas Murphy once remarked, then discerning car lovers had better shop elsewhere.

Aristotle's second concern is with insatiability. Use-values have, as we have seen, a controlling end: the good life. To pursue them beyond this point is senseless. Money, by contrast, has no controlling end. As a blank, all-purpose instrument, its uses are as multifarious as human desire itself, and as limitless. If there is good reason to progress from £1,000 to £10,000, then there is equally good reason to progress to £10,000 to £100,000. Of course, concrete goods can also be accumulated without end, but such behavior is either clearly irrational (viz. Mrs. Marcos) or else a sign that the goods in question are being treated as stores of monetary value. Money is the one thing of which there is never enough, for the simple reason that the concept "enough" has no logical application to it. There is perfect health and happiness, but there is no perfect wealth.

Aristotle's worries about insatiability were widely shared in ancient

Greece. "No bounds to riches have been fixed for man," declared the poet and lawgiver Solon. The legendary King Midas was granted power to turn all he touched into gold, with the result that he starved to death in the midst of luxury—a striking image of the sacrifice of use- to exchange-value. Aristophanes' play *Wealth* deals wittily with the same theme. "Nobody ever has his fill of you," says Chremylus to Plutus, the god of money.

> Anything else one can have too much of—for example, love, or bread, or culture, or dried fruit, or honour, or cakes, or valour, or figs, or ambition, or barley buns, or power, or soup. But no one ever has enough of you. If a man has eighty thousand drachmas, he's all the more set on getting a hundred thousand; and once he's got that, he says life's not worth living unless he makes a quarter of a million.[8]

Mistrust of the boundless and infinite was characteristic of ancient Greek thought in general, astronomy and mathematics included. Aristotle held that the stars, as perfect bodies, must follow a circular, that is, a finite motion. Pythagoras hated the irrational numbers so much that he is said to have murdered their unfortunate discoverer. The Greeks had yet to discover the romance of infinite tasks and boundless yearnings, of which modern capitalism is just one striking manifestation. They were a supremely "un-Faustian" people.

All ancient Greek philosophers shared Aristotle's insistence on limiting wants to needs, though their interpretation of those needs varied widely. At one extreme was Diogenes of Sinope, the fourth-century BC Cynic, who lived in a barrel and threw away his only bowl after seeing a child drink water from his bare hands. (Asked by Alexander the Great whether he could do anything for him, Diogenes is said to have replied: "Yes, get out of my sunlight.") Diogenes' contemporary Epicurus was a more amiable ascetic. A vegetarian and teetotaller rather than the "epicure" of popular legend, he taught that pleasure lies not so much in the satisfaction of desire as in its reduction to a bare minimum. His followers gathered in a garden, far from the bustle of the marketplace, where they passed their time in conversation and learning.

Philosophical contempt for riches migrated from ancient Greece to Rome, where it merged with the tradition of Republican austerity mentioned in the last chapter. Denunciations of *avaritia* (avarice) and *luxuria* (luxury) became part of the standard arsenal of satire, alongside accusations of sexual excess. "Neither burning heat, nor winter, fire, sea, sword, can turn you aside from gain," declaimed Horace to the miser. "Nothing stops you, until no second man be richer than yourself."[9] Roman philosophers of all schools extoled *parsimonia* or frugality; the unphilosophical, meanwhile, were held in check by sumptuary laws. The governing model was dietary: just as we must train ourselves to stop eating once we are full, so we must school ourselves, individually and collectively, to stop accumulating once we have enough.

What would Aristotle and other ancient philosophers make of our modern predicament? Individual cases of avarice and extravagance would not surprise them; the ancient world had its share of Midases and Croesuses. Nor would they be surprised by the dynamic of want-creation outlined in Chapter 1; this too existed in the ancient world, if on a much smaller scale. But they would be astonished beyond measure that we view such things, not as vile deformations, but as a normal and indispensable part of the social mechanism, even as marks of vitality. Aristotle knew of insatiability only as a personal vice; he had no inkling of the collective, politically orchestrated insatiability that we call growth. The civilization of *toujours plus*, as the French philosopher Bertrand de Jouvenel termed it, would have struck him as moral and political madness.

Economic Attitudes
in Europe and Asia

Aristotle is often, and with some reason, dismissed as the ideologist of a slave-owning oligarchy. His vision of the good life is very much of its time and place. It has no room for the joys of nature, of solitude, of artistic creation or religious ecstasy, for all the things that Christianity and romanticism have taught us to appreciate. And of course it is reserved for Greek gentlemen; women, barbarians and slaves are excluded. How can this apologia for the social order of fourth-century BC Athens hold any interest for us today?

Such criticisms of Aristotle are all very well, but they miss what is deepest and most enduring in his thought. Aristotle's vision of the good life may be parochial, but his assumption that there *is* a good life, and that money is merely a means to its enjoyment, has been shared by every great world civilization except our own. By articulating this assumption rigorously, Aristotle created an intellectual framework adaptable to widely differing ethical ideals. Followers of Judaism, Christianity and Islam were all able to make use of this framework; parallels to it can even be found in civilizations as radically alien to the West as India and China. In the face of this massive agreement, it is our own devotion to accumulation as an end in itself that stands out as an anomaly, as something requiring explanation.

The birth of Christianity signalled a shift, not a revolution in economic attitudes. Christ's call to consider the lilies of the field could easily be assimilated to classical denunciations of avarice and luxury. Christians differed from their pagan forebears only insofar as they viewed world-rejection as a collective project, not an expression of personal independence. *Agapē*, or brotherly love, replaced *autarkia*, or self-sufficiency, as the motive for renunciation. Christians also had a special tenderness for the poor, the "inheritors of the earth," and a quasi-ritual horror of money, filthy lucre.[10] It was money, after all, that had tempted Judas to betray Christ. But such anti-commercialism fell well within the normal range of classical and Jewish sentiment. The real novelty of Christianity lay elsewhere.

Christianity's debt to the classical past is nowhere more evident than in the famous dualism of *vita activa* and *vita contemplativa*: the active life and the contemplative life. The contrast between these two ideals was, as we have seen, central to much ancient debate, but it was medieval Christianity that fixed it with typological precision. Firm precedence was now given to the *vita contemplativa*, identified with monasticism, while the worldly *vita activa* fell automatically into second place. Work, meanwhile, remained the province of the menial "third estate." The Middle Ages thus inherited both classical assumptions outlined above, namely, that a certain way of life is good in itself, and that it is not one of work. It differed from the ancient world only in its dogmatic certainty as to what the good life actually is.

These continuities between the ancient and medieval worlds

ensured that, when the works of Aristotle returned to Christian Europe via Muslim Spain in the early thirteenth century, they found minds ready to receive them. "The desire for material things as they are conducive to an end is natural to man," runs a quintessentially Aristotelian passage from St. Thomas Aquinas's *Summa Theologica*. "Therefore it is without fault to the extent that it is confined within the norms set by the nature of that end. Avarice exceeds these limits and is thereby sinful."[11] Needless to say, the Angelic Doctor had a conception of the "end" that was very different from that of Aristotle, and hence a different (and more modest) conception of the goods required to support it. But structurally speaking, the two accounts are identical. Both agree that the *telos* of human life imposes limits on the pursuit of wealth, and both recognize powerful forces in human nature tending to exceed these limits.

Above all, it was Aristotle's condemnation of usury that captured the medieval mind. At the heart of his argument is a play on words: interest (*tokos*) is so called because it is the offspring (*tokos*) of money. But since money is by nature sterile, to make it breed is unnatural and hateful. This vision of interest as a kind of monstrous birth proved irresistible to the theological imagination. "Repeatedly, by the most vile cunning of usury, gold is born from gold itself," runs a typical passage from Gratian's twelfth-century corpus of canon law. "Never is there satisfaction; never will there be an end in sight for the greedy."[12] As a perversion of the procreative instinct, usury was often coupled with sodomy. Dante placed sinners of both types together in the seventh circle of his hell. Meanwhile, figures representing avarice and usury—grim, squat men clasping moneybags, often hook-nosed, sometimes excreting coins—sprang up in manuscripts and cathedrals across Europe. All this was grotesque, certainly, but not without a grain of psychological truth. Throughout the ages, artists and writers have contrasted the artificial productiveness of money with the natural fertility of the womb. It is poetically apt that Midas, in Nathaniel Hawthorne's version of the legend, should turn his own daughter into gold. Henceforth, his only "offspring" will be monetary.

Rhetoric aside, however, the basic tendency of late medieval Christianity was towards reconciliation with commerce. This was the first great era of capitalist expansion, and the Church was powerless to restrain it. The doctrines of usury and the just price were progressively qualified and diluted, falling finally into disuse. Yet unlike its Protestant counterparts, the Catholic Church never entirely abandoned the project of subordinating economic activity to a higher purpose. "The feeling was never quite overcome," writes Max Weber, "that activity directed to acquisition for its own sake was at bottom a *pudendum* which was to be tolerated only because of the unalterable necessities of life in this world."[13] An economic order subservient to human ends—one in which riches exist for man, not man for riches, as St. Antoninus of Florence put it—remains the goal of Catholic economic thought to this day.

No purely secular discussion of the good life took place in ancient India, a culture in which ethical questions were not sharply distinguished from ritual and religious ones.* Nonetheless, a clear set of attitudes to wealth and trade emerge from the Dharmasūtras, the ancient law codes of the Brahmins—attitudes not unlike those we have already encountered in Aristotle and the Scholastics. The Dharmasūtras speak of three aims in life: *dharma* (law or righteousness), *artha* (wealth) and *kama* (pleasure). All three are good, but not equally so: *dharma* is to be preferred to *artha*, *artha* to *kama*. Severe penances are enjoined for the man "who, when Law (*dharma*) and profit (*artha*) are in conflict, chooses profit." Almost as bad is the exploitation of *dharma* as a means to *artha*. "Let him not follow the Laws for the sake of worldly benefits," runs the text, "for then the Laws produce no fruit at harvest time. It is like this. A man plants a mango tree to get fruits, but in addition he obtains also shade and fragrance. In like manner, when a man follows the Law, he obtains, in addition, other benefits. Even if he does not obtain them, at least no harm is done to the Law."[14] We are reminded of Aristotle's scorn for men "who turn every quality or art into a means of getting wealth." Like Aristotle, the Dharmasūtras are anxious to protect the integrity of

* Ancient India did not lack a secular intellectual life, as Amartya Sen has recently reminded us (in *The Argumentative Indian* [London: Allen Lane, 2005]). There were important achievements in mathematics, astronomy, metaphysics and logic, as well as treatises on administration written from a secular standpoint. Yet ethical as opposed to theoretical and political thought remained closely intertwined with myth and ritual.

higher ends against money's relativizing power—its capacity to make everything tradable with everything else.

This conception of a hierarchy of ends, with wealth in subordinate position, is also implicit in the caste structure of ancient India. The Dharmasūtras list four castes in order of precedence: first, the priestly Brahmins; next Kshatriyas, warriors and kings; third Vaishyas, farmers and merchants; and fourth, Sudras, laborers and artisans. How far this hierarchy ever corresponded to social reality is debated, but, as the ideal self-image of traditional Hindu civilization, it has always exercised an important normative influence.

The Indian caste system embodies a social vision strikingly similar to the three estates of medieval Europe. In both cases, there is a rank ordering of classes, with priests in first place, warriors in second, and workers in third. The main difference between the two lies in the position of merchants: in India, they rank above peasants; in Europe, their status is undetermined.[15] But there is perfect agreement as to the inferiority of work *in general* compared to both religious contemplation and political action. Brahmins are permitted to farm or trade only in times of need and are forbidden to lend money at interest altogether.* Their duty is to support themselves by teaching and officiating at sacrifices, or else to become hermits or wandering ascetics. That, at any rate, was the ideal; in reality, the Brahmins' monopoly of ritual power enabled them, like their monastic counterparts in Europe, to become immensely rich. But a neglected ideal is an ideal nonetheless. The presence at the apex of the caste system of a nominally ascetic and contemplative class prevented the emergence of an openly commercial world-view along Western lines. Money could never be the ultimate arbiter of value in India, however much weight it might carry in practice.

Finally, the Dharmasūtras echo the familiar Western concern with insatiability. The desire for wealth is as tenacious as the desire for life itself, and as vain: "As a man gets old his hair and teeth show signs of age. The yearning for life and wealth, however, shows no sign of aging even as a man grows old. Yearning! Fools find it difficult to give up.

---

* The Dharmasūtras are divided on the subject of interest. The Dharmasūtras of Apastamba, Baudhayana and Vasistha forbid it; that of Gautama permits it.

It does not weaken with age. It is a lifelong disease. A man who gives it up finds happiness."[16] Here, however, the parallel between West and East breaks down. For the Western tradition, avarice is a perversion or misdirection of desire; for the Brahmins, it is an expression of the slavery inherent in desire itself. Thus, while Aristotle and Aquinas counsel us to proportion desire to its object, the Hindu scriptures urge us to extinguish it altogether. "He who is without desire, who is freed from desire . . .—he goes to Brahma."[17] This ideal, better known to us under its Buddhist name of *nirvana*, bears some resemblance to the Stoic concept of *apatheia* or tranquillity, but is otherwise without parallel in the West.

India and China have often appeared, to lazy European eyes, as bearers of a common "oriental wisdom." In reality, the two civilizations were almost as alien to each other as each was to the West. The high culture of old China, like that of Greece and Rome, and unlike that of Brahminical India, was unified and this-worldly. It was thus able to produce something like an "ethics" in the Western sense—a free, rational inquiry into the human good. Where Chinese thinkers differed from both their Western *and* Indian counterparts was in their indifference to logic. The epigram, fragmentary and poetic, was their preferred mode of expression. They had no patience for those long, involved chains of reasoning beloved of the Scholastics and the Indian metaphysicians.[18]

China also differed from both the West and India in its lack of—indeed, its deep mistrust of—the ascetic impulse. Here there was no stigma attached to trade or usury, no religious contempt for the pursuit of wealth. On the contrary, money was frankly and (in our residually Christian eyes) shamelessly celebrated. This gulf in attitudes remains palpable today. Shops and restaurants across China are decorated with images of the god of wealth and the jolly, pot-bellied Buddha, so very different from his austere Indian prototype. Money is given to children in pretty red envelopes and pinned festively to shrines and idols. Strangest of all, from a Western perspective, is the Chinese custom of burning "spirit money" for the use of souls in paradise. We can be sure that no filthy lucre exchanges hands in the heavenly Jerusalem.

But for all its plutophilia, old China was not a civilization devoted to accumulation for its own sake. Here too, if less explicitly than in Europe and India, the pursuit of wealth was subordinated to ideal ends. For the Confucian literati, wealth was a means to education and public office; for philosophically inclined Taoists, it bought leisure for the cultivation of experience.* These two ideals correspond roughly to the Western *vita activa* and *vita contemplativa*, only they were seen not as rivals or members of a hierarchy but as belonging to separate, complementary spheres of life. "In office, a Confucian, in retirement, a Taoist," runs a well-known Chinese saying. A logical contradiction was thus resolved into aesthetic harmony, a typically Chinese solution.

Confucius's ideal was that of the educated official. The "gentleman," as his term is usually translated, should study calligraphy, music, poetry and above all *li*, the rules of ritual propriety, so as to be able to serve the state with integrity and wisdom. All-round cultivation, not technical expertise, is his goal. "A gentleman," as Confucius famously put it, "is not an instrument."[19] The Confucian ideal of learned dilettantism was later enshrined in the imperial examination, the sole route to public office from 605 to 1905. This monument to bureaucratic centralism ensured that for over a thousand years the highest offices of state went to men steeped in ancient poetry and philosophy and little else besides—an important factor in the collapse of China during the final years of the Qing.

The education of a Confucian scholar-official was no small undertaking. Decades were required to memorize the classics and to master the intricacies of the "eight-legged" essay, and even then success was rare. Nevertheless, to get a son through the exam was the dream of every merchant and gentry family, for public office ranked immeasurably higher than any private situation, however remunerative. "The ten thousand careers are all base," runs a well-known proverb; "only studying is high." Here again is the notion, already encountered in the West and India, of a qualitative gulf between "higher" and "lower" ways of life, a gulf unbridgeable by any quantity of money. Needless to say, in reality state office was often sought less for its intrinsic luster than for the opportunities it offered for graft, while education was

---

* Buddhism is usually counted as the third traditional teaching of China, but in terms of its influence on the culture at large, it can be grouped together with Taoism.

viewed merely as a tedious outlay. Nonetheless, the *ideal* of the disinterested scholar-official remained perpetually bright, ensuring that commercial values could never dominate Chinese society entirely.

When the Chinese mandarin was ousted from office, as he often was, he turned for consolation to the alternative Taoist tradition. If Confucianism is sober and realistic, Taoism is poetic and idealistic. "Ah, this floating life, like a dream," runs a line of the poet Li Bai. "True happiness is so rare!"[20] The Taoist mood is wistful, not tragic, though, for even if nothing endures, moments of beauty can still be wrested from the flux. To savor such moments is the Taoist art of life. Its spirit is nicely captured in the "thirty-three happy instants" recorded by the seventeenth-century critic Jin Shengtan while cooped up for a few days with a friend in a temple. Here are five:

> I have nothing to do after a meal and try to go through the things in some old trunks. I see there are dozens or hundreds of I.O.U.s from people who owe my family money. Some of them are dead and some still living, but in any case there is no hope of their returning the money. Behind people's backs, I put them together in a pile and make a bonfire of them, and I look up to the sky and see the last trace of smoke disappear. Ah, is this not happiness?
>
> I wake up in the morning and seem to hear some one in the house sighing and saying that last night some one died. I immediately ask to find out who it is, and learn that it is the sharpest, most calculating fellow in town. Ah, is this not happiness?
>
> To cut with a sharp knife a bright green watermelon on a big scarlet plate of a summer afternoon. Ah, is this not happiness?
>
> To open the window and let a wasp out of the room. Ah, is this not happiness?
>
> To see someone's kite line broken. Ah, is this not happiness?[21]

Here is a vision of the good life unlike any we have looked at so far. Jin's list reflects no philosophical or religious ideal, no striving after self-perfection or self-sacrifice. It is just a record of a few inconsequential moments of bliss—some generous, some whimsical, some downright *schadenfreudig*. It would be another two centuries before romanticism would teach Western readers to let their minds wander as freely and aimlessly as this.

The experiences listed by Jin cost little or no money, and this fact is important to their appeal. Had Jin written about the delights of bear-paw soup or mutton-fat jade he would strike us as merely exotic. It is because he writes about basic, universal things that he comes over as human. Taoism, like Epicureanism, was a philosophy of simple pleasures. Its ideal was the *yinshi* or hermit, the man who withdraws from society to write poetry or paint or simply drink tea with old friends. The *yinshi* was no ascetic, though. Fishermen and herders might decorate his paintings, but there could be no question of him taking up such menial occupations himself. In China, as elsewhere, rustic poverty was to be meditated on, not lived.

Ancient Chinese literature contains nothing quite as precise as Aristotle's discussion of the corrupting effects of money, but the underlying idea was expressed with great panache by the first-century BC historian, Sima Qian:

> The desire for wealth does not need to be taught; it is an integral part of all human nature. Hence, when young men in the army attack cities and scale back walls, break through the enemy lines and drive back the foe . . . it is because they are spurred on by the prospect of rich reward . . . In like manner, when the women of Chao and the maidens of Cheng paint their faces and play upon the large lute, flutter their long sleeves and trip about in pointed slippers, invite with their eyes and beckon with their hearts, considering it no distance at all to travel a thousand miles to meet a patron, not caring whether he is old or young, it is because they are after riches . . . When officials in the government juggle with phrases and twist the letter of the law, carve fake seals and forge documents, heedless of the mutilating punishments of the knife and saw that await them if they are discovered, it is because they are drowned in bribes and gifts . . . Thus men apply all their knowledge and use all their abilities simply in accumulating money. They never have any strength left over to consider the question of giving some of it away.[22]

Like Aristotle and the Dharmasūtras, Sima is appalled by money's power to twist all human enterprises to its own purpose. And, as a good Confucian, he is particularly upset to see public service reduced to the level of prostitution and warfare. Yet at the same time, he seems to think that there is little to be done about all this, that it is simply the way of the world. His tone is one of resigned irony, not reformist zeal.

The old civilizations of Europe, India and China all shared a basically Aristotelian outlook, even if it was not drawn from Aristotle. All viewed commerce as properly subordinate to politics and contemplation, while at the same time recognizing and fearing its capacity to subdue these other activities to its own end. All regarded the love of money for its own sake as an aberration. Such agreement between three great and largely independent cultures ought to give us pause. In matters concerning the human good, the opinion of the world cannot err entirely. We too are more Aristotelian than our official thinking allows us to admit. We know implicitly, whatever the votaries of growth may tell us, that money is essentially a means to the enjoyment of the good things of life, not an end in itself. After all, to sacrifice health, love and leisure to a mere bundle of paper or electrical impulses—what could be sillier than *that*?

The Eclipse of the Good Life

For all its vestigial resonance, the idea of the good life no longer forms part of public discussion in the Western world. Politicians argue their case in terms of choice, efficiency or the protection of rights. They do not say, "I think this policy will help people lead fruitful, civilized lives." Private discussion has tended to follow suit. How many teachers have tried to interest their students in some question of ethics or aesthetics, only to be told, with an air of weary condescension, that it is all just a matter of opinion?

The effect of this development has been to release the acquisitive instinct from all fixed bounds. If there is no such thing as the good life, then acquisition has no absolute goal, only the relative one of "as much as" or "more than" the others; a goal that, since it is shared by those others, must recede forever into the distance. Imagine, by way of analogy, two men walking to a certain town. On their way they get lost, yet keep on walking, now with the sole aim of staying ahead of their fellow walker. Here is an image of our situation. The vanishing of all intrinsic ends leaves us with only two options: to be ahead or to be behind. Positional struggle is our fate. If there is no right place to be, it is best to be ahead.

How can we explain the eclipse of the good life? In the last chapter, we traced the history of the idea that evil motives may be licensed for the sake of their good effects. But the writers we examined—Mandeville, Goethe, Marx, Marcuse and Keynes—were under no illusion that evil motives are indeed evil. They did not themselves believe that fair is foul and foul is fair, though they may have encouraged such a belief in others. The last few decades, however, have seen the triumph of two movements of thought whose combined tendency has been to erode the very language of "fair" and "foul"— modern liberal theory on the one hand, neoclassical economics on the other. Between them, these two movements have established a virtual monopoly on public discourse, forcing older ethical traditions into a marginal, counter-cultural position.

Ever since the publication of John Rawls's *A Theory of Justice* in 1971, liberal thinkers have insisted on public neutrality between rival conceptions of the good.* The state, they claim, should not throw its weight behind this or that ethical outlook; rather, it should leave citizens free to follow their own moral lights, insofar as is compatible with a similar freedom for others. Needless to say, this philosophical ideal has never been fully realized in practice. The French state is not neutral in its treatment of hijab wearers, nor is any liberal state neutral with regard to heroin. But at the level of argument, the Rawlsian ideal has triumphed. Today, even manifestly paternalist policies are defended on the grounds that they promote choice or prevent harm to third parties. For instance, pornography is condemned on the dubious ground that it exploits women or incites men to rape, while its real offence—that of degrading taste and feeling—goes unmentioned. Here as elsewhere, the principle of neutrality has had a chilling effect on public debate, diverting what should be ethical arguments into sterile technical byways.[23]

---

* Prominent "neutralists" include, alongside Rawls, Ronald Dworkin and Robert Nozick. Other liberal philosophers, notably Joseph Raz, have been critical of the idea. But in the broader political arena, it is the neutralists, and not their critics, who have had the greater influence.

The principle of state neutrality is now so well established that we sometimes forget how revolutionary it is. Until the 1960s, liberalism was primarily a doctrine of tolerance, not neutrality. The distinction is significant. Tolerance is not mere absence of bias but a positive ethical virtue; it implies forbearance, serenity, good humor and a respect for privacy. Tolerance does not rule out public preference for one moral or religious doctrine over others; it insists only that rivals be treated with consideration and respect. Finally, tolerance need not extend to the intolerable, whereas neutrality must in all consistency be universal. The tolerant state does not face the dilemma of the neutral state when dealing with necrophiliacs, neo-Nazis and the like.

The shift from tolerance to neutrality has two main causes. The first is the decline of liberal Protestantism, the mainstay of the old culture of tolerance. The second is the fact of increasing ethnic and cultural diversity. From the 1950s onwards, European states opened their doors to large numbers of non-white, non-Christian immigrants, while in America, the WASP ascendancy came under attack from blacks, Catholics and Jews. As a result of these developments, any public preference for one religious or cultural tradition over others, however slight or symbolic, has come to be felt as demeaning. Ironically, the demand for neutrality has come as much from guilt-ridden members of former elites as from the minorities themselves, many of whom would prefer to live under the shadow of a tolerant rival confession than under an impartial but despotic secularism.[24]

Of even greater significance for the de-moralization of public life is the discipline of economics, especially as that is now taught in universities and business schools across the world. Economists—we generalize, but not grossly—conscientiously abstain from passing judgment on wants. "Nothing in economics so quickly marks an individual as incompetently trained," wrote J. K. Galbraith, "as a disposition to remark on the legitimacy of the desire for more food and the frivolity of the desire for a more elaborate car."[25] Economists are all for the *satisfaction* of wants, at least within certain limits. But as to the wants themselves, they maintain a fastidious indifference.

This peculiarity of economics is a product of the discipline's roots in the empiricist revolt against Aristotle. "The philosophers of old did in vain inquire," wrote John Locke, a leader of that revolt, "whether summum bonum consisted in riches, or bodily delights, or virtue, or contemplation: and they might have as reasonably disputed, whether the best relish were to be found in apples, plums, or nuts."[26] Locke prudently concedes that the existence of heaven and hell gives us an overriding interest in acting virtuously, but adds that, were it not for this, no one way of life would be preferable to another. This skeptical standpoint has passed into mainstream economics under the slogan "the givenness of wants." Desire is no longer, as it was for the ancients, an arrow capable of hitting or missing its mark; it is a bare psychological fact, guiltless and inerrant. There is no intrinsically desirable life, only a range of *desired lifestyles*.

Once this keystone of pre-modern economic thought is removed, the other blocks fall rapidly to the ground. First to go is the distinction between needs and wants. Needs, on the classical conception, are objective; they refer to the requirements of life or the good life. Wants, by contrast, are a psychological phenomenon; they are "in the mind" of the wanter. Needs and wants are independent of one another. The child needs, but does not want, his medicine; the bibliophile wants, but does not need, a first edition of Blake. A need for x establishes a moral claim to x, whereas merely wanting x does not. Beggars talk about their needs, never about their wants.[27]

Having discarded the concept of the good life, modern economics can make no sense of the distinction between needs and wants. "Arthur needs a jacket" must be read as shorthand for "Arthur needs a jacket *in order to* . . . ," where the dots spell out some desire on the part of Arthur. Economists might, at a push, admit the existence of subsistence needs, but would probably add that even these are conditional upon the (normally reliable) desire to stay alive. Another common strategy is to interpret needs as a special class of wants— namely, those that are relatively impervious to changes in price, or "price-inelastic" in the jargon. But this amounts to a revision, not a clarification, of our normal concept of need. Heroin is price-inelastic, but addicts do not *need* heroin. They may talk about "needing a fix," but except in cases where their life is at risk, this is not literally true. They just want a fix very much.

Along with the distinction between needs and wants falls the closely related distinction between necessities and luxuries. Necessities in the classical sense are things one needs for life or the good life. "No man can live well, or indeed live at all, unless he be provided with necessaries."[28] Luxuries, by contrast, are things one wants but does not need. Again, the two terms are morally freighted: necessities are items to which one has some claim, if not always an overriding one; luxuries are an optional and possibly corrupting extra. A necessity should never be sacrificed to a luxury. But if there is no such thing as the good life, then "necessities" can refer only to subsistence goods such as food and shelter, or to the requirements of a particular social role. And in this latter sense, they are only conventionally, not naturally, distinct from luxuries. First-class travel is a necessity to the executive but not to the backpacker. Indoor toilets are regarded as a necessity in Britain today but were not so fifty years ago.

Next to fall is the concept of "enoughness" or sufficiency. If for the Aristotelian "enough" means "enough for the good life," for the modern economist it can mean only "enough to satisfy wants." (It is in this spirit that Billy Bunter might exclaim, as he casts a gleaming eye over the hams in his larder, "there's not enough.") Understood in this desire-relative sense, our question "how much is enough?" can be answered only with a shoulder-shrugging "how much do you want?" And of course, if enough means merely "enough to satisfy wants," there can be no such thing as wanting more than enough. Avarice as a vice disappears from view.

Last not but least, modern economics has dispensed with the central concept of use-value. For Aristotle, as we saw, the use-value of an object is its particular contribution to the good life. Wine, for instance, enhances food and friendship, both central human goods. It therefore has use-value, whereas crack cocaine (which enhances neither food nor friendship nor any other good thing) does not. That I prefer crack to wine does not alter this fact; it simply shows me to have corrupt taste.

Aristotle's concept of use-value was taken over by Smith, Ricardo and of course Marx, who put it to sturdy critical work. But in the late nineteenth century, and partly in reaction to Marx, economists set about dismantling it. "Value," wrote Carl Menger, a pioneer of the new approach, "is nothing inherent in goods, no property of them, nor an independent thing existing by itself. It is a judgement economizing men make about the importance of the goods at their disposal."[29] This new conception of value, better known by its English name of "utility," has since become standard in the discipline. Utility is a purely descriptive concept; it expresses what I want, not what I ought to want. If I prefer to spend my money on crack rather than wine—well, then, crack has more utility for me.

The discovery of utility was hailed as a great advance in economic analysis, not least because it seemed to solve Aristotle's old problem of the relation of use- to exchange-value. Aristotle had puzzled over how a pig and a bed, which both contribute to the good life in very different ways, could nonetheless be valued on a single monetary scale. But from the new perspective, the problem disappears. If use-value is just "utility in consumption," and exchange-value "utility in exchange," the two appear, in Menger's words, merely as "different forms of a single general phenomenon of value."[30] There is no longer a metaphysical problem of transforming one kind of value into another, but only a technical problem of determining at what point consumption goods will be exchanged rather than used. However, as so often in the history of ideas, Aristotle's problem had not really been solved so much as replaced by another, more tractable problem. Understood in its original sense, as real *usefulness* rather than mere utility in consumption, use-value can no more be transformed into exchange-value than color into length.

The dissolution of the distinction between use- and exchange-value was pregnant with consequence. From Aristotle to Keynes, exchange-value—or money, its pure embodiment—has been regarded as a distinct and questionable object of pursuit. Virgil spoke of the *auri sacra fames*, the accursed lust for gold. For Keynes, the love of money "as a possession" and not just "as a means to the enjoyments and realities of life," was "one of those semi-criminal, semi-pathological propensities which one hands over with a shudder to the specialists in mental disease."[31] But if the modern orthodoxy is correct, the distinction drawn here by Keynes has no substance. Money itself, as distinct from the goods it commands, cannot be a special object of love. The passion of Midas and Shylock turns out to be not a positive passion at all, but simply a preference for future over present consumption, or a certain degree of risk-aversion. Some see this as a mark of intellectual progress. We are inclined to see it as a regression in economic thought.

Let us pause and take stock. The various distinctions drawn by pre-modern economic thought—between needs and wants, necessities and luxuries, use- and exchange-value—all rest on the assumption that some ways of life are intrinsically superior to others. Modern economics has dispensed with this assumption. It no longer aspires to realize the Good but only to create conditions in which people can realize "the good" as they conceive it. "Given the multitude of competing conceptions of the good life," writes economist Robert Frank, summarizing the orthodox view, "perhaps the most we can hope for in our social institutions is that they grant each of us the widest possible latitude to forge lives that suit us."[32] Economists have no ambition to remake human nature. They take people as they are, not as they should be. After all the horrors committed in the name of heaven and utopia, this seems to them a suitably modest stance.

But why—a critic might at this point interject—should we privilege what economists say? After all, they are just one group of academics among others, and not even a very popular group. But such a dismissal would be foolish. Economics is not just any academic discipline. It is the theology of our age, the language that all interests, high and low, must speak if they are to win a respectful hearing in the courts of power. Economics owes its special position in part to the failure of other disciplines to impress their stamp on political debate. Philosophy was a powerful force in public life until the early twentieth century, when it retreated into linguistic hair-splitting. Sociology made a bid for influence under Weber and Talcott Parsons, but was never able to develop a systematic body of theory to rival economics. History succumbed to the worship of power. Poets and critics once boasted of being "unacknowledged legislators of the world," an ambition briefly rekindled by T. S. Eliot and F. R. Leavis but now quietly abandoned. Economics has been left in sole possession of the field.

The triumph of economics over its academic rivals reflects a broader social change, which might be labelled the breakdown of institutional authority. Ideals of the good life, enshrined in the Church and the landed aristocracy, and promoted by a "clerisy" of writers, artists and dons, exerted a powerful force in Britain well into the twentieth century. In industrial towns, shared patterns of work gave rise to ways of life that, if not exactly "good" in Aristotle's sense, were at least more than purely maximizing. All that is now gone. The aristocracy, deprived of its political role, has merged into the rich; the clerisy is a small and uninfluential coterie; the old Churches are shadows of their former selves; and the working class is scattered and powerless. Neoclassical economics, atomistic and subjectivist, has swelled to fill the vacuum.

The two traditions of thought examined here, post-Rawlsian liberalism and neoclassical economics, both forbid any *public* preference for this or that way of life. Neither has any objection to individuals deciding for themselves that a certain lifestyle is "good" and working no harder than they need to support it. (If their "utility function" is shaped that way, who are we to gainsay them?) But this concession is less generous than it might appear. For a social species such as ours, the good life is essentially a life in common with others. Its home is not in the brains of individuals but in groups of people doing things together. My desire may be to play boules in the town square all day, but if no one else plays boules, or if there is no town square, it will come to nothing. Collective participation is essential to all but the most solitary visions of human fulfilment.

Of course, there is nothing to prevent individuals in a liberal society getting together to live the good life. Utopians and sectarians typically do just that. However—and this highlights a second, deeper sense in which the good life is essentially public—such groupings depend for their continuing vitality on the recognition of the surrounding culture; without it, they are liable to implode in mistrust and resentment. (Compare the fate of most modern communes with that of the medieval monasteries, sustained as they were by the whole society, morally and materially.) In a world devoted to the satisfaction of private wants, the good life can be at best a marginal concern, an affair of eccentrics and enthusiasts. Its adherents are liable to be plagued by the thought that they are not "up to" the pressures of competition, that their ideals are a mere mask for failure. Thus, although it is true that a liberal society permits any number of visions of the good life, it is by the same token hospitable to none of them.

The idea of the good life is a universal of human thought, cropping up independently the world over. We alone have seen fit to eliminate it.

Not the good life, but life itself—its comfort, convenience and prolongation—has become our overriding goal. Ours is the age foreseen by Nietzsche, when "man will no longer shoot the arrow of his longing beyond man, and the string of his bow will have forgotten how to whir!"[33]

The eclipse of the good life explains the endless expansion of wants outlined in Chapter 1. A tendency to insatiability has always been recognized, but was previously held in check by prohibitions and countervailing ideals. Those prohibitions and ideals have now vanished. Detached from any vision of the human good, and fomented by envy and boredom, wants multiply like the heads of the mythical Hydra.

The gloom is not unrelieved, however. The visions of the good life described in this chapter were confined to small elites living off the labor of others, often of slaves. Traditional economies were unable to support any greater number at above subsistence level. Now, for the first time in history, we are in a position to rectify this secular injustice. We have the material ability to extend the good life, or at least, the possibility of the good life, to all. The requirements of human flourishing no longer conflict with the demands of human justice.

But what if the good life is not just contingently but in principle unavailable to all members of a society, much as the epithets "best" and "highest" are unavailable? What if it is an inherently snobbish or contrastive concept, one premised upon the existence of ways of life that are *not* good? The suspicion is uncomfortably plausible. Much of classical ethics exudes contempt for the base and ill-born, and even the Christian virtue of charity seems wrapped up with the assumption that (as Jesus put it) the poor are always with us. If the idea of the good life rests on what Nietzsche called "the pathos of distance," it seems irreconcilable with the democracy that most of us cherish.

A full response to this objection must wait until Chapter 6. But let us just note, by way of reassurance, that our vision of the good life is not premised on a contrast with other, lower ways of life. The pleasures of mastery and condescension play no part in it. This restriction rules out a good deal of pre-modern ethics. We would not wish to resurrect Aristotle's ideal of the "great-souled" man, basking in the consciousness of his own superiority. Not all pre-modern ethics deserves suspicion, though. Just because an idea of the good life has been historically bound up with privilege, it does not follow that it logically entails privilege. Gentlemen were a small elite, but gentlemanly manners are in principle available to all. Nietzschean pessimism must be resisted.

Our task, then, is to retrieve such fragments of wisdom as still exist, whether in past traditions or in our own deep-buried intuitions, so as to reconstruct from them an image of the good life. If we can succeed in this, we may be able to revive, in democratized form, something of the *douceur* of the great civilizations of the past, if not their creative vigor. Mephistopheles will be cheated of his victory.

Before outlining our vision of the good life, we must look at a couple of other influential attempts to halt the growth juggernaut. The first appeals to the concept of happiness, the second to that of sustainability. We are in sympathy with the goals of both movements, but believe they mislocate the real basis of our objection to endless growth, which is ethical, not utilitarian.

4

The Mirage of Happiness

It is indeed a strange thought that the end should be amusement, and that the busyness and suffering through- out one's life should be for the sake of amusing oneself.

—Aristotle

Intellectuals have long indicted economic growth for failing to make us happy. "The progress of the sciences and the arts has added noth- ing to our genuine felicity," wrote Jean-Jacques Rousseau in 1751.[1] Rather, it has kindled envy, ambition and idle curiosity—passions that cannot in their nature be fully or universally satisfied. Real happiness is the fruit of simple tastes and rugged virtues. Its symbol is ancient Sparta, not modern Paris.

Rousseau's complaint has recently been resurrected, now armed with the weapons of statistical science. "Happiness economics," as the new field is called, claims to show that citizens of the developed world, although on the whole pretty happy, are not getting any happier. Reported British happiness levels have hardly budged since 1974, while real per capita GDP has increased almost twofold. Other developed countries show similar patterns. Above a certain level, it seems, absolute income and happiness are unrelated. Happiness econ- omists have accordingly urged advanced nations to shift their focus from GDP to GDH—"Gross Domestic Happiness." Their strictures have not gone unheeded. In 2010, David Cameron unveiled a new "well-being index" to supplement the traditional macroeconomic indices. Happiness is now serious politics.

Happiness economists have the best of intentions. They are rightly alarmed by the divorce of economic growth from any humanly intelligible end; they wish to remind us of the old truth that riches exist for man, not man for riches. Sadly, their emancipation from orthodoxy is far from perfect. Like their more conventional colleagues, they view the economic problem essentially as one of maximization; they depart from convention only in their choice of what to maximize. The shortcomings of this approach are manifold. For a start, it rests far too much faith on the accuracy of the survey data. More disturbingly, it treats happiness as a simple, unconditional good, measurable along a single dimension. The sources or objects of happiness are disregarded. All that matters is whether you have more or less of the stuff. These are false and dangerous ideas. Generally speaking, happiness is good only where it is due; where sadness is due, it is better to be sad. To make happiness itself, independent of its objects, the chief goal of government is a recipe for infantilization—the prospect memorably dramatized by Aldous Huxley in *Brave New World*. We do not want to banish the engineers of growth only to see them replaced by the engineers of bliss.

A Very Brief History of Happiness

We all know what the word "happiness" refers to—that fond, familiar thing that parents wish for their children and romantic heroines look forward to in marriage. Yet when it comes to spelling out what it means, we confront a bewildering array of conflicting definitions. Happiness is one of those "essentially contested concepts," debate over which can be neither resolved nor abandoned. In short, it is a philosophical concept.

The first extended discussion of happiness in the Western world appears at the beginning of Herodotus's *Histories*, with the visit of Solon of Athens to Croesus, the fabulously rich king of Lydia. Croesus asks Solon whether in the course of his travels he has come across anyone "happier than everyone else." Pointedly ignoring this invitation to pay his host a compliment, Solon instead names a certain

Tellus as the happiest of men. Croesus, insulted, demands an explanation. This is how Solon answers him:

> In the first place ... while living in a prosperous state, Tellus had sons who were fine, upstanding men and he lived to see them all have children, all of whom survived. In the second place, his death came at a time when he had a good income, by our standards, and it was a glorious death. You see, in a battle at Eleusis between Athens and her neighbours he stepped into the breach and made the enemy turn tail and flee; he died, but his death was splendid, and the Athenians awarded him a public funeral on the spot where he fell, and greatly honoured him.[2]

The conception of happiness revealed in this passage is both familiar and strange to us. We can understand why Solon should mention Tellus's wealth, his fine sons, and his grandchildren. Naturally such things make a man happy! Harder to understand is his stress on Tellus's glorious death and funeral. Surely all this did nothing for Tellus himself, even if it cheered his surviving relatives? (Of course, Tellus might have had a happy few final moments contemplating his noble death, and his soul, if it survived, might have enjoyed the spectacle of his posthumous renown, but this does not seem to be what Solon has in mind.) The crux of the mystery is that *eudaimonia*, the Greek word conventionally translated as "happiness," does not refer to a state of *mind* at all, but to an admirable and desirable state of *being*. It is a matter of public appraisal, not private awareness. If this concept strikes us today as strangely amphibious—part happiness, part success, part virtue—it is because we are heirs to the conceptual revolution to be described in more detail below. That revolution has placed beyond our grasp a notion that, through most of Western history and still today in many non-Western parts of the world, has appeared perfectly transparent.

Solon's story highlights another feature of the pre-Socratic conception of happiness: its dependence upon fate. Tellus's death is crucial to his happiness not only because it is glorious but because it secures him against all further loss. "Call no man happy till he is dead," is how Solon famously puts it—words later recalled by Croesus as he is burnt to death by his Persian vanquishers. Herodotus's moral is clear:

in an uncertain world, ruled over by jealous gods, to boast of happiness is hubris and folly.

Solon's vision of happiness as a gift of fate, precarious and revocable, was a central theme of ancient Greek literature, most memorably of tragedy. But from the late fifth century BC onwards, it came under attack from that elite, countercultural movement known as philosophy. Happiness, proclaimed the philosophers, is an achievement of wisdom and virtue, both of them within our power. Socrates and Plato went so far as to claim that nothing, not even torture, could take away a good man's happiness. Aristotle was typically more sensible. Even if happiness lies in virtue, he retorted, it is still vulnerable to chance, for virtue itself, or at least its exercise, requires favorable circumstances. Certainly no one would call Priam happy, who lost both his sons and his kingdom, while those who describe a man broken on the wheel as happy are simply "talking nonsense."[3]

All ancient visions of happiness, with the important exception of Epicureanism, are objective in character; they address the question: "what is the good life for man, the most complete, most fully human life?" They are not concerned with the attainment of certain states of mind. Christianity remained within this framework while straining it to a paradoxical limit. Happiness is still man's end, but it is not to be found in any worldly goods, nor even in the moral and intellectual goods extolled by philosophers. Rather, it lies in those very conditions identified by common sense as *unhappiness*, in poverty, loneliness, persecution and death. "Blessed are ye," says Christ, "when men shall revile you, and persecute you, and shall say all manner of evil against you falsely." This is still *eudaimonia* in the ancient sense, though at the furthest possible remove from Solon's homely conception of it.

The English word "happiness," like its European cognates, was originally synonymous with *eudaimonia*. To be happy was to enjoy good "hap" or fortune, to be in a blessed, enviable condition. "We few, we happy few," says Shakespeare's Henry V to his troops before Agincourt, fully expecting that they will be killed or maimed. This old usage survives in stock phrases such as "happy returns" and "happy chance," but has been more or less displaced in modern English by the new meaning, dating back to the sixteenth century, of a pleasant or contented state of mind. Philosophical developments played a role in this linguistic shift.

If consciousness is the essence of personhood, as Descartes and Locke maintained, then happiness must be something internal to it. The goods once held to *constitute* happiness—wealth, honor, fame and so forth—now appear only as so many *causes* of happiness, varying from person to person. To argue over which one "really is" happiness is absurd; one might as well, as we saw Locke quip in Chapter 3, dispute "whether the best relish were to be found in apples, plums, or nuts."[4]

The consequences of this transformation were profound. If happiness is the Good, as tradition taught, and if it is a pleasant state of mind, as philosophy now proclaimed, it follows that *the Good itself is a pleasant state of mind*. This thought was to blossom into utilitarianism, the dominant tradition in British public ethics since the nineteenth century. In its classical, Benthamite form, utilitarianism defines right action as that which maximizes general happiness or pleasure, these two states being regarded as equivalent. The objects of happiness or pleasure are of no account; what matters is the *quantity*. "Pleasure being equal," said Bentham famously, "pushpin is as good as poetry."[5] This drear doctrine appealed strongly to the technocratic imagination. In place of the anarchy of opinion, it promised a mechanical rule for resolving moral and legal conflict, a "felicific calculus," as Bentham called it. How such a calculus might work in practice was never fully explained. Bentham's own formulation, with its seven vectors of intensity, duration, certainty, propinquity, fecundity, purity and extent, is a pantomime of scientific reasoning. The problem of measurement bedevils utilitarianism to this day, as we shall see.

Utilitarianism sprang from the same soil as classical political economy. Bentham was a close associate of Ricardo and James Mill; his ideas were taken up with important modifications by James's son, John Stuart. The marginalist revolution of the late nineteenth century if anything strengthened this connection. Whereas earlier economists had focused on the expansion of production, the marginalists emphasized the pleasures of consumption. "To satisfy our wants to the utmost with the least effort," wrote William Stanley Jevons, a pioneer of the new approach, "to procure the greatest amount of what is desirable at the expense of the least that is undesirable—in other words, *to maximise pleasure*, is the problem of Economics."[6] F. Y. Edgeworth, the brilliant if eccentric author of *Mathematical Psychics*, went even further. To make sense of the economic project, he argued, we must postulate a "hedonimeter," an "ideally perfect instrument" for measuring quantities of pleasure:

> From moment to moment the hedonimeter varies; the delicate index now flickering with the flutter of the passions, now steadied by intellectual activity, low sunk whole hours in the neighbourhood of zero, or momentarily springing up towards infinity. The continually indicated height is registered by photographic or other frictionless apparatus upon a uniformly moving vertical plane . . . We have only to add another dimension expressing the number of sentients, and to integrate through all time and over all sentience, to constitute the end of pure utilitarianism.[7]

We have certainly come a long way from ancient Greece. Tellus, one suspects, would have shown up none too well on a hedonimeter.

In the early decades of the twentieth century, economists started to feel uneasy about the psychological underpinnings of their discipline. Behaviorism was all the rage; speculation about mental states was tabooed as unscientific. Luckily, it turned out that the bulk of economic theory could be reconstructed without reference to such states. All that is required, it was shown, is the assumption that consumers have a coherent set of preferences, revealed in their behavior. To the extent that these preferences are satisfied, they are said to possess "utility." For instance, if I am offered an apple and a pear, and choose the pear, then by hypothesis the pear gives me more utility than does the apple. But to say all this is to say nothing about my mental states, only about my propensities to behavior. Hedonimeters and the rest can be set aside as irrelevant.

This theoretical reconstruction—the work of a series of great economists from the 1900s to the 1930s—has allowed the profession to maintain an attitude of cheerful indifference to the facts of human psychology. It does not matter, from the economic point of view, whether people are altruists, egoists, hedonists, masochists or anything else; all that matters is that they have certain preferences and act on them. This formalism has come at a cost, however. The nineteenth century assumed that greater wealth would lead to greater happiness, in the full-blown Benthamite sense. But all modern economists can say is that it maximizes utility, meaning "satisfaction of consumer preferences." Whether satisfaction of consumer preferences itself spells *happiness* is a question on which they are necessarily silent. The project of economic growth has come to look like Bugs Bunny running over the edge of a cliff—its feet keep moving, but there is nothing there to support them.

In the 1930s and 1940s, amidst global recession and war, such worries could be set aside as academic. Two decades later, however, they felt increasingly urgent. A slew of influential books—*The Affluent Society* by J. K Galbraith, *One-Dimensional Man* by Herbert Marcuse and *The Joyless Economy* by Tibor Scitovsky—questioned the equation of "utility" and happiness. Rousseauesque anxieties were rekindled. What if technological progress creates new wants as fast as it satisfies old ones? What if humans crave relative rather than absolute advantage, making market competition a zero-sum game? Such questions took economists outside the remit of their discipline into the previously forbidden territory of psychology.

Meanwhile, psychology itself was undergoing a revolution. The behaviorist veto on introspection was lifted, allowing self-reports to be admitted as evidence. Happiness surveys were first conducted in America in the 1940s and have been repeated, in increasing bulk and sophistication, every decade since. This data has come as a godsend to economists dissatisfied with the purely formal concept of utility, for it promises a measure of well-being independent of consumer choice, a hard standard against which to assess the benefits of growth. Economics can once again become what it originally hoped to be: the science of how to achieve the greatest happiness of the greatest number.

Happiness Economics

In 1974, the economist Richard Easterlin published a famous paper, "Does Economic Growth Improve the Human Lot?" The answer, he concluded after a thorough survey of happiness and GNP in a number of countries across the world, is probably "no." Happiness economics has since mushroomed, but the central finding of Easterlin's paper, the

Chart 6. GDP per Head and Life Satisfaction

Source: Eurobarometer; *World Database of Happiness*
(http://worlddatabaseofhappiness.eur.nl/index.html); ONS

so-called Easterlin paradox, remains largely uncontested. It can be illustrated with three simple charts (Charts 6–8). Chart 6 plots GDP and life satisfaction levels in the UK from 1973 to 2009. It shows an almost constant rise in GDP but no change in life satisfaction. Data from other developed countries shows a similar pattern. These findings are certainly striking. It looks as if the huge improvement in living standards over the last thirty-six years has brought us no extra happiness at all. Perhaps Rousseau was right all along. More money does not make us happier.

Chart 7 is based on a poll taken in 2005–8. It shows the percentage of people in both the top and bottom decile of the UK income distribution who rate themselves as "very happy," "quite happy," "not very happy" and "not at all happy." Clearly, there are more "very happy" people among the rich and more "not at all happy" people among the poor. Again, similar findings have been duplicated in countries across the world, developed and undeveloped.

These two sets of statistics seem at first glance to contradict one

Chart 7. Happiness According to Income Position in the UK

	Bottom decile	Top decile
very happy	43.9%	55.0%
quite happy	44.0%	43.1%
not very happy	7.1%	1.8%
not at all happy	5.0%	0.0%

Source: World Values Survey, 2005–8

another. The second suggests that more money does make us happier, the first that it does not. But there is no real contradiction. To make sense of the figures, we must assume that happiness is affected by relative, not absolute, wealth. In other words, the happiness of the rich is an expression of their satisfaction at being top of the pile, the unhappiness of the poor their frustration at being bottom. Since the rich remain at the top and the poor remain at the bottom whatever the income of society as a whole, average happiness levels do not change. (Imagine, by way of analogy, a queue on an escalator; the woman at the back of the queue remains at the back, even as the queue itself moves forwards.)

Psychological experiments appear to confirm that relative, not absolute, income is what matters most to people. When Harvard students were asked to choose between two imaginary worlds—one in which they earned $50,000 a year against an average of $25,000, the other in which they earned $100,000 a year against an average of $200,000—the majority opted for the former.[8] This may look like an expression of vanity, and no doubt it is in part, but there are reasons aside from vanity for wanting to be top of the pile. Many of the best things in life—beautiful country houses, unspoilt holiday resorts, top schools—are essentially limited in supply and so accessible only to the richest. Such positional or oligarchic goods are, as we saw in Chapter 1, one reason why the lust for gain remains powerful even in the wealthiest societies.

But even when all concessions are made to relative income, the stubbornly flat line in Chart 6 remains a mystery. Is absolute income

Chart 8. Happiness and Income by Country

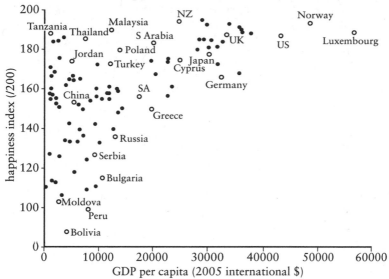

Source: World Values Survey, 2005–9

irrelevant to happiness? Have laptops, Kindles, foot spas, foreign holidays, takeaway sushi boxes and all the rest added *nothing* to our collective well-being? Happiness economists like to remind us of the power of adaptation. Most material gains have only a fleeting effect upon mood, after which it reverts to its customary level. Income can thus rise steadily while happiness rises not at all. Another popular explanation for the failure of happiness to rise in tandem with wealth is inequality. As we saw in Chapter 1, average incomes in the UK have doubled over the past thirty years, but the *median* income—that is, the income of the person in the middle of the distribution—has shifted much less. The gains have been predominantly at the very top. Thus even if absolute income does matter for happiness, the statistics may reflect the feelings of the majority whose absolute income has stagnated.

Chart 8 shows GDP and happiness for a wide variety of countries at various points in the 1990s. As can be seen, the unhappiest countries all have average incomes of less than $15,000 a year, after which point there seems to be little correlation.[9] These data suggest a modification of Easterlin's original thesis. Beneath a certain threshold, it seems, absolute income does matter for happiness. This should come as no surprise. Lack of adequate nutrition, sanitation, education and housing might well be expected to have a depressing effect. Chart 8 also suggests that the standard against which people judge their relative material well-being is a national, not a global, one. Otherwise, middle-income countries would score consistently lower than high-income ones, which they do not. It is sometimes pointed out, in this connection, that East German workers felt less happy after reunification than before, even though their real wages rose. Presumably they started comparing themselves with their new and very much richer compatriots.[10]

How, then, do happiness economists propose to boost our flagging happiness levels? There are, as they see it, two problems: one of individual, the other of collective, irrationality. The first problem arises because people overestimate the long-term happiness they will derive from consumption goods and underestimate the satisfactions of leisure, education, friendship and other intangibles. The second problem arises because, even if people are rational in wanting to be top of the pile, the logic of positional competition dictates that not all of them can be. A's success must be at the expense of B's failure, so that overall happiness remains constant. Indeed, it may even fall, since positional struggle is itself unpleasant. By analogy, when one person starts shouting at a party, others are better off shouting too, though everyone would be better off speaking in a murmur. We are in a familiar game-theoretical quandary.

Happiness economists respond to both these problems in predictable ways. If certain goods generate no lasting improvements in happiness, either for their owners or for society at large, why not tax them? This would both divert resources into goods that do generate such improvements, such as leisure, and raise revenue for happiness-boosting public projects. Thus, for instance, economist Robert Frank has advocated a progressive consumption tax as a curb on luxury spending and an encouragement to saving.[11] We propose something similar, though without reference to happiness, in Chapter 7. Other commonly proposed measures include restrictions on working hours and on certain forms of advertising. Generally speaking, the preference of happiness economists is for a European over an American way of life, although as Will Wilkinson of the Cato Institute has pointed out, America scores better on happiness league tables than most of the big European social democracies.[12] With little firm evidence on either side, this argument looks set to continue for some time.

What's Wrong with
Happiness Economics

Happiness economics is in one sense nothing new. Sound moralists since Solomon and Socrates have told us over and again that happiness lies in love and virtue, not riches. "Better is a dinner of herbs where love is," says the Book of Proverbs, "than a stalled ox and hatred therewith." What is new is the attempt to deck this old wisdom up in statistical garb, complete with graphs and formulas. We cannot, it seems, admit to knowing what we know without the stamp and seal of science. This exercise in self-reassurance is dangerous for two reasons: it exaggerates the usefulness of happiness surveys and requires us to attach an unconditional value to happiness itself, independent of the various things we are happy about. Let us take these two errors in turn.

Measurement Problems

Look again at Chart 6. That resolutely flat line ought to trouble happiness economists more than it does. For it implies not only that rising incomes have had no effect on happiness, but that none of the great social changes that have taken place in Britain over the last thirty years has had any effect on happiness. Other countries for which time-series data is available, including the USA and Japan, display an identical pattern. One of two things must be true. Either happiness is extremely insensitive to changes in the social environment, or happiness measurements are extremely insensitive to changes in happiness. Neither conclusion is particularly comforting to happiness economists.

There are reasons to think that the problem lies with the way happiness is measured. Chart 6 was compiled using data from a survey in which respondents had to identify themselves as (4) "very satisfied," (3) "fairly satisfied," (2) "not very satisfied," and (1) "not at all satisfied."

Since the initial average in 1973 was 3.15 out of a maximum of 4, happiness could have risen by 28 per cent at most during this period, three to four times less than GDP. But even such a modest rise would have required an amazing 100 percent of the population to declare themselves "very satisfied." In fact, even a 10 percent rise would have required 31.5 percent of the population to jump up a category, i.e., to go from "not very" to "fairly" or from "fairly" to "very" satisfied—a significant rise in national felicity. Furthermore, "bounded" surveys such as this cannot register changes at the two ends of the spectrum. They cannot represent a situation in which, say, the happiest 10 percent become still happier, since these people already fall into the top category of "very happy." By contrast, if the richest 10 percent grow richer, the effect on national income may be profound. In short, the touted contrast between static happiness and rising GDP is probably no more than an artifact of the way the two things are measured.[13]

Other happiness surveys use a 10- or 11-point numerical scale. Participants are asked questions such as: "Taking all things together on a scale of 0 to 10, how happy would you say you are?" Such surveys are slightly more sensitive than the verbal one described above, but they create further problems of their own. The categories "very happy," "pretty happy" and "not too happy" are, if rough, at least meaningful. But what could it mean to score 7 out of 10 for happiness? Even if we assume, charitably, that it makes sense to assign cardinal values to states of feeling, we still lack the information necessary for such an assignment. What, for a start, do the two extremes stand for? Is 0 being boiled alive in oil together with your family? Is 10 a state of perfect bliss—"God having an orgasm in your brain," as a certain drug dealer was heard to say, referring to the effects of his merchandise? And what about the 5? Does it designate a state midway between the two extremes? Or a state of emotional indifference? (These are not necessarily the same thing; absolute pain might be more painful than absolute pleasure is pleasant.) Or does 5 refer to average happiness? Clearly, many survey designers take it in that sense, hence their surprise that a large majority rate themselves 6 or above. And if 5 refers to average happiness, what is the reference population? The nation? The world? Participants in happiness surveys are given no answers to any these questions.

When it comes to international comparisons, problems multiply. One difficulty is that expressions of happiness are highly conventional, with protocols varying from nation to nation. Ask an American how he is doing and the chances are he will say, "great, thanks." Ask a Russian the same question and he is likely to shrug his shoulders and say, "*normalno,*" suggesting that things could be worse. If the American and Russian differ only in how they *express* their happiness, then a private questionnaire might get at the truth of the matter, but if they differ in how they *perceive* their own happiness, then no survey, however sensitively conducted, can hope to unearth their real feelings. Happiness researchers overlook this second possibility. They assume that people know how happy they are, or at least that errors of optimism and pessimism are evenly distributed across the globe. But why assume this? Those brought up to view happiness as a mark of success may well be reluctant to admit, even to themselves, that they are sad. Might the high happiness levels of America and other Western nations reveal nothing more than the prevalence of "positive thinking"—a fierce determination to look on the bright side of life? And we should not forget, of course, that most Western nations contain large non-Western minorities, often concentrated at particular socio-economic levels. Cultural biases may therefore compromise the accuracy not just of international but of national surveys too.

Then there is the problem of translation. Happiness researchers must assume that the English word "happy" has synonyms or near-synonyms in other languages across the globe; otherwise, comparisons are meaningless. But this is not always the case. Take *xingfu*, the word used in the Chinese version of the World Values Survey. *Xingfu* implies a favorable condition of life, with an emphasis on strong family relations. One is not *xingfu* while playing tennis or eating an orange. And it would be an abuse of terms, not just a psychological error, to call a prostitute or ageing playboy *xingfu.** *Xingfu*, in short, is closer in meaning to the ancient Greek *eudaimon* than to the modern English

---

* Linguistic intuitions seem to differ on this last point: some Chinese native speakers allow the prostitute and ageing playboy to be *xingfu*, others do not. Perhaps there are regional or generational differences. But as long as a significant number of Chinese native speakers use *xingfu* in the objectivist sense, no equivalence with "happy" can be assumed.

"happy."[14] Other languages raise similar difficulties. Generally speaking, "happy" is a far lighter, less demanding term than its foreign equivalents—this perhaps reflects the influence of utilitarianism in Anglo-Saxon cultures. Anna Wierzbicka, a leading authority on the semantics of emotion, has bemoaned "the glibness with which linguistic differences are at times denied in the current literature on happiness."[15]

Happiness researchers are in general untroubled by the exact wording of their questionnaires or the meaningfulness of their scales. They are content to observe that, whatever it is they might be measuring, it is strongly correlated with other things associated with happiness: low blood pressure, high levels of left-hemisphere brain activity, good health and plenty of smiling. Their results are, in the jargon, "valid." But this now raises a perplexity of a more philosophical kind. If happiness surveys must be checked for validity against what we already know about happiness, what new information can they contain? Either they tally with existing knowledge, in which case they are redundant, or they do not, in which case they are flawed. At most, happiness surveys might flesh out in greater detail what we already know. But they cannot tell us anything radically new; if they did, we would not believe them.

The correlates of self-reported happiness are of two sorts: physiological and circumstantial. On the physiological side, it has been shown that people who rate themselves happy tend to have high levels of electrical activity in the left forebrain and robust immune systems.[16] But how do we know that these things themselves track happiness? (The answer clearly cannot be that they track self-reported happiness, since that is the very item in question.) Other studies show a correlation between self-reported happiness on the one hand and the actions and circumstances associated with happiness on the other. It has been shown, for instance, that people who rate themselves happier are also rated happier by their friends and relatives, and that they smile more frequently.[17] Andrew Oswald and Stephen Wu have established a correlation between quality of life in US states, as measured by sunshine hours, commuting times, crime figures, etc., and the self-reported happiness of their inhabitants. (New York comes out bottom on both counts.)[18]

If these studies are credible, they show that those who say they are happy are indeed, on average, happy. Yet this result is not the vindication that it at first appears, for it presupposes that we already have a measure of how happy people are, independent of what they say on the subject, namely, our common-sense understanding of what makes humans tick, of what is good for them. Self-reports cannot be the ultimate criterion of happiness, however useful they might be as supplementary evidence. A simple thought experiment bears this out. Imagine a woman whose children have been killed in a violent accident, and whose every action radiates misery, yet who nonetheless declares herself happy. We would assume that she is either lying, self-deceived or using words in an unusual way. (Perhaps she is a philosopher with an idiosyncratic understanding of "happy.") We would not insist, against all appearances, that she really is happy. Happiness, in short, is not an item in the mind's inner theatre, visible only to its owner; it is essentially manifest in acts and happenings. If it were not, it would be mysterious how we could talk about it at all. The assumption underlying the survey method—that we are authoritative judges of our own happiness—is false.

These confusions are clearly visible in the above-mentioned article by Oswald and Wu. "Although it is natural to be guided by formal survey data," they write,

> it might be thought unusual that Louisiana—a state affected by Hurricane Katrina—comes so high in the state life-satisfaction league table. Various checks were done. It was found that Louisiana showed up strongly before Katrina and in a mental-health ranking done by Mental Health America and the Office of Applied Studies of the U.S. Substance Abuse and Mental Health Services Administration . . . Nonetheless, it is likely that Katrina altered the composition of this state—namely, those who were left were not a random sample of the population—so some caution in interpretation is called for about this state's ranked position, and that position may repay future statistical investigation.[19]

This is a revealing admission. While recognizing that they should, in all consistency, "be guided by formal survey data," Oswald and Wu allow themselves to be swayed by what they intuitively know about the effects of hurricanes on happiness. When it comes to the crunch, they question the data; they do not revise their views on what makes people happy. In a similar manner (though in this case with a critical intent), Helen Johns and Paul Ormerod point to a *positive* relationship between happiness and violent crime in the USA. They rightly take this as evidence for the unreliability of the statistics; they do not entertain the possibility that violent crime makes people happier.[20] And even if the data in these two cases turned out to be sound—that is, drawn from sufficiently large and representative samples—we would still query it. We would suspect the survey participants of being dishonest or deluded, or of having misunderstood the question. We would not abandon what we all know about the conditions of happiness.

This, then, is the bind. Happiness surveys are dubitable, both because of the above-mentioned obscurities of wording and measurement and also, more fundamentally, because we are not authorities on our own happiness. They therefore require external validation, whether in the shape of formal correlations or our own intuitive sense of how happy people are. Yet to the extent that they receive such validation, they drop out as redundant. Their function, it seems, is essentially ceremonial: it is to bestow the blessing of science on the deliverances of common sense.

Are happiness surveys useless, then? Not quite. Even if they cannot radically revise our common-sense understanding of what makes people happy, they may be able to flesh it out in places where it is uncertain or vague. It is sometimes claimed, for instance, that homosexuals are less happy than heterosexuals. Surveys, by contrast, indicate that there is no difference between the two groups.[21] This looks genuinely informative, though note that we accept it only because nothing in our experience contradicts it. (If gay people habitually wore long faces and drank heavily, we would tend to skepticism.) Similarly, surveys can help us rank the various causes of happiness and unhappiness in order of importance, where this is not already obvious. We all know that unemployment makes people unhappy, for instance, but it is perhaps interesting to learn that its impact is even greater than divorce.[22] Finally, happiness surveys can be useful in places where information about living conditions is difficult or expensive to obtain. But where statistics on health, employment, education, marriage and so forth are readily available, as they are in the UK and most other developed nations, there is no reason not to appeal to them directly rather than taking a detour via happiness. This will be our own approach in Chapter 6.

When it comes to international comparisons, the above-mentioned cultural and linguistic differences make any conclusions very uncertain. Even the prominent champion of happiness economics, Derek Bok, has admitted that "efforts to compare the average levels of well-being of different countries should be treated with considerable caution."[23] It is no doubt not an accident that Zimbabweans and Haitians rate themselves as less happy than Britons; we might have predicted as much. But we should not attach any great significance to the superior happiness of the Danes, nor lose sleep over the secret of their success. The attempt to create "national accounts of well-being" as a supplement or rival to GDP is an exercise in futility.[24] We should never forget that such accounts measure only what people say about their happiness; they do not, and cannot, measure happiness itself.

Ethical Problems

Let us suppose the methodological problems described above to be overcome. Let us suppose ourselves in possession of an infallible instrument for measuring happiness, a super-hedonimeter. Can we now press ahead with the project of maximizing happiness? The answer is no. Happiness as understood by happiness economists is not a proper goal of policy, quite apart from any problems of measurement, for the simple reason that it is not necessarily good. To make it a goal of policy is to open up the disturbing prospect of what LSD guru Timothy Leary termed "hedonic engineering."

How do happiness economists understand happiness? Few of them give the matter much thought. Yew-Kwang Ng, a leader in the field, is content to repeat Henry Sidgwick's classic Benthamite definition: happiness is a "surplus of pleasure over pain; the two terms being used, with equally comprehensive meanings, to include respectively all kinds of agreeable and disagreeable feelings."[25] Happiness, in other words, is a subjectively agreeable state of mind, not an objectively desirable condition of being. Other happiness economists are less forthright, but we must assume that they share this psychological understanding of happiness, otherwise their reliance on self-reports is a mystery. Solon did not need to ask Tellus to know that he was the happiest of men.

Sidgwick's psychological conception of happiness has become standard in the modern West. To many, it looks like the merest common sense. Yet on deeper analysis, our understanding of what it is to be happy turns out to contain many residues of the older idea of *eudaimonia* or "good hap." Or at least, so we shall suggest. We do not insist on the point. But we do insist that, taken in the psychological sense, happiness cannot be the supreme good. We cannot think that all our suffering and labor has as its end something as trivial as a buzz or tingle. Our argument, then, has the form of a dilemma. *Either* happiness is understood in the pre-modern sense, as a condition of being, in which case it is not the kind of thing that could be measured by happiness surveys, *or* it is understood in the modern sense, as a state of mind, in which case it is not the supreme good. Either way, the project of happiness economics fails.

The understanding of happiness implicit in modern happiness research has two main elements. Both are questionable, in the sense that they are in tension with what we really think about happiness, as opposed to what we may at first blush *think* we think. Let us take them in turn.

Happiness is aggregative. In other words, the happiness of a whole life is the sum (or possibly average; this leads to rather different conclusions) of the happiness of its individual moments. This contrasts with what might be called a "holistic" view, which sees the happiness of a life as irreducible to that of its momentary parts. Researchers disagree about how best to measure aggregate happiness. Psychologist Daniel Kahneman has argued, much in the spirit of Edgeworth, that we should try to measure happiness moment by moment and then integrate the results.[26] Most researchers are content, by contrast, to rely on subjects' own assessment of their overall happiness level. But these are differences of method only. All happiness researchers must agree that happiness is aggregative, not holistic in character, otherwise we should have to obey Solon's injunction to call no man happy till he is dead.

This aggregative understanding of happiness draws some support from the surrounding culture. Modern English (in contrast to many other languages) allows us to talk of being happy for a few hours or even minutes; this makes it possible to think of a happy life as a string of happy moments. But do we really believe this? Compare the life of a man who overcomes early suffering to achieve great things with that of a golden youth who loses everything. We would naturally describe the first as happy, the second as unhappy. Yet the two lives may contain an equal number of happy moments. Why then the distinction? The answer, surely, is that suffering at the beginning of a life is felt to be made good by subsequent achievement. It can be seen in retrospect as a trial or apprenticeship, as part of a larger story of success. By contrast, suffering at the end of a life remains unredeemed—unless of course we look beyond this world. This is the permanent truth in Solon's dictum. It is only with death that the overall shape or meaning of a life comes into view. Calling a life happy or unhappy before the end is like calling a play tragic or comic before it has run its course.

Unredeemed suffering is not the only thing that can mar the shape of a life. A life packed with happy moments from beginning to end may nonetheless be unhappy if those moments fail to coalesce into a greater whole.[27] The playboy meandering from harbor to harbor and girlfriend to girlfriend springs to mind. Lord Glenconner, who died in 2010 after dissipating his fortune in lavish entertainments, was one such type. "Nothing much has happened to me," he is reported to have said towards the end of his life. "It's like a party—gone the day after."[28] We might resist calling Glenconner happy, though his life was doubtless full of happy moments. And even if he had died before the regrets set in, we might still hesitate to call him happy. At any rate, it's a moot point.

A more stark example of the same scenario is offered by philosopher Fred Feldman. Imagine, he suggests, a case such as that described by Oliver Sacks in *The Man Who Mistook His Wife for a Hat*. Jamie, a victim of Korsakoff's syndrome, cannot keep anything in mind for more than a few minutes. His life is utterly fragmented—"an incoherent sequence of fleeting and unrelated episodes," as Feldman puts it.[29] Yet Jamie himself is unaware of his condition. He takes pleasure in each moment as it comes, watching butterflies, playing draughts and so forth. Is he happy? Feldman himself, faithful to his hedonistic theory of happiness, must maintain that he is. We are inclined to say that he is not. When parents wish their children happiness, it is not usually a life like Jamie's that they have in mind. Thoughts such as this nudge us in the direction of a more objectivist theory of happiness. Jamie's misfortune, even if it lies in the way his conscious states are organized, is not present to his consciousness. It is necessarily visible only to others.

Happiness is one-dimensional. Happiness economists hold, together with Bentham and Sidgwick and against Mill, that all conscious states can be ranked according to how happy they are. (Some furthermore hold that they can be assigned a cardinal value expressing their *degree* of happiness, but this is controversial.)[30] There is, in the jargon, a single "currency" of happiness. The distinctions drawn by ordinary language between happiness, joy, pleasure, contentment and their various negative counterparts are disregarded. Richard Layard offers an ingenious analogy: just as all sounds can be rated as more or less noisy, whatever their differences of pitch, tone, etc., so all states of mind can be rated as more or less happy.[31] If they could not, the project of measuring happiness would founder at the outset.

These assumptions may be necessary for reasons of methodological convenience, but they are nonetheless deeply flawed. Positive feelings come in many kinds, of which happiness is just one. And within happiness itself there are distinctions of quality irreducible to differences of degree. Let us look, as illustration, at the differences between *pleasure*, *happiness* and *joy*, noting in passing that there may be other, equally fundamental distinctions to be drawn here.

Take pleasure first. Economists in the Benthamite tradition are quick to identify happiness with pleasure, hoping thereby to eliminate its obscurities. Pleasure—so runs the thought—is a special kind of feeling, varying only in quantity. Thus if happiness is pleasure, it too can be treated quantitatively. But pleasure is not in fact a special feeling, as Aristotle demonstrated long ago. Imagine, he suggested, a couple of friends thick in conversation who hear in the background the playing of a pipe. Were pleasure a special feeling, we would expect the pleasure of the music to combine with that of the conversation in a straightforwardly additive fashion, like the heat from two fires. But that is not what happens. The music tears the friends away from their conversation; they cannot enjoy both at once.[32] Readers may remember the Haagen Dazs campaign of a few years back, in which naked lovers were shown smearing themselves rapturously with ice cream. Neither of us have tried this, but we suspect it would confirm Aristotle's thesis: the pleasure of sex would distract from that of ice cream, or vice versa. In short, pleasure is not a distinct feeling, generated now this way, now that; it is thoroughly bound up with its objects. To reduce happiness to pleasure with the aim of revealing it as one-dimensional is to get things wrong from the start.

In any case, happiness is not pleasure. The logical grammar of the two concepts is quite different. Pleasure is often (though not always) localizable in the body; think of foot spas, head massages, etc. Happiness, by contrast, has no physical location. One is not happy in one's big toe, or anywhere else. Pleasure takes up a precise stretch of time, from twelve till one, say. Happiness in modern English is sometimes "clockable" in this way, though its boundaries are never quite so precise ("I woke up happy this morning, but it soon faded"). Yet there is also, as we have seen, a kind of happiness without temporal dimensions. To say that John had a happy life is not to say that he was happy at certain times or a certain proportion of the time. Pleasure is never atemporal in this manner. A "life of pleasure" is just a life full of pleasurable episodes. Pleasure punctuates life; it does not characterize life as a whole.

These contrasts between happiness and pleasure are rooted in a more fundamental, phenomenological difference between the two states. Happiness is not just an inner feeling but a stance, an outlook on reality. It is the glad apprehension that such-and-such is the case: that my daughter has got into university, that my country has been liberated. There are some exceptions to this rule. Babies and animals can be happy without being happy about anything; adults too sometimes feel happy "for no particular reason." But even in these cases, happiness typically manifests itself as a certain comportment towards the world. The happy animal is at ease in its surroundings; the happy baby is open and communicative; the happy man looks on the world as bright, hopeful, full of novelty. "The world of the happy is quite another than that of the unhappy," said Wittgenstein.[33] The drug Ecstasy achieves its effects by changing the face of the world in this way, by transforming it, temporarily, into a kinder, lovelier place. This is why its after-effects are so depressing. Not only do you feel nauseous, you realize that your feelings have been duped.

Pleasure also has objects, as Aristotle recognized, yet these differ from the objects of happiness in being primarily experiential. One cannot take pleasure in things that will happen after one's death, or on the other side of the world, though one can take pleasure in the thought of them. Unlike happiness, pleasure is not centrally bound up with beliefs about the world; it can subsist on fantasies and illusions. (A virtual woman could give a man pleasure, but only a real one, or one believed to be real, could make him happy.) And even where pleasure is taken in real states of affairs, it draws them subtly into the orbit of experience. Compare "I am happy that Arsenal is top of the league" with "I take pleasure in the fact that Arsenal is top of the league." The former suggests a state of contented awareness, the latter a lip-smacking perusal of newspapers, television footage and so forth. This explains pleasure's dubious reputation. To "live for pleasure" implies a deliberate cultivation of experience, a gourmandising attitude to the world. And this remains true whether the pleasures in question are of the "high" or "low" variety.

Then there is joy. This is a state more exalted than either pleasure or happiness yet also more elusive. Pleasure and happiness can be pursued, but one would be hard put upon to pursue joy. Joy is paradoxically congruent with suffering, hence its prominence in Christian writing. Philippa Foot mentions a Quaker woman who after much hardship and persecution spoke of her "joyous life" preaching the Word. "She did not speak of her life as a happy life," adds Foot; "it would have been puzzling if she had."[34] And if joy is compatible with the absence of happiness and pleasure, happiness and pleasure are likewise compatible with the absence of joy. In his poem "The Deserted Village," Oliver Goldsmith lambastes the pleasures of the idle rich:

> But the long pomp, the midnight masquerade,
> With all the freaks of wanton wealth array'd—
> In these, ere triflers half their wish obtain,
> The toiling pleasure sickens into pain;
> And, e'en while fashion's brightest arts decoy,
> The heart distrusting asks if this be joy.

Goldsmith does not mean to deny that the revellers are enjoying themselves, at least up to the point at which "toiling pleasure sickens into pain." They are having "fun"—a word coined, not by accident, at around this time. But such fun does not amount to joy. Nor, presumably, would more fun amount to joy; the difference is one of quality, not degree.

Happiness, then, is distinct from both pleasure and joy. But even within the field of happiness there are distinctions to be drawn. We have said that happiness has objects, that it is about something. We can now add that happiness *takes its character* from what it is about. Deep happiness, for instance, is characterized as such not by palpitations or tremors—the mistake made by so many high-school story writers—but by its relation to certain centrally important human goods: love, childbirth, the completion of an important piece of work. "It does not make sense," writes Philippa Foot in her excellent discussion of the subject,

> to suggest that someone found deep happiness in, say, a victory in a running dispute with a neighbour over a morning newspaper or a milk bottle, however much we think of "fizzy" behaviour and elation. Whereas deep happiness and joy over the birth of a child? That is a different matter! ... We are tempted to think of deep happiness as explicable psychologically *in a way that makes it possible to separate it from its objects.* But why should this be possible? Why shouldn't the communality of meaning not depend here on a shared reaction among human beings to certain things that are very general in human life?[35]

If states of happiness take their character from their objects in the way Foot describes, there is no reason to suppose that they can all be ranked in order of intensity. Of course, we can, if we like, separate out the "fizz" and make that the measure of happiness, just as, in Layard's analogy, we can single out the loudness of a sound from its various other attributes. But why would we want to do that? What makes fizz so important? It would be as if—to turn Layard's analogy against him—we were to assess speeches purely on the basis of their volume, overlooking their content. The mistake can also be compared to that of people who rate sexual acts on the strength or frequency of orgasm, ignoring all the other ways in which they can succeed or fail.

As further illustration of this point, consider the figure of General Wynne-Candy, the Blimp character in Powell and Pressburger's marvellous 1943 film, *The Life and Death of Colonel Blimp*. As a young man, Candy falls in love with a woman who goes on to marry his best friend. He never gets over her, and all his subsequent love interests (played in the film by the same actress, Deborah Kerr) bear her a remarkable resemblance. Yet we are not given to suppose that the General spends much time brooding over his romantic disappointment; he is not, as he says, a "long-haired poet type." He has a successful military career, hunts big game, and generally exudes high spirits. Is Candy happy, then? On any "fizz" test, he surely is. He would show up proudly on a hedonimeter. Our grounds for thinking that he is not happy, or at least not deeply so, have to do with our belief in the centrality of love, as opposed to shooting tigers, in the scheme of human purposes. But this is not, perhaps, a perception shared by Candy himself. Here again, we find ourselves pushed towards a more objectivist understanding of happiness.

We have tried to show that a happy life, as most of us really understand that phrase, is not just a string of agreeable mental states but one that embodies certain basic human goods. *Eudaimonia* lurks under the surface of the modern, psychological understanding of happiness; it is not just a case of "smuggling in by the back door a particular philosopher's idea of a worthwhile life," as Samuel Brittan and others have claimed.[36] But to those unconvinced by this suggestion (of whom there will be many) we now present the second horn of our dilemma: if happiness is just a state of mind, how can it at the same time be the supreme good, the ultimate object of all our striving? To labor for years on a work of art or on bringing up a child simply so as to enjoy the resultant mental buzz is to betray a very peculiar attitude to life. Yet it is precisely this attitude that underlies the current cult of happiness.

The problem can be stated a bit more precisely. Happiness economists believe that states of mind are good in proportion as they are happy. The happier, the better; the sadder, the worse. The objects or occasions of happiness and sadness are of no moral significance. "No good feeling is bad in itself," writes Layard; "it can only be bad because of its consequences."[37] Other happiness economists are less forthright, but they must believe something similar if their project is to make moral sense. If happiness is not intrinsically good, what on earth are we doing trying to maximize it?*

Yet the plain fact is that happiness, conceived psychologically, is not good in itself but insofar as it is *due*, or at least not undue. To be happy that x is the case when x does not warrant happiness, or does not obtain at all, is not necessarily a good thing. Imagine someone smiling rapturously at the news of a disaster in which hundreds have died. "Why are you so happy?" we might ask. "What is there to be happy about?" Or think of a student who, thanks to a double dose of Prozac, is serenely indifferent to his impending failure—in a fool's paradise, as we say. We might well think it better for this student *not* to be happy, for he would then at least be in touch with the reality of his situation. (An Aristotelian would make the same point by saying that the student is not really happy at all, but that is not an option open to happiness economists.) Not all unwarranted happiness is bad; we do not want to snuff out the child's gratuitous joy in living, or the dying man's illusions. But clearly, the value of a happy state of mind hinges at least in part on the worthiness or otherwise of its object. And if this is granted, then the project of maximizing happiness itself, independent of its objects, assumes a sinister aspect.

Just as there is unwarranted happiness, so there is warranted sadness. Sadness is often unwarranted, of course, being rooted in false beliefs or irrational mental mechanisms, but in other cases it is simply the lucid perception of things to be sad about. So long as such things exist—and they surely always will—sadness can be eliminated only by (a) screening them from view or (b) altering our sensibilities so that we are no longer care about them. Ways of doing this can easily be imagined. Scientists might develop a drug—a kind of psychic aspirin—to erase all memory of grief or heartache. Newspapers and broadcasters might stop reporting famines, earthquakes and so forth. Some of these

---

* It should be added, in all fairness, that most happiness economists are not proposing to maximize happiness just anyhow, including, say, by compulsory lobotomization. They are, in the jargon, "constrained maximizers"; they seek to maximize happiness within a framework of basic rights and justice. How these constraints might be justified on their own utilitarian premises is not generally explored.

measures might actually work. But none of them strikes us as remotely desirable.

Many religious and philosophical traditions have seen sadness as the proper response not just to individual tragedy but to the tragedy of human life as such. This perception has faded from Western Christianity but remains strong in the Orthodox East. "If you are really aware of things, of how tragic life is, then there is restraint in your enjoyment," said Archbishop Bloom, the former head of the Russian Orthodox Church in Britain. "Joy is another thing. One can possess a great sense of inner joy and elation, but enjoying the outer aspects of life with the awareness of so many people suffering . . . is something which I find difficult."[38] Similar thoughts can be found in other religious traditions. Even that pagan life-affirmer Nietzsche had little time for any happiness not born of suffering. "Man does not strive for happiness," he wrote famously; "only the Englishman does that."[39]

Happiness economists will no doubt dismiss all this as so much mystic misery-mongering. Yet one does not have to be a Russian monk or a German philosopher to find something disturbing in the project of maximizing happiness itself, regardless of its objects. For the logical conclusion of such a project is to dispense with external objects altogether and act directly on the brain. Some happiness economists have already drawn this conclusion. Yew-Kwang Ng has called for research into brain stimulation, an operation with the power to generate "intense pleasure without diminishing marginal utility." The only potentially more effective method, Ng adds cheerfully, is genetic engineering.[40] Richard Layard speaks enthusiastically about mood-altering drugs, not just as remedies for depression but as general welfare-enhancing devices. Perpetual euphoria is rejected by him only because "part of the time we should need our minds to be sharp enough to organise our existence."[41] Otherwise, presumably, we would be better off in a state of permanent idiotic bliss.

Brave New World is not upon us quite yet. Layard and Ng do not want to force us to take soma or have our brains stimulated. They are, as we said, constrained maximizers; they seek to maximize happiness within the established framework of legal rights. But this qualification is not greatly reassuring, for the deepest and most troubling aspect of Brave New World is not coercion but infantilism—the disappearance of any desire or attachment that could disrupt the machinery of pleasure. A system of this kind is only incidentally coercive; it could just as easily come into being as a result of free private choices, without anyone pointing a gun at anyone. After all, if pleasures of the sort described by Ng were to become available on the market, would any of us be able to resist them?

Only in the very special case of depression is unhappiness an unequivocal evil and a legitimate target of state action. But depression is a class apart. It is not just extreme unhappiness but inapt, disproportionate unhappiness, and it is this that constitutes its peculiar badness. (A grieving widow might be no less unhappy than a man with depression, but her unhappiness is a fitting response to loss, not a problem to be cured.) Depression is a medical matter, to be dealt with under the rubric of mental health. It is not, as Layard presents it, part of a general crisis of unhappiness, nor should the fight against it be seen as part of a broader campaign to make people happier.

To go from the pursuit of growth to the pursuit of happiness is to turn from one false idol to another. Our proper goal, as individuals and as citizens, is not just to be happy but to have reason to be happy. To have the good things of life—health, respect, friendship, leisure—is to have reason to be happy. To be happy without these things is to be in the grip of a delusion: the delusion that life is going well when in fact it is not. Such a delusion is known by Marxists as an ideology and it serves to conceal the fact of oppression and degradation. Paradise and gin were the traditional instruments for reconciling the wretched to their lot. The endorsement of "happiness" by the Cameron government suggests that it too may soon play a similar role.

Of course, most happiness economists have no such design. They only wish, like us, to steer policy away from the blind pursuit of wealth towards the improvement of real living conditions. But they have adopted a language that points—"objectively," as Marxists say—in quite another direction. For if happiness is a mere private sensation, with no intrinsic connection to living well, then soma or brain stimulation might well turn out to be the cheapest, most effective means of achieving it. Why not admit up front that our concern is with the good life—and let happiness look after itself?

5

Limits to Growth:
Natural or Moral?

*Nature has good intentions, of course, but, as Aristotle
once said, she cannot carry them out.*

—Oscar Wilde

As well as failing to improve the human lot, economic growth has
been accused of violating the innocence of nature. This second charge
is almost as old as the first. Wordsworth in 1814 lamented the "out-
rage done to nature" by machine production; others following him
have bemoaned the destruction of forests and wildernesses, the
extinction of flora and fauna, and the fouling of rivers, lakes and seas.
But in the last two decades, one spectre above all has gripped the
public imagination: that of a catastrophic, irreversible rise in the
earth's temperature. To avert this disaster, we are urged to abandon
economic growth, perhaps even civilization as we have known it.

The environmentalist case against growth likes to present itself as
a rational response to established facts. Yet its secret spirit remains
that of romanticism. It is not self-evident, to dispassionate eyes, that
global warming requires us to abandon growth. It might rather
require us to *persevere* with growth, so as to finance the technologies
needed to mitigate its consequences. Facts alone cannot decide this
argument. The clash is rather one of worldviews: Promethean optimism on the one hand, piety before nature on the other. But the
utilitarian cast of our public discourse requires us to talk instead of
offsets and emissions.

The covertly religious character of the Green movement is often
viewed, by friends and foes alike, as an embarrassment, a scandal,

even. In our public culture, science is the supreme arbiter of truth and falsehood; the rest is chit-chat. This is not our view. We respect and share the religious feeling at the heart of environmentalism. But we believe that this feeling is best expressed openly rather than hidden under the fig leaf of science. Concealment is not only dishonest, it creates hostages to fortune. For if growth turns out to be sustainable after all, as it well might, then those whose opposition to it was based solely on its *un*sustainability will have nothing left to say. They will be in the position of those early Christians whose faith was founded on the conviction of Christ's imminent return.

There is something else that environmentalists might remember. Prophecies of plague and tempest are a time-honored yet unlovely way of encouraging a spirit of renunciation. It is kinder (and probably more effective) to show people that a less cluttered life is a good life, one desirable in and of itself. The art historian Kenneth Clark spoke of the German Rococo, with its ravishing domes and ornaments, as persuading "not by fear but by joy." Extremists have always relied on the exploitation of fear to achieve their ends. Our own aspiration is to persuade by joy, to present a vision of the good life as one to be pursued not from guilt or fear of retribution but in happiness and hope.

Limits to Growth

Keynes looked forwards to a final *end* of growth, a point at which all material wants are definitively satisfied. Others, more pessimistic, have postulated a *limit* to growth, an external barrier to further progress. Thomas Malthus's *Essay on the Principle of Population*, mentioned in Chapter 2, is the first and classic statement of this point of view. Malthus's argument is beguilingly simple. It starts from two certainties: the finitude of the earth and the existence of a certain "passion between the sexes." The earth's ability to bring forth food is inherently limited. Field can be added to field, but sooner or later a point of maximum capacity will be reached. The multiplicative power of the human race, by contrast, is without bounds. If each generation were to double its numbers—and remember that in Malthus's day, four or more offspring was the rule—the universe would soon be teeming with humanity. Collision is inevitable. As Malthus puts it, "the power of population is so superior to the power of the earth to produce subsistence for man, that premature death must in some shape or other visit the human race."[1]

The Malthusian spectre was avoided by most (although not all) European countries in the nineteenth century, through a combination of rising agricultural productivity, falling birth rates and mass emigration to the New World. But it has been raised many times subsequently. The 1972 bestseller *Limits to Growth* predicted that world population would hit 7 billion by the end of the twentieth century, leading to shortages of grain, oil, gas, copper, aluminium and gold.[2] These prophecies turned out to be predictably alarmist. Specifically, the "green revolution" in agriculture, which greatly increased cereal yields per hectare, staved off the threat of mass starvation, despite the close-to-projected growth of population. The other scenarios of depletion also failed to materialize.[3] The "population bomb," to borrow the title of an influential 1960s tract, turned out to be a damp squib.[4]

This turn of events comes as no surprise to economists. The basic flaw in Malthus's argument has long been known to them: it ignores the joint force of prices and technological innovation. As existing reserves of any raw material dwindle, its price goes up, creating an incentive to (a) seek out new reserves, (b) exploit existing reserves more efficiently and (c) explore alternatives. For example, the recent rise in oil prices has prompted the opening up of new fields in Alaska and the Gulf of Mexico as well as investment in wind, solar and other forms of power. Given a technologically progressive civilization, *which controls population growth*, it is highly unlikely that our planet will run out of food, energy or the other requirements of life. The quality of life in such a planet is, of course, another matter.

But the Malthusian argument can take another, more powerful form. What if the ultimate limit to growth lies not in "sources" but in "sinks," not in the earth's supply of oil and other industrial resources but in its capacity to absorb their waste products? Pollution is recalcitrant in relation to the usual market mechanisms. It is what economists call a "negative externality": its ill-effects are not reflected in its price, so it tends to be overproduced relative to its true cost. If pollution is to be controlled, it must be by collective action. And this action must be global, since the effects of pollution are often felt a long distance from its source.

One particular pollutant has come to dominate public discussion. Carbon dioxide is released into the air by the combustion of coal, gas and oil, fuels that between them account for about 80 percent of global energy. Its atmospheric concentration has risen steadily since the Industrial Revolution and continues to rise. This is worrying, because carbon dioxide is one of a number of gases that prevent heat from the sun escaping back into the atmosphere. As its concentration increases, the earth gets warmer. This is the "anthropogenic (or man-made) greenhouse effect," believed to be the chief cause of global warming.

Global warming is quite unlike previous Malthusian scares, in scale and in character. Its anticipated effects include flooding, drought, plague and, on a worst case scenario, the total destruction of human life. Its elimination requires the abandonment not just of this or that luxury but of coal, gas and oil—the lifeblood of industrial civilization. This provides a convenient platform to those who never liked industrial civilization to begin with. Climate campaigner George Monbiot has urged the governments of the rich world "to keep growth rates as close to zero as possible."[5] In a similar spirit, sustainability adviser Tim Jackson argues that only the *complete* elimination of growth can save us from planetary disaster, adding hopefully that it will make us happier too.[6]

We agree that, for the affluent world, growth is no longer a sensible goal of long-term policy. But we regard this as an ethical truth, not as a conclusion from scientific fact. The problems of global warming, serious as they are, do not on their own require us to abandon growth. It is only on the additional assumption, usually unacknowledged, that beyond a certain point growth is inherently undesirable that the inference becomes compelling. An ethical ideal has been smuggled in under the cloak of a pragmatic necessity, a familiar ruse in our utilitarian political culture.

The term "climate change denier"—modelled on "Holocaust denier," and with similar overtones—is often applied to those who dispute the scientific consensus on global warming. We are not deniers. Our doubts concern the economic implications, not the science of global warming. That said, the science is not as settled as is often claimed. Climatology is a young field, in which much remains uncertain and disputed. It is also fiercely politicized, with powerful commercial and bureaucratic interests on either side of the debate. Not even the Inter-governmental Panel on Climate Change (IPCC), the world's chief assembly of climate scientists, is entirely above suspicion. "There remains a risk," claims a 2005 House of Lords report on climate change, "that IPCC has become a 'knowledge monopoly' in some respects, unwilling to listen to those who do not pursue the consensus line."[7] Faced with this barrage of accusation and counter-accusation, the best we can do as non-scientists is to accept the majority view, which is that global warming is indeed mainly the result of human activity. Nothing in what follows hinges on its not being true.

The argument from global warming to growth reduction typically takes a utilitarian form. A degree of suffering is required today, it is claimed, in order to prevent much greater suffering in the future. But this argument is valid only if (a) the future costs of global warming can be known with some degree of certainty and (b) these costs carry equal weight whether they are felt now, fifty years hence, or two hundred years hence. Both assumptions are questionable. Let us take them in turn.

Forecasting is a hazardous business, especially in fields as complex and ill-understood as this. That does not prevent people trying though. The IPCC has been putting out estimates of the costs of global warming since 1990. These estimates are generated on powerful computers and stretch decades into the future. They radiate technocratic authority. But how much can they really tell us? The IPCC's models are based on long-term projections not only of climate but of population, economic growth and technological change, all highly uncertain. Compound these uncertainties, and you have what the IPCC itself calls a "cascade of uncertainty."[8] This seems a weak basis on which to adopt measures that will *certainly* have a drastic effect on our standard of living.

Technology is central to estimating the costs of global warming, because it determines how well we can respond to the flooding, drought and disease forecast to follow in its wake. Yet technological change is in principle unpredictable, for the reasons spelt out by Karl Popper: if we could predict what we will know, we would already know it.[9] (This might be dubbed the *Star Trek* effect, in honor of the well-known tendency of old sci-fi films to tell us only about the fantasies of their own epoch.) The IPCC is aware of the difficulty, admitting that technologies "in use 100 years hence could have unimagined effects on climate sensitivity and vulnerability."[10] Yet it is precisely because these effects are unimagined—and unimaginable—that they cannot be incorporated into a formal predictive model. Our Edwardian ancestors could not have foreseen the genetic technologies that enable us to feed 7 billion people today. Should we be surprised if our descendants devise technologies that enable them to cope with three, four or even more degrees of warming?

To its credit, the IPCC does not attach probabilities to its various scenarios, presenting them simply as alternative "story lines." Inevitably, though, it is the most extreme of these story lines that is seized on by politicians seeking to bolster their Green credentials and by advisers hoping to curry favor with them. The process is the familiar one of "sexing up": expert statements are gradually stripped of their caveats, emerging finally as easy-to-digest sound bites. Thus, for instance, it was the bleakest of the IPCC's six scenarios that became the basis of the influential 2006 Stern Review, which in turn inspired Tony Blair's statement, in an open letter to EU heads of state, that "we have a window of only 10–15 years to take the steps we need to avoid crossing a catastrophic tipping-point."[11] (That was in 2006. We now have only five to ten years left.)

The idea of a catastrophic "tipping point" or "point of no return" is rejected by most serious scientists as lacking sufficient empirical foundation. "The language of catastrophe is not the language of science," writes Mike Hulme, former director of the Tyndall Centre for Climate Research at the University of East Anglia.[12] But that has not stopped its use by some who should know better. Veteran geochemist James Lovelock (of whom more later) sees the world approaching a state "that could easily be described as Hell: so hot, so deadly that only a handful of the teeming billions now alive will survive."[13] Passages like this present us with a secular version of Pascal's famous wager: they conjure an evil so fearful that its avoidance is worth *any* sacrifice, however great. This argumentative strategy (now dignified as the "strong precautionary principle") is one calculated to inspire panic. On any sober reckoning, the dangers of global warming, though real, are on a scale commensurable with those of war, plague and many other potential disasters. They do not demand the *total* concentration of effort and resources called for by climate radicals.

The environmentalist case for growth reduction presupposes not only that the ravages of global warming are foreseeable with some degree of accuracy but that they carry equal weight regardless of their remoteness in time. Even if the disaster lies two hundred years ahead, we must make sacrifices of up to the same level *now* in order to avert it. This is counterintuitive in the extreme. Most people value the happiness of the living more than that of the as yet unborn. They are "present-centric." Most environmental economists register this fact by applying a "discount" to future welfare: they stipulate, in effect, that jam tomorrow shall count for less than jam today. They furthermore assume that since future generations are likely to be richer than ourselves, they will be better able to bear the cost of global warming. Together, these two assumptions lead to the conclusion that "despite the serious threats to the global economy posed by climate change, little should be done to reduce carbon emissions in the near future; that controls on carbon should be put into effect in an increasing, but gradual manner, starting several decades from now."[14]

Climate radicals are strongly opposed to discounting future welfare. Why should the mere fact that an individual is born in 2100 rather than 2000 diminish his claim on our regard? Isn't this "presentism," analogous to racism and sexism? The Stern Review operates with a pure time discount rate of close to zero, meaning that it attaches almost equal weight to the welfare of all individuals, present and future. (The only reason the discount rate is not zero is to allow for the small possibility that the human race may cease to exist.) This generates the conclusion that an immediate reduction in carbon emissions, small at first but increasing to 1 percent of global GDP by the year 2050, is necessary in order to avoid the still greater costs of global warming.[15] Stern has subsequently doubled his estimate of the cost of tackling climate change, and even higher figures have been proposed by authors following him, amounting to a complete elimination of growth.[16]

The ethics of the Stern Review are those of a celestial egalitarian, to whom all ages are contemporary and all human beings, past, present and future, count equally for one. But our standpoint, the human standpoint, is sub-celestial. We see the world from a particular location in time and distribute our sympathies accordingly. We value our children's welfare higher than our grandchildren's and our grandchildren's higher than our great-grandchildren's, and we would be remiss not to. Nigel Lawson reminds us of the figure of Mrs. Jellyby, the "telescopic philanthropist" in Charles Dickens's *Bleak House*, who is so devoted to the poor of Africa that she neglects her own children. "The self-proclaimed ethical basis of the Stern Review's discount rate is little more than intertemporal Jellybyism," he adds.[17] But Stern's position is even odder than this. Mrs Jellyby treats her nearest and dearest on a par with strangers. Stern treats existing people on a par with non-existing people. He throws the welfare of mere *possibilia* into the scales together with that of flesh-and-blood human beings. We can reject this bizarre philosophy without embracing Louis XV's *après moi le déluge*. We need only say that the welfare of the unborn counts for *less* than that of the living, though it still counts for something.

The argument from global warming to growth reduction is so weak that one reaches for deeper explanations of its persistent appeal. Such explanations are not hard to come by. Most climate radicals are also passionate haters of greed and luxury, people who in previous ages might have been Cromwells or Savonarolas. Infusing a good deal of environmentalist literature is a love of the hair shirt. The puritan accent is unmistakable in George Monbiot's announcement that his is a campaign "not for abundance but for austerity. It is a campaign not for more freedom but for less. Strangest of all, it is a campaign not just against other people, but also against ourselves."[18] Here, and not in the dreary reams of computer-generated cost-benefit analysis, lies the beating heart of climate activism.

To sum up: the environmentalist case for growth reduction cannot be explained as a pragmatic response to known facts. It betrays a passion, a will to believe, to which the facts are incidental. When Marx's economic predictions were falsified by events, his followers remained unshaken. Similarly, if current fears about global warming turn out to be baseless, climate radicals will not abandon their opposition to long-distance flying and four-by-fours; rather, they will find new arguments to justify their austerities. It is as faith, not science, that environmentalism stands or falls. Where does this faith come from? To answer that, we must look to history.

The Ethical Roots of Environmentalism

The scientific revolution of the seventeenth century strove to establish what its prophet Francis Bacon called the *regnum hominis*, the empire of man. Nature was reduced to inert material, serviceable to human ends, God to an abstract "first mover," remote and indifferent. Man alone was left sovereign of the world. Locke and others reinterpreted the Book of Genesis in the light of this new philosophy, as a God-given mandate to strip, plough and quarry, thereby forging a link between Protestant Christianity and environmental exploitation that endures to this day. The nineteenth-century American economist H. C. Carey was voicing the common sense of his age when he described the earth as "a great machine, given to man to be fashioned to his purpose."[19]

The Baconian project and its industrial aftermath provoked an impassioned reaction from poets and writers. Wordsworth's protest against the rape of nature was taken up by John Ruskin and William Morris in England, Henry David Thoreau and Ralph Waldo Emerson in America and numerous others. What moved these writers was not any scientific theory of pollution or resource depletion but a primal, semi-pagan sense of nature as sacred and a corresponding horror of human meddling. "All is seared with trade, bleared, smeared with toil," wrote Gerard Manley Hopkins, contemplating the effects of man's activity on the earth. This disgust was directed as much against farming as it was against industry. Romanticism fostered a new taste for *wild* nature, for moors and mountains as opposed to the pastures and vineyards favored by earlier generations of poets and painters.

The earliest environmental groups—the National Trust in Britain, the Homeland Protection League in Germany, the Sierra Club in America—were products of the romantic cult of old buildings and "unspoilt" landscapes. Their members were middle-class enthusiasts with conservative, patriotic leanings. They had no quarrel with industry as such, so long as it remained hidden tactfully away. The rambling clubs that sprang up in the late nineteenth century were more proletarian and leftist in character, yet they too aimed only at temporary holidays from industrial civilization, not at its overall dismantlement. Workers knew very well on which side their bread was buttered.

But early environmentalism harbored other, more radical tendencies, for which the enemy was technology itself, not just its occasional abuses. Ludwig Klages, a charismatic German philosopher and poet, sounded the characteristic note. "Progress is bent on the *destruction of life*," he wrote in 1913. "It attacks it in all its forms, cuts down forests, extinguishes species, wipes out indigenous peoples, smothers and disfigures the landscape with the varnish of commerce and degrades such living creatures as it spares, like 'livestock,' into mere merchandise."[20] The philosopher Martin Heidegger was similarly absolutist. His 1953 essay on modern technology presents it as an all-pervasive "enframing" of nature, which co-opts even attempts to escape it:

> The hydroelectric plant is not built into the Rhine River as was the old wooden bridge that joined bank with bank for hundreds of years. Rather, the river is dammed up into the power plant. What the river is now, namely, a water-power supplier, derives from the essence of the power station ... But, it will be replied, the Rhine is still a river in the landscape, is it not? Perhaps. But how? In no other way than as an object on call for inspection by a tour group ordered there by the vacation industry.[21]

Klages, an anti-Semite, and Heidegger, an unrepentant Nazi, are among the unacknowledged forefathers of the modern Green movement. Their ideas were made over for the left by Theodor Adorno and Max Horkheimer after the Second World War and exported to America by Adorno's old colleague, Herbert Marcuse. ("The ecological movement," said Marcuse with typical intransigence, "must seek not the mere beautification of the existing Establishment but a radical transformation of the very institutions and enterprises which waste our resources and pollute the earth."[22]) In recent decades, environmentalism has come to be seen as a wholly "progressive" movement. It is only a few old-school Marxists who harbor a suspicion that it conceals a design to keep the poor in their place.

Until the 1960s, the radical critique of technology remained confined to a fringe of students, artists and intellectuals. Two developments brought it into the mainstream. One was the emergence of ecology, the science of living creatures in their natural habitat. Ecology fostered a new awareness of the interdependence of life and the hazards of human intervention. It lent scientific support to the old mystical idea that nature embodies a "balance" that we disturb only at our own cost. Rachel Carson's *Silent Spring*, a 1962 polemic against the misuse of pesticides, was an influential expression of this line of thought. The 1960s also saw a revival of Malthusian worries about population growth and resource scarcity. Paul Ehrlich's *The Population Bomb* was published in 1968, followed shortly by *Limits to Growth* (1972) and economist E. F. Schumacher's *Small is Beautiful* (1973). This new wave of environmentalist thinking retained an aura of radicalism, but its real object was the long-term "sustainability" of industrial society, not its abolition. It could make a dent on practical men and women to whom alienation and enframing meant little or nothing.

Since the 1970s, mainstream environmentalism has continued to frame its case in the utilitarian language of sustainability, though its profounder impulses remain ethical, aesthetic or even religious. This has led to a tension in the movement between so-called deep and shallow ecologists, the former valuing nature as an end in itself, the latter valuing it as an instrument of human purposes. (The campaign against global warming positions itself in the "shallow" camp, though as we have seen, many of its supporters harbor "deeper" leanings.) There is a parallel tension between environmentalism's originally Luddite instincts and its new reliance on computer forecasting. The same people who forty years ago might have spoken of "techno-fascism" now find themselves staunch defenders of the scientific orthodoxy.

The two sides of the environmental movement, romantic and

scientific, are united in the person of James Lovelock, inventor of the electron capture detector and author of the famous Gaia hypothesis. A scientist with broad interests in geochemistry, ecology and cybernetics, Lovelock came to the view that living creatures play a crucial role in maintaining the earth's temperature and atmosphere in a state hospitable to life. This led him to wonder whether the earth as a whole might not be thought of as a self-regulating system, akin to an organism. He mentioned his hunch to the novelist William Golding, a neighbor of his, who "without hesitation . . . recommended that this creature be called Gaia, after the Greek Earth goddess."[23] A new myth was born.

Gaia was first proposed by Lovelock as a purely heuristic device, a way of framing hypotheses, not a literal statement of fact. "Occasionally it has been difficult, without excessive circumlocution, to avoid talking of Gaia as if she were known to be sentient," he wrote in 1978. "This is meant no more seriously than is the appellation 'she' when given to a ship by those who sail her."[24] But in Lovelock's more recent writings, the caveats have vanished. "What if Mary is another name for Gaia?" he asks rhetorically in *The Ages of Gaia*. "On Earth she is the source of life everlasting and is alive now; she gave birth to humankind and we are part of her."[25] Lovelock is playing a double game here: on the one hand, reassuring his scientific colleagues, on the other, giving the nod to the neo-pagans. Gaia, respectably naturalistic yet rich in mythical undertones, is a divinity tailor-made for an age incapable of transcendent faith.

Gaia's message is ambiguous. If she is robust ("a tough old bitch," as Lovelock's collaborator Lynn Margulis has called her), then perhaps she can accommodate all we throw at her. After all, she has been accommodating disturbances throughout her long history. But perhaps she is not so robust any more. Or perhaps her "accommodation" of this particular disturbance will take the form of removing its source—namely, ourselves. Lovelock's recent book, *The Revenge of Gaia*, favors this latter possibility. Here, Gaia is no longer the Virgin Mary, mild and tender, but a pagan fury. "We now see that the great Earth system, Gaia, behaves like the other mythical goddesses, Khali and Nemesis; she acts as a mother who is nurturing but ruthlessly cruel towards transgressors, even when they are her progeny."[26]

With this, prophecy has finally triumphed over science. Lovelock's catastrophic vision has no empirical or theoretical foundation. Its logic is mythopoeic: man's misdeeds call out for vengeance, and, God being dead, Nature must wield the sword. It was in this spirit that Wordsworth, in the poem quoted at the start of this chapter, called on nature to "avenge her violated rights," and the Victorian naturalist G. P. Marsh spoke of nature "avenging herself upon the intruder."[27] Such rhetoric is not only bad science; it is also, more importantly, bad religion. Nature as conceived by her modern devotees cares only for her own "balance," not for the good of man. She inherits God's wrath, but not his mercy. Gaia marks a retrogression, not an evolution, in religious consciousness.

This brief history confirms the conclusion arrived at earlier: sentiment, not science, has driven and continues to drive the environmentalist movement. Why are modern Greens reluctant to admit as much? Partly because they worry about undermining the credibility of their purely "positive" arguments; partly, too, because they fear that a frank airing of their motives would expose much that is unsavory. They may not be wrong. The pity of it is, however, that amidst all the silliness and nastiness environmentalism harbors the germ of a marvellous ideal, acknowledgement of which would not weaken but greatly *strengthen* its cause. It is to this ideal that we turn now.

Harmony with Nature

Modern ecological ethics divides into two broad groupings, which we have identified as "shallow" and "deep." The former sees nature as a human resource, to be managed with an eye to the interests of future generations. The latter views it as valuable in and of itself, independently of its utility to us. Neither captures the true character of our concern for nature. It is by dissecting the shortcomings of both that we can arrive at a more adequate formulation.

The "shallow" wing of the Green movement, as exemplified by the Stern Review and many subsequent publications, simply extends the standard cost-benefit analysis over a longer than usual timeframe. Its rationale is the familiar egalitarian one: we should not privilege our own welfare over that of the as yet unborn, just as we should not privilege the welfare of whites over blacks, or of men over women. We should not be "presentists."

This argument takes us some way. We have already made the case that the welfare of future generations should count for *something* with us, if not as much as the welfare of the living, and that we should therefore take pains not to leave the world a desert. But welfarist considerations do not exhaust our interest in nature. The philosopher Mary Midgley asks us to imagine Robinson Crusoe blowing up his island, together with all its plant and animal inhabitants, as he sets sail for home. No human interests are at stake, yet the act still strikes us as wanton.[28] Or to take a real-life example, we care strongly about the fate of the polar bear and the snow leopard, neither of them of any utility to us. (Some might say that the pleasure we take in their existence *is* their utility to us, but were that true, we could obliterate this utility simply by ceasing to care about them, thus releasing ourselves from any obligation to ensure their survival.) It is clear that we value the existence of the polar bear and the snow leopard "for its own sake," independent of any benefit we may derive from it. And the same is true of the vast majority of endangered species across the globe.

Thoughts such as these give encouragement to the alternative, "deep" wing of the Green movement. Deep ecologists regard the "shallow" argument outlined above as a mere variant on the discreditable old Lockean idea that the earth exists solely for our benefit. They urge us to view "the flourishing of non-human life" as an end in itself, independent of any interest, long-term or otherwise, that we might have in it.[29] But this now raises an intractable problem. What can "the flourishing of non-human life" possibly *mean*? For plainly, there is no single entity called "non-human life," only a myriad of non-human organisms and species, many of them in competition with others. The flourishing of the grey squirrel is at the expense of the red squirrel. The flourishing of the tick is at the expense of the dog. What could it mean to promote the "flourishing of non-human life" as a whole?

Perhaps promoting the flourishing of non-human life means promoting the flourishing of all non-human species equally. Arne Naess, the original deep ecologist, speaks of an "equal right to live and blossom."[30] But this now raises a host of further problems. Who are the bearers of this "equal right"? Are plants, fungi and bacteria all included? Does a life form acquire it on being classified as a species and lose it on being reclassified as a subspecies (a common occurrence in biology)? That seems rather harsh. Does the "equal right to live and blossom" imply that we should devote equal resources to saving the snow leopard and the *acanthomyops latipes*, one of many hundreds of endangered insects? What about the smallpox virus, now confined to two laboratories in the world? Surely we need consult only our own interests here. But for "biospherical egalitarians" such as Naess, any favoring of one species over others on self-interested, sentimental or aesthetic grounds reveals the cloven hoof of "anthropocentrism." We must be as disinterested in our dealings with nature as a Cato or a Brutus.

An only somewhat more sensible proposal is utilitarian in inspiration. If our goal is to maximize pleasure and minimize pain, animal pleasures and pains must be given equal consideration. To disregard them is "speciesism": an arbitrary prejudice in favor of our own kind.[31] But quite apart from the general problems of utilitarianism, some of them touched on in the last chapter, this proposal misrepresents the character of our concern with nature. For a start, it gives us no non-instrumental reason to care for plants, which cannot feel pleasure or pain. Moreover, many animals, wild herbivores in particular, lead lives shot through by disease, hunger and fear. A consistent utilitarianism would require us to shelter them in large parks, safe from predators, with easy access to food and medical treatment. The predators meanwhile might be fed chunks of ethically farmed meat, or some soya-derived substitute. The fantasy can be developed at length. The point is that this is not a proposal that could possibly be endorsed by anyone concerned with the flourishing of our *natural* habitat.

Another tack for deep ecologists is suggested by Aldo Leopold, an early pioneer of environmental ethics. "A thing is right," wrote Leopold, "when it tends to preserve the integrity, stability, and beauty of the biotic community. It is wrong when it tends otherwise."[32] Here, the unit of concern is not all species taken individually but the *community* of species. We are called on to maximize the good of the whole, even if this requires the injury or destruction of some of its parts. James Lovelock is in this holistic tradition. He talks of Gaia as sick, feverish, senile and so on, urging us to do whatever we still can to restore her to health. He even appears to take a grisly relish in the thought that our destruction might benefit Gaia, like the elimination of a cancer or a virus.

Such language is morally dangerous, as we said earlier. It is also confused. The biotic community, or Gaia, is neither an organism nor anything like an organism. It cannot be healthy or sick, flourish or founder. Organisms belong to *kinds*, whose characteristic functioning and way of life defines their norms of sickness and health.[33] A camel with only one hump is a defective camel, unless of course it is a dromedary. Gaia, by contrast, is *sui generis*. There are no "gaias." It is therefore misleading, even as a metaphor, to talk of Gaia as sick or feverish. (What is the correct temperature for "a gaia" to be?) Promoting the health of Gaia is a task without meaning—which is just as well, otherwise it might oblige us to commit collective suicide.

What has gone wrong? Deep ecologists are quite right to insist that nature's value is intrinsic, not instrumental; their mistake is to conclude from this that it is *independent of our point of view*. That does not follow, and is not true. All value, instrumental and intrinsic, is relative to the human point of view, for the simple reason that we are the one and only valuing animal. Other animals have goods, but they do not grasp those goods *as* goods, as things worthy of pursuit. They are not moral agents. "Anthropocentrism" is not a prejudice but a simple corollary of this fact. As Bernard Williams puts it in his discussion of the subject, "a concern for nonhuman animals is indeed a proper part of human life, but we can acquire it, cultivate it, and teach it only in terms of our understanding of ourselves."[34]

It may seem strange to say that nature's value is both anthropocentric *and* intrinsic. How can both ascriptions be true? Yet we are all familiar with another item whose value is both anthropocentric and intrinsic, namely, art. "One day," wrote Oswald Spengler, "the last portrait of Rembrandt and the last bar of Mozart will have ceased to be—though possibly a coloured canvas and a sheet of notes will remain—because the last eye and the last ear accessible to their message will have gone."[35] Art, in other words, has value only to creatures sharing our sensibilities and concerns. But it does not follow that art's value is merely instrumental, that we prize it solely as a source of pleasure, cultural capital, or whatever. Art's value is clearly intrinsic, though it enters the world only through the window of our perceptions. And if this is true of art, why should it not be true of nature as well?

Another way of putting the point that nature's value is both anthropocentric and intrinsic is to say that *harmony with nature is part of the good life for man.* This formulation captures both sides of the picture. It makes it clear that nature's value is intrinsic (to live in harmony with something is not to manipulate it for one's own ends) yet at the same time anthropocentric (harmony with nature is part of *our* good). It preserves what is true in both shallow and deep positions while discarding what is false.

A practical illustration of "harmony with nature" is provided by the activity of gardening. A good gardener knows and respects the potentialities of nature. He does not (unless he is French) see trees and bushes as mere "material" to be twisted into any desired shape or form. Yet neither are his interventions entirely disinterested. He waters some plants, digs up others. He lops trees when they grow too large. He lays down poison for slugs and snails. In short, he channels nature's inherent tendencies in accordance with a human ideal of comfort and beauty. His relation to nature is neither vulgarly instrumental nor grimly sacrificial. It is a relation of harmony.[36]

Gardening's unique power to reveal what it means to live in harmony with nature explains why it figures prominently in depictions of the good life the world over. The Bible places Adam and Eve in a garden. The Koran promises the faithful a place in "the garden of delights," where water flows perpetually and the fruit is never out of season. Chinese philosophers are typically depicted strolling amidst mountains or bamboo groves, far from the bustle of the city. "If you have a garden and a library," wrote Cicero, "you have everything you need." The recurrence of such imagery in cultures across the world suggests that harmony with nature is a universal need of the soul—a "basic good," as we put it in the next chapter.

This being the case, why does the idea of harmony with nature feature so little in the literature of modern environmentalism?

The answer, presumably, is that it assumes a picture of nature as something we *could* be in harmony with, as summoning us to certain ways of life and not others. That picture is now seen as "metaphysical" in the bad sense. Nature, in the standard modern conception, is just there: factive, hard, impermeable to human understanding. It is not the kind of thing we could be (or fail to be) in harmony with. To care for nature can only mean to manage it in our long-term interests or else let it go its own strange way—the standpoints of shallow and deep ecology respectively.

Yet the fact remains that most people—even those who have been through the positivist mill, when they are not on philosophical best behavior—*do* make a distinction between activities that are and are not "in harmony" with nature. They find the gardens of Versailles artificial compared to those of Stowe, though they know that both are products of human art. They are nauseated by factory farming, though they know full well that all farming involves the deliberate modification of life. Common sense, the supreme arbiter in matters of practice, tells us that some activities go "with," others "against," the grain of nature. We will need more than a philosophical theory to convince us otherwise.

What would an environmentalism remodelled along these lines— "good-life environmentalism," we can call it—look like in practice? Very different from current environmentalism, both deep and shallow. It would promote "green" ways of life not for nature's sake or for future generations' sake but for *our* sake. It would encourage us, for our own good, to acquire a knowledge of local plants and animals, to eat local food, and, where possible, to take part in its production, through fishing, horticulture and other activities. Many environmentalists are already moved by such "good-life" considerations, though most would blush to admit it. (How many English allotment owners would say, as a Russian lady once said to us, that growing vegetables is "good for the soul"?) Other environmentalists are more consistent in their disregard for human interests. James Lovelock, for instance, suggests scrapping agriculture entirely in favor of artificially synthesized foods—a course of action that, whatever its benefits for Gaia, would surely not add to *our* joy in living.[37]

Second, good-life environmentalism has no use for the prejudice, foisted on us by romanticism, against farming and gardening. On the contrary, it respects them as attempts to bring man and nature into closer harmony with each other. It shares the feeling for nature classically expressed by Virgil, who wrote verses in praise of grafting and breeding and urged husbandmen to "tame with culture the wild fruits, lest earth lie idle." This is not to say that all farming is innocuous. Battery cages and monocultures are abominations. But they should be seen as perversions of a normally healthy practice rather than expressions of any depravity inherent in agriculture itself. There is no merit in the view of ecologist J. Baird Callicott that "a herd of cattle, sheep or pigs is as much or more a ruinous blight on the landscape as a fleet of four-wheel-drive off-road vehicles."[38]

Does good-life environmentalism have any place then for "the weeds and the wilderness" beloved of Hopkins and other romantics? Possibly. But it is a place determined by our own concerns, not by the good of nature itself, whatever that could mean. The vision of man transforming the earth into a vast garden that so stirred Victorian progressivist Herbert Spencer fills us moderns with claustrophobia. We tend to agree with Spencer's more romantic contemporary John Stuart Mill, who argued for preserving wildernesses on the grounds that "it is not good for man to be kept perforce . . . in the presence of his species."[39] But whether or not desirable in theory, the preservation of wilderness is in practice a paradoxical undertaking, for a wilderness that can be preserved in its current state only through human intervention is no longer truly a wilderness. The savannahs of Africa, carefully monitored and manipulated as they are by scientists, are in effect vast parks, differing only in scale from those of rural England. And if we additionally strive, as justice requires we should, to make wildernesses accessible not just to scientists and explorers but also to ordinary vacationers, their wild character will be compromised still further. So it seems that we may be fated to turn the world into a garden, whatever our intentions.

Third, a good-life environmentalist will not be embarrassed to admit to preferring the survival of the snow leopard to that of the *acanthomyops latipes*. If pressed to explain why, he will say simply that the leopard is a beautiful beast with a long and distinguished place in art and heraldry. This is anthropocentrism, to be sure, but what alternative do we have? Deep ecologists imagine that stripping nature of human significance will reveal the full depth of its intrinsic value. The opposite is true. If we could strip nature of human significance—which we cannot—we would be left with something of no intrinsic value at all, like coal or oil reserves. All value is mediated through the veil of human symbolism. Remove this veil, and we have only "the drear and naked shingles of the world."

Finally, good-life environmentalism will take seriously the problem of population growth. As we write in 2011, world population has just passed the 7 billion mark and continues to rise, though at a diminishing rate. Whether this increase triggers a Malthusian crisis or not, it will certainly diminish our quality of life. The prospect of humans living stacked on top of one another like battery hens, even if "sustainable," is not one to be welcomed. Keynes himself made the advent of "bliss" conditional upon our "power to control population." How to achieve such power is a pressing technical problem, though one that lies beyond the scope of this book.

What are the economic implications of good-life environmentalism? Protection of agriculture, restrictions on the building of supermarkets, encouragement of artisan food production—these are just some of the policies that would help maintain links with the soil. They have been advocated by environmentalist economists such as E. F. Schumacher for decades, though often for misleading utilitarian reasons. What would their impact on growth be? Possibly negative, although both France and Italy have maintained their agricultural traditions more successfully than England without any noticeable diminution of growth. Either way, it is not crucial. For good-life environmentalism, growth reduction is not a goal but an indifferent side effect of measures desirable in and of themselves.

An environmental movement reformed along these lines would no longer be dependent on scientific claims that are both uncertain and irrelevant. Natural limits to growth, even if they do exist, will come into play far too late to meet the requirements of the good life. To pin our hopes on ultimate scarcity is to condemn ourselves to decades, possibly centuries, of mindless consumerism. Good-life environmentalism would moreover dispel the atmosphere of po-faced moralism that has recently hung about the movement. It would remind us that a life in harmony with nature is not a sacrifice but something ardently to be desired. Nature is neither raw material to use as we please nor a strange god demanding sacrifice. She is "slumbering spirit," as the German romantics liked to put it—the mute bearer of the same life that has come to consciousness in us. When we wrong her, we strike at the roots of our own existence.

6

Elements of the Good Life

I need a jug of wine and a book of poetry,
  Half a loaf for a bite to eat,
Then you and I, seated in a deserted spot,
Will have more wealth than a Sultan's realm.
                    —Omar Khayyam

We have argued that our continuing addiction to consumption and work is due, above all, to the disappearance from public discussion of any idea of the good life. Those fixed objects of ambition and desire gestured to by Keynes and Virginia Woolf—the £500 a year, the room of one's own—have long since melted away, leaving nothing but the shifting fortunes of "the Joneses" to guide us. If we are to recover an understanding of what it means to have enough, we must relearn to ask the question: what is it to live well?

The good life, as mentioned in Chapter 3, is a life that is desirable, or worthy of desire, not just one that is widely desired. We cannot identify it by counting heads or going around with a questionnaire. But neither can the good life differ utterly from the aspirations of most people across the world and across time. In ethics, unlike science, universal error is not a coherent possibility, since the subject of ethics, the human good, is one on which all humans have something to say. There are no experts in morality. Aristotle understood this, which is why he broached ethical questions by first of all gleaning "the opinions" about them, popular as well as educated. He realized that there was wisdom in ordinary experience, however concealed or distorted. Today we can pursue the same enterprise on a much broader front, drawing on the opinions not just of our compatriots but of all civilized peoples through the ages.

At this point in the discussion, it is usual to point to the vast diversity of moral beliefs and practices. How, in the face of such diversity, can we talk about any such thing as "the good life"? Isn't such talk just chauvinism, or even worse, "cultural imperialism," the arbitrary imposition of our own preferences on those who disagree? Should we not limit our ambitions to constructing a neutral framework of rules allowing people of diverse beliefs to live together in harmony? As we saw in Chapter 3, this approach typifies most modern liberalism, economic liberalism in particular.

Two responses are in order. First, it does not follow from the mere fact that moral opinions differ that they are all of equal worth. The truth is that some cultures—including, of course, our own—might be *wrong* about ethical matters. Even dogmatic value-relativists are usually brought up short by mention of such stock examples as female circumcision in North Africa or foot-binding in China. Nor is it impossible for one culture to persuade another of the wrongness of its ways—not, to be sure, with knock-down arguments, but by awakening hitherto dormant feelings of indignation or sympathy. Examples include the liberalization of family structures in Tang China under Buddhist influence, and in twentieth-century India under Western influence. It is not true, as Milton Friedman claimed, that about differences of basic value "men can ultimately only fight."[1]

Second, although moral variety undoubtedly exists, it is less extensive than is often supposed. All cultures across the world encourage more or less stable unions between men and women for the purpose of getting and rearing children, although exact arrangements vary widely. All humans live in groups that extend beyond the immediate family, with some settled form of political organization. All possess some notion of property and of exchange. All engage in activity over and above the procuring of necessities, whether religious, aesthetic, recreational or otherwise. All revere the surrounding world and its plant and animal inhabitants, through worship, painting or poetry. All, or almost all, cover their genitals. All treat their dead with ritualized forms of respect, and not just as decaying flesh.[2]

These and other communalities define the distinctively human form of life. They reveal broad agreement on what might be called the "basic goods"—the goods that constitute living well. Health, respect, security, relationships of trust and love are recognized everywhere as part of a good human life; their absence is recognized everywhere as a misfortune. These goods appear in a multitude of guises. It is one thing to pay respect to a Javanese prince, another to a London cabby. But the concept of respect itself is universal, as is shown by our ability to respond sympathetically to depictions of humiliation in stories from around the world.[3] "It is ultimately the 'same' human being," writes German philosopher Ernst Cassirer, "who meets us again and again in a thousand manifestations and in a thousand masks."[4] We have, then, the materials for a universal inquiry into the good life, transcending limits of time and place. We are not doomed to a chauvinistic "clash of civilizations," mediated only by the rules of the market or international treaties.

What is the relationship of our enterprise to other recent discussions? In *A Theory of Justice* and subsequent works, John Rawls outlined a category of "primary goods," goods that a rational individual will want whatever else he wants, "since they are in general necessary for the framing and the execution of a rational plan of life."[5] Rawls's list of primary goods includes civic and political liberties, income and wealth, access to public office, and "the social bases of self-respect." Primary goods are not themselves elements of the good life, but rather the means to achieving any possible version of the good life. They are the external conditions of autonomy. A liberal state must ensure that they are fairly distributed among its members, but should not take a view on the uses to which they are put, for that would be to violate its cardinal principle of neutrality.

Amartya Sen and Martha Nussbaum—the one coming from development economics, the other from moral philosophy—have criticized Rawls for overlooking the varying degree to which individuals are able to translate the primary goods into actual opportunities. A handicapped person will need more money to attain the same level of physical mobility as an able-bodied person; a girl in a patriarchal culture will need more educational resources to reach the standard of her male counterparts. Our focus, then, should not be on goods but on *capabilities*—concrete powers of thought and action. The question should be not "how much in the way of resources is so-and-so able to command?" but "what is so-and-so able to do and be?" Nussbaum has advanced a list of ten central human capabilities, including bodily health and integrity, imagination, thought, practical reason, affiliation and play.[6] Such capabilities, she and Sen argue, define the space within which quality of life should be assessed. Their ideas have been highly influential in the development community, prompting a shift of focus from GDP to other, more specific indexes.

For all their disagreements with Rawls, Sen and Nussbaum share with him an overarching concern for autonomy. It is this very concern that prompts them to go beyond his list of primary goods. As Nussbaum writes, summarizing her relationship with Rawls:

> We want an approach that is respectful of each person's struggle for flourishing, that treats each person as an end and as a source of agency and worth in her own right. Part of this respect will mean not being dictatorial about the good, at least for adults and at least in some core areas of choice, leaving individuals a wide space for important types of choice and meaningful affiliation. But this very respect means taking a stand on the conditions that permit them to follow their own lights free from tyrannies imposed by politics and tradition.[7]

The desire to safeguard autonomy explains Sen and Nussbaum's focus on capabilities rather than actual functionings. This focus is at first blush rather odd. Why should we care whether individuals are *capable* of health, education and so forth? Surely what matters is that they are *actually* healthy and educated. But taking a public stance on this latter question would mean, for Nussbaum, being "dictatorial" about the good. "Where adult citizens are concerned, capability, not functioning, is the appropriate political goal."[8]

Our approach is quite different. The basic goods, as we define them, are not just means to, or capabilities for, a good life; they *are* the good life. Moreover, we regard such goods as an appropriate goal not just of private but of political action too. If what matters, in most cases, is not just the capacity to lead a good life but the actual leading of it, then why should we deny ourselves all the powers at our disposal to bring this about? Imagine two societies, one in which there are no hospitals, the other in which there are hospitals that no one uses. In one there is a capability for health, in the other not, but what matters, surely, is that both populations are equally *unhealthy*. And both, surely, present us with a political problem, a problem of state action.

Furthermore, a focus on ends rather than capabilities is required by our particular problem, which is one of wealth, not poverty. Sen and Nussbaum are primarily concerned with poor nations, in which many people lack the resources to live well. But in the affluent world, we face the very different problem of making good use of resources that already exist. If the goal of policy is defined solely in terms of capabilities, this problem disappears from view. "A person who has opportunities for play can always choose a workaholic life," writes Nussbaum, implying that so long as the choice is free, its outcome is of no public interest.[9] But if the workaholic life is an impoverished one, as most people who have thought about the matter agree it is, then its adoption over finer lives, whether freely chosen or not, is surely something to worry us.

At this point, our opponent will brandish the dread spectre of *paternalism*. In suggesting that ends rather than means or capabilities should be the goal of policy, are we not being "dictatorial about the good"? Two reflections may help allay this suspicion, or at least rob it of its sting. First, until recently, all Western nations had on their statute books large numbers of laws explicitly intended to make people better than they would otherwise have chosen to be. (Until the 1960s, pornography was defined in British and American law as matter tending to "deprave and corrupt.") Many of these laws are still in force, and indeed have been extended, although now usually on the pretext of preventing harms to third parties. Examples include the laws against drugs, incest and bestiality, restrictions on the sale and use of pornography, alcohol and cigarettes, and much health and safety legislation. It is only in the rarefied world of academic philosophy that liberal states are not "dictatorial" about the good.

Second, since the good life is on any reasonable definition an autonomous or self-determined one, there is only so much that the state, as a coercive body, can do to promote it. It is plainly self-stultifying to *force* people to be civilized, like Peter the Great, who ordered his nobles to attend *salons* and discuss philosophy on pain of torture. But there are many things the state can do without going to such extremes. The use of economic incentives to encourage people towards the good is not usually felt as dictatorial, except perhaps by a few libertarians. In fact, all liberal states already use such incentives, although their official rationale is usually utilitarian rather than ethical. (For instance, tax breaks for married couples are often justified on the grounds that children born in wedlock perform better in later life, which, while true, does not get to the heart of the matter.) In the next chapter, we suggest several ways in which the existing instruments of economic persuasion might be deployed in service of the good life. The state can make it easier for people to live well rather than badly, but the ultimate choice must remain their own.

The notion of the good life might also be queried on deeper, metaphysical grounds. The modern scientific image of nature as devoid of inherent ends encourages the thought that man, too, has no inherent end, that each individual's good is as his fancy paints it. This thought is one source of the economists' doctrine of "the givenness of wants," discussed in Chapter 3. But is it true? A full answer to this question would take us into deep waters, so a peremptory response must suffice. Even if science forbids us to speak of purposes—which, incidentally, is less obviously true in biology than it is in physics and chemistry— why should this constrain our thinking in matters that concern us more intimately? Science is a marvellous instrument for the exploration of external nature, but where the subject is the human good, it is our own intuitions, broadened by reading, travel and conversation, that must be our guide.

The Basic Goods

An air of arbitrariness hangs over lists of basic goods, to dispel which we must make clear our criteria of inclusion. There are four:

1. Basic goods are *universal*, meaning that they belong to the good life as such, not just some particular, local conception of it. To see the universal through the particular requires strong

philosophical intuitions, guided by the testimony of different ages and cultures. This latter proviso is frequently forgotten. Too often, the "intuitions" of modern philosophers simply repeat the platitudes of early twenty-first-century liberalism. Nussbaum's catalogue of central human capabilities includes, for example, "protection against discrimination on the basis of race, sex, sexual orientation, religion, caste, ethnicity, or national origin"—an impeccably progressive list, but hardly a universal one.[10] A more philosophical caste of mind might question the equation of universal with modern liberal values. After all, from the standpoint of eternity, our own civilization is just as parochial as any other.

2. Basic goods are *final*, meaning that that they are good in themselves, and not just as a means to some other good. (This distinguishes our basic goods from Rawls's primary goods and from Nussbaum and Sen's capabilities.) The standard philosopher's way of uncovering final goods is to ask "what for?" over and over, like certain annoying small children. When no further answer is forthcoming, we know we have hit upon a final good. "What is that bicycle for?" "To get me to work." "And what is work for?" "To make me money." "And what is money for?" "To buy me food." "And what is food for?" "To keep me alive." "And what is life for?" Blank stare. Life is not "for" anything. In our terms, it is part of the basic good of health.

All basic goods are final, but not all final goods are basic. An explanatory chain might conceivably come to an end with "in order to complete my collection of Soviet stamps." Completing a stamp collection is a final good—it is not usually for the sake of anything else—but it is not basic, since it fails the test of both universality and indispensability, to be discussed in more detail below.

Many philosophers would want to add an additional last term to any given sequence of explanations, namely "in order to make me happy." We think this is a mistake. Outside psychiatric clinics and philosophy seminars, people do not generally explain their actions by saying "this will make me happy." As we have already argued in Chapter 4, this is a strong reason not to treat happiness as the ultimate good.

The requirement of finality rules out many goods that appear at first glance to be basic. Food, for instance, features in many traditional lists of basic goods, but as the above chain of questions shows, it is in fact instrumental to the basic good of life or health. Indulged in beyond this point, it ceases to be useful, and may even be harmful. (This is not to say that all spices and relishes superfluous to health are not good, just that they are not *basic* goods. We do not wish to reduce everyone to a diet of salad and tofu.) More relevantly to our theme, money cannot be a basic good, since it is essentially an instrument for obtaining other things. Other goods are more ambiguous. Health, security and leisure are on some accounts final, on others instrumental. We return to this issue below.

3. Basic goods are *sui generis*, meaning that they are not part of some other good. The good of "freedom from cancer" is certainly universal and final, but not basic, because it can be subsumed under the larger good of health. Whether a good is *sui generis* or not is often hard to decide. For instance, family relationships, which we have included under the good of "friendship," might be thought to merit a separate heading of their own. However, since what makes family and non-family relationships good is very much the same set of things—love, trust, stability—we decided that two categories would be superfluous.

4. Basic goods are *indispensable*, meaning that anyone who lacks them may be deemed to have suffered a serious loss or harm. The qualification "anyone" is important. That missing, set-completing stamp might cause the stamp fanatic much genuine anguish, but this does not make a basic good. Nor need the loss or harm in question be perceived as such by its victim. Harms are frequently so taken for granted that they no longer register, but they are still harms.

Another way of highlighting the indispensability of basic goods is to think of them as needs. The term "need" captures

more clearly than "good" the idea that these are the sine
qua non of a decent human existence, and a priority in any distribution of scarce resources. At first, we considered talking
about basic needs rather than basic goods, but in the end stuck
with goods on the purely stylistic grounds that "need" has an
unpleasantly puritanical ring to it. "You don't need that" often
carries the additional implication, "and therefore you shouldn't
have it." ("O reason not the need," says King Lear, when
confronted with an argument of this sort by his horrible
daughters.) Talk of basic goods makes it clear, by contrast, that
there is nothing remotely shameful about pursuing goods over
and above the basic ones—provided, of course, that they do not
subtract from the basic ones.

The criterion of indispensability distinguishes our list of
basic goods from other similar lists. The legal philosopher
John Finnis, for example, defines basic goods or values as
"the basic purposes of human existence" but not as things
whose absence in an individual constitutes serious harm or
loss. As a result, he is able to include "religion" (defined very
broadly as concern for the ultimate order of things) and
"aesthetic experience" in his list of basic values.[11] Now, while
we might consider a culture devoid of religion or aesthetic
experience to be impoverished, we would not call an individual who lacked either of these two things seriously
harmed. There are many people who are simply "tone-deaf"
to art or religion but lead otherwise healthy, flourishing lives.
Finnis's definition makes perfect sense in view of his purpose,
which is to establish the first principles of natural law, but
our own goal, which is to work out a criterion of sufficiency,
requires us treat as basic only those goods whose lack
constitutes a serious loss or harm, for it is only such goods
whose possession could be thought to constitute "enough."

Which goods meet our criteria of basicness? We have identified
seven. Our list makes no claims to finality. Some of the goods on it
overlap at the margins or encompass a number of interrelated concerns;
others might arguably be left off it altogether. "Harmony with nature"

is often claimed—wrongly, in our view—to be a peculiarly Western fixation, a product of romanticism and environmentalism. And some have queried whether "health" and "security" are good in themselves rather than for the sake of other things. So there is some fuzziness here, and some room for argument. But that needn't be an objection. In subjects that are inexact by nature, honest roughness is better than spurious precision.*

Health. By health we mean the full functioning of the body, the perfection of our animal nature. Health includes all things needed to sustain life, or a reasonable span of life, but is by no means limited to them. It implies vitality, energy, alertness and that ruddy beauty favored by Tolstoy and other moralists over more decadent ideals. Health is generally associated with absence of bodily pain, but its value is not purely utilitarian, for a comfortably ill person (on a morphine drip, say) is still worse off than a healthy one. Above all, health means a happy obliviousness of one's own body, as of a tool perfectly fitted to its tasks. In the words of French physician René Leriche, it is "life lived in the silence of the organs."[12] Health looks outwards. Illness throws one back upon oneself.

Many philosophers have ranked health lower than the other goods, on the grounds that it belongs to our animal as opposed to our distinctively human nature. "It is for the sake of the soul," wrote Aristotle, setting the tone, "that . . . goods of the body are desirable at all, and all wise men ought to choose them for the sake of the soul, and not the soul for the sake of them."[13] If this is true, then health is not final in our sense, and so has no place on a list of basic human goods. But why deny health the status of a final end simply because animals can enjoy it too? Is that not just an intellectual's prejudice? Our admiration of a young man's vitality need not involve the further thought that it will help him walk to work, serve his country or whatever. We can admire it for its own sake, just as we do that of a playing dolphin or leopard cub.

---

* Aristotle famously said that "it is the mark of an educated person to look for precision in each kind of enquiry just to the extent that the nature of the subject allows it" (Aristotle, *Nicomachean Ethics*, tr. Christophe Rowe and Sarah Broadie [Oxford: Oxford University Press, 2002], p. 96). In a similar spirit, Keynes is alleged to have said, "it is better to be roughly right than precisely wrong."

Today, health is the one good on which liberal states feel entitled to take a positive stance, for, unlike the goods of the soul, it carries the authority of science. But is there really a distinction here? Science can tell us whether drug x treats condition y, but not that condition y itself constitutes "ill-health." This latter presupposes a *pre*-scientific, common-sense understanding of what it is for human beings to flourish. We all know a healthy baby when we see one, just as we all recognize blindness and lameness as disabilities. Other cases are more controversial. How fat does one have to be to count as overweight? How bodily capable to count as fit? Our answer to these questions will depend on what we think of the martial virtues, of sport, sex and much else besides. In short, judgments of health are objective in the same sense and to the same degree as ethical judgments: they too rest on an idea of human flourishing.

Given this relationship, it is not surprising to find that the eclipse of teleological thinking in our culture has proceeded hand in hand with an unravelling of the concept of health. The process is similar to that we have already traced in connection with money. An earlier notion of health as being in "tip-top condition," with everything "working as it should," has given way to a new ideal of perpetual improvement. One symptom of this slippage is our obsession with longevity. Older medical traditions aimed to help individuals realize their natural lifespan; dying "of old age" was not deemed a calamity. But if there is no such thing as a natural lifespan, only a shifting, culturally relative norm, then death at *any* age can be seen as a regrettable and remediable failing. Modern science has rekindled the old alchemical promise of eternal youth; meanwhile, people who a few decades earlier would have died swiftly and relatively painlessly are kept alive in a state of chronic, debilitating sickness.*

---

* The gerontologist Aubrey de Grey has claimed that we will very soon be able to enjoy thousands of years of good health. Guy Brown, a Cambridge neuroscientist, sounds a more sober note. "We are adding years to life," he writes, "but they are poor quality years at the extremity of life" (Guy Brown, "No Way to Go," *Guardian*, November 13, 2007). Our goal is not to hurry people to their graves, but to allow them grow old gracefully. "A man able to celebrate his eighty-first birthday," wrote the Chinese philosopher Lin Yutang, "is actually looked upon as one specially favored by heaven."

Another symptom of this disorientation is the disappearance of any sharp distinction between *curing* the sick and *enhancing* the already healthy. Once the dividing-line was clear-cut: vital operations fell on one side, cosmetic improvements on the other. But if there is no such thing as perfect health, then *any* undesirable condition can be defined as illness and made an object of medical treatment. (And, as we saw in Chapter 1, there is no limit to the number of things that people can find undesirable.) This whole process is hastened along by the drugs companies, who have a strong interest in identifying the illnesses that their products will cure. The role of Pfizer, manufacturer of Viagra, in transforming what was once part and parcel of the human comedy into the fearsome new ailment of "erectile dysfunction" is a case in point.

Ultimately, this assimilation of medicine to the economic rat race destroys the very idea of good health. If every state of the body can be seen as defective relative to some other, preferred state, then we are all in a sense perpetually ill. The world becomes, as Goethe said it would, a vast hospital, in which everyone is nurse to everyone else. What is more, where the demand for health is insatiable, medical costs expand in tandem with or faster than income, keeping us tethered to the work/growth treadmill. It is thus crucial to our purpose that health *not* be defined in this demand-relative sense, but retain the older meaning of the body's natural perfection. For it is only in this sense that it can function as part of a criterion of enoughness.

Security. By security we mean an individual's justified expectation that his life will continue more or less in its accustomed course, undisturbed by war, crime, revolution or major social and economic upheavals. Security is a necessary condition for the realization of other basic goods on our list, in particular personality, friendship and leisure. But it is also a good in itself. Like any creature, a human being has an environment, a set of taken-for-granted objects against which his life runs its course. If this environment is changed abruptly or frequently, he will feel perplexed and threatened, like a cat in a new house or a caged animal released into the wild. Of course, as intelligent beings, we have in us that which transcends any environment—which sees "the stars above the roof," as the philosopher Josef Pieper puts it.[14] Nonetheless, roofs and all that they imply are still necessary, not least as providing a stable location from which to gaze upon the stars. Across the world, the word "peace" has a soothing ring, while "turmoil," "chaos" and their equivalents bode ill.

To be sure, there are types—tyrants, speculators, romantic poets— who thrive on chaos. Chairman Mao, a tyrant and a romantic poet, loved chaos so much that he renamed it "permanent revolution." In the West, security has so long been vilified by bohemian artists and intellectuals that admitting to a fondness for it now is almost like admitting to a fondness for garden gnomes. Yet the truth is that security is cherished by all creative spirits—including poets, when they are honest with themselves—as a condition of their own productivity. W. B. Yeats, writing in 1919, as Ireland descended into war, prayed that his young daughter would grow up to enjoy security:

> And may her bridegroom bring her to a house
> Where all's accustomed, ceremonious;
> For arrogance and hatred are the wares
> Peddled in the thoroughfares.
> How but in custom and in ceremony
> Are innocence and beauty born?
> Ceremony's a name for the rich horn,
> And custom for the spreading laurel tree.

Yeats was not immune to the romanticism of disorder. He had written rapturously about the "terrible beauty" of the Easter 1916 uprising. Yet faced with real chaos, his choice was clear. He knew that extreme civil disorder is destructive of the arts of civilization.

What are the effects of capitalism on security? Nineteenth-century liberals argued that *le doux commerce* would have a pacifying influence on international relations, since nations that traded with each other would have no good economic reasons to go to war. This argument has something to it, though of course trading nations can still go to war for bad economic or *non*-economic reasons, as they did in 1914. Internally, the effect of free markets on security is less salutary. "All that is solid melts into air," wrote Marx famously, referring to the endless revolution of technologies, skills and ways of life under capitalism. This perpetual ripping up of the social fabric is wearisome for both workers and consumers. It is particularly taxing for those over the age of 40 or 50, who may have lost their taste for novelty. Free-market fundamentalists respond to such discontents with thinly veiled contempt. Those who cannot find work locally are urged to relocate, those whose talents have become redundant to "retool." This is to get things precisely backwards. It is not human beings who need adapting to the market; it is the market that needs adapting to human beings. That was the guiding principle of the early twentieth-century social liberals, whose enlightened efforts to minimize the insecurities of capitalism have now largely been jettisoned, as we shall see in the next chapter.

Respect. To respect someone is to indicate, by some formality or otherwise, that one regards his views and interests as worthy of consideration, as things not to be ignored or trampled on. Respect does not imply agreement or liking: one can respect an enemy. It does not imply any special admiration. But it does imply a certain recognition or "taking account" of the other's point of view, an attitude fundamentally different from that shown towards animals. One can have great affection for a pet dog, but not respect or disrespect.*

Respect is a necessary condition of other basic goods, friendship in particular. But it is also a good in itself. Everywhere, slavery—that is, the complete withdrawal of respect—is regarded as a calamity second only to or worse than death. Indeed, as has often been said, slavery is a kind of social death, since the slave, though still human in the biological sense, has lost the *status* of a human being. "That look was not one between two men," writes Primo Levi, a survivor of Auschwitz, recalling his cross-examination by a Nazi scientist.[15] Those exposed regularly to such looks soon come to assimilate their perspective. Self-respect cannot long survive the withdrawal of respect.

Respect need not be equal or reciprocal. I can respect someone who respects me less or not at all. Nonetheless, reciprocal respect is uniquely satisfying to both parties, for our deepest wish is for the respect of those whom we ourselves respect. (The adoration of a

---

* What we here call respect is also often called "dignity," especially in religious discussions. We prefer the term "respect" because it brings out more clearly its interpersonal dimension. Respect is conferred; dignity is inherent. Still, our ability to respect a human being presupposes that there is something in him worthy of respect, and this something could, if desired, be called dignity.

sycophant or a mob leads more often to self-contempt than to self-respect.) In all ages, we find groups of "peers" or "equals" respecting each other while looking down on everyone else. The citizenry of ancient Athens was one such group, as was the medieval nobility. Modern democracy extends the circle of peers to all adults in a given territory. Whether or not its triumph is guaranteed by History, as Francis Fukuyama has claimed, it now has the support of almost all the world, at least on paper. No modern vision of the good life can be such as to thwart it. This rules out, as we noted in Chapter 3, values such as mastery and "greatness of soul," which cannot in principle be universalized.

Respect has many sources, varying from culture to culture. Strength, money, land, nobility, education and office have all figured prominently at one time or another. In modern bourgeois societies, the two basic sources of respect are civil rights and personal achievement. Civil rights confer what one might call "formal" respect; they guarantee their possessor protection against the worst forms of arbitrary power. But because they are bestowed on all citizens regardless of their merits, they are powerless to create real respect. For this, an individual must make something of his life; at the very least, he must earn an "honest crust." Rank and title no longer automatically confer respect. The modern-day duke must prove his worth by sitting on charitable boards and so forth; otherwise he appears little better than a parasite.

Equality of formal respect can coexist with inequality of real respect, but only up to a point. If the gulf grows too gross, formal equality will come under strain. Suppose (what is not too implausible) that persistent unemployment were to lead to the division of society into two hereditary castes, a working majority and a jobless minority. It would then be all too easy to enshrine this de facto distinction in law, with differential civil and voting rights. Democracy as we know it would cease to exist. It is also important for mutual respect that inequality not exceed certain bounds.[16] An elite that lives, plays and learns entirely separately from the general population will feel no bond of common citizenship with it. A more equal—not a completely equal—distribution of wealth and income is a requirement of democratic solidarity.

It is a feature of our approach, in contrast to most recent liberal discussions, that the requirements of justice are not seen as fixable in isolation from the good but as flowing from a particular conception of it. Equality is founded on fraternity, not vice versa. It follows that there can be no abstract, a priori answer, of the kind attempted by Rawls, to the question "how much inequality is too much?" One must look to the effects of inequality on the moral fabric of society, and on the political system in particular. Where the rich behave with lawless arrogance, the poor with impotent resentment and politicians with obeisance to money, inequality has exceeded the mark.

Personality. By personality we mean first of all the ability to frame and execute a plan of life reflective of one's tastes, temperament and conception of the good. This is what Kantians call autonomy and Aristotelians practical reason. But the term personality implies something else as well, an element of spontaneity, individuality and spirit. Many philosophers—Kant himself springs to mind—have been models of rational self-government yet sadly lacking in personality.

Why distinguish personality and respect? Are the two concepts not correlative: respect is paid to personality; personality calls forth respect? But there is a subtle difference. One can picture a community—a monastic order, say, or a revolutionary phalanx—where all property is shared, all affairs open to scrutiny, and all wills bent on the common good. Members of this community might hold each other in the highest respect yet would lack personality. Personality implies a private space, a "room behind the shop" as Montaigne called it, in which the individual is at liberty to unfurl, to be himself. It denotes the inward aspect of freedom, that which resists the claims of public reason and duty.

Personality is pre-eminently a post-medieval, European ideal; it corresponds roughly to what the French liberal Benjamin Constant called "modern liberty." But its appeal is not just local. All cultures have their holy fools and star-crossed lovers, honored in verse and song if not in real life. A society devoid of personality, where individuals accepted their social role without tension or protest, would scarcely be human. It would be more like a colony of intelligent social insects, of the sort envisaged in certain science-fiction films.

There is a tendency in modern liberalism to elevate personality—or autonomy, as it is usually called—into the *ur*-good from which all others derive. Something like this underlies, as we saw, the reluctance of Rawls, Sen and Nussbaum to discuss final ends. We think this is a mistake. Autonomy is one good among others, with no special precedence. (It can, without obvious absurdity, be sacrificed to love.) Detached from any broader background of ethical concern, autonomy degenerates into that "liberty of indifference" for which all things are possible and nothing matters. The modern rhetoric of "choosing values" is one symptom of this confusion. Properly understood, choice *responds* to value. Where it is allowed to *create* value, its exercise becomes arbitrary—like firing arrows into a barn door and drawing targets around them.

Private property is an essential safeguard of personality, for it allows individuals to live according to their own tastes and ideals, free from the tyranny of patronage and public opinion. "Stable fortunes . . . are an invisible social asset on which every kind of culture is more or less dependent," wrote the French economist Marcel Labordère in a letter to Keynes. "Financial security for one's livelihood is a necessary condition for organised leisure and thought. Organised leisure and thought is a necessary condition of a true, not purely mechanical, civilisation."[17] Note that it is specifically *property*, not income, that has this liberating influence. Soviet apparatchiks, with access to consumables of all sorts but not to capital, were not free to develop their personalities. Neither are those Wall Street traders whose huge pay packages vanish immediately in "necessary" expenses.* Independence is distinct from opulence, and vastly more important.

This "personalist" defense of property is central to modern Catholic social teaching, where it forms part of a subtle, two-pronged attack on both free-market capitalism and state socialism. The foundation was laid in Pope Leo XIII's Encyclical of 1891, *Rerum Novarum*. Every householder, argues Leo, should possess the means of providing for himself and his family now and in perpetuity. To be without such means is to be forced into a degrading dependence on the managers of capital, be they private individuals or state servants. "The law,

---

* Sherman McCoy, the "master of the universe" in Tom Wolfe's novel, *Bonfire of the Vanities*, consumes his salary in rents, school fees, etc., with the result that bankruptcy follows within a few weeks of his losing his job. He is in effect a wage-slave, if a rather well-heeled one.

therefore, should favour ownership, and its policy should be to induce as many as possible of the people to become owners."[18] These ideas were to flow into the "distributionist" movement of early twentieth-century England, as well as into Christian Democratic thought in Germany and Italy, as we shall see in the next chapter.

The personalist argument for private property is distinct from the standard free-market one, and has different implications. For mainstream economics, property is simply part of the legal infrastructure of capitalism. Its distribution is not fundamentally a matter of concern, except insofar as it leads to monopoly pricing. By contrast, from a personalist point of view, the concentration of property in a few hands violates its essential function, which is to provide individuals and families with an independent livelihood. Property must be broadly distributed, or it cannot do its ethical job. How such a distribution might be brought about will be a central theme of the next chapter.

Harmony with Nature. The case for treating harmony with nature as a basic human good was argued for in the last chapter. But the issue remains controversial. Martha Nussbaum reports that some of her South Asian colleagues dismissed the whole idea as "a romantic Green Party flourish."[19] We have encountered a similar reaction from Chinese friends. There is no denying the proneness of modern Westerners to wax sentimental over nature, sometimes to the extent of overlooking the weightier demands of human suffering. Nonetheless, a sense of kinship with animals, plants and landscapes is hardly a Western peculiarity. The abundance of nature poetry in Sanskrit, classical Chinese and other languages around the world is sufficient proof of that.

Harmony with nature has often been understood to favor rural over urban life. Ever since the days of Babylon and Rome, cities have appeared as sinks of squalor and vice. But the opposite point of view has also had its defenders. Socrates found all the wisdom he needed within the walls of Athens. Marx spoke of the idiocy of rural life. There is no need for us to enter into this old debate; both sides have some truth to them. What is new, however, is the sheer scale of the modern city. An inhabitant of eighteenth-century Paris, then the largest city in the world, had only to walk thirty minutes to find himself in farmland. His modern equivalent would have to walk six hours through crowded traffic. Here is the source of that typically modern feeling of urban malaise and that yearning, often comic in its effects, to "get back to nature." The ill-effects of urban overcrowding on behavior and mood have been well documented by psychologists.

Should we abolish the modern city, then? With current population densities, such a policy would only succeed in transforming the country into a vast suburb. But we *should* strive to ensure that cities are not entirely alienated from their rural surroundings. For millennia, local food markets served as the main point of contact between town and country. These are now largely gone, and with them all sense of place and season. The modern British foodie can tickle his jaded palate with Japanese tempura, Sichuan chili, Moroccan couscous and a host of other pickings from the global storehouse, all equally detached from any context of meaning. Alienation from nature is just one of the unpriced costs of consumer choice.

Friendship. This is a necessarily inadequate translation of the ancient Greek *philia*, a term encompassing all robust, affectionate relationships. A father, spouse, teacher and workmate might all be "friends" in our sense of the term. As mentioned above, this might seem to blur a crucial distinction between family relations, which are unchosen, and friendships in the strict sense, which are elective. But examined closely, the distinction is not so clear-cut. All family relationships have an elective element—beyond a certain point, one has to *work* at being a mother or a sister—and all deep non-family relationships have a binding force, often expressed by the extension to them of family terms: blood-brother, mother superior and so forth. Family and other personal relations vary in structure and importance from culture to culture, but some such relations are clearly essential to any conceivable version of the good life. "No one would choose to live without friends," noted Aristotle, "even if he had the other good things."[20]

Why do we speak of "friendship" instead of "community," a word that has become horribly popular in recent decades? Our concern has to do with reification. It is all too easy to talk about the "good of the community" as though this were something over and above the good of its constituent members. The term "friendship" is not open to this kind of abuse. My friendship with Paul is clearly a *relation* between me and Paul; it does not float above us, ghost-like, with interests and rights all of its own. If we could learn to think of communities in this fashion, as networks of friends, one notorious source of political oppression would be removed.

Friendship was taken seriously in the ancient world. Aristotle, in his classic discussion of the subject, distinguishes friendship proper from utility-friendship (based on a coincidence of interests) and pleasure-friendship (based on shared amusements). True friendship exists when each party embraces the other's good as his own, thereby bringing into being a new *common* good. It is a relationship possible only between people of virtue, who love one another for what they are, not for what they can offer. Friendship is both personal and political. It binds together members of a family and, by extension, citizens of a *polis*. It is "the greatest good of states and what best preserves them against revolutions."[21] These words sound strange to modern ears. We are used to thinking of the state as an alliance of self-interested individuals, and of friendship as a purely private relationship, of no political significance. But from Aristotle's point of view, a state without friendship is no state at all. A state is not "a mere society . . . established for the prevention of mutual crime and for the sake of exchange." It is "the union of families and villages in a perfect and self-sufficing life, by which we mean a happy and honourable life."[22]

Writing a hundred and fifty years before Aristotle, on the other side of the world, Confucius nonetheless shared his belief in the political importance of personal relationships. "Those who in private life behave well towards their parents and elder brothers, in public life seldom show a disposition to resist the authority of their superiors."[23] But the resemblance is superficial only. Confucius' focus is on deference to authority, not participation in shared goods. And whereas Aristotle subsumes the family under the broader heading of *philia*, the Chinese philosopher singles it out for special commendation. "Surely proper behaviour towards parents and elder brothers is the trunk of Goodness?"[24] These differences of attitude are still visible today. Western children often grow up to view their parents as "friends" in the narrow sense, whereas in China the relationship remains one of mutual love and sacrifice throughout life.

Friendship is not primarily an economic good, but it has economic prerequisites. Social trust does not flourish in times of famine. And an economy marked by continual restructuring, downsizing and outsourcing will not be hospitable to deep, long-lasting relationships. "You need to rid your life of Leeches and replace them with Energizers," writes American lifestyle coach Robert Pagliarini, a message reiterated in countless self-help books and websites.[25] In Aristotelian terms, friends acquired with the specific aim of "energizing" oneself are not real friends at all, but utility friends. Still, they are a predictable feature of a culture that prizes autonomy and mobility above almost all else.

Leisure. In contemporary parlance, leisure is synonymous with relaxation and rest. But there is another, older conception of leisure, according to which it is not just time off work but a special form of activity in its own right. Leisure in this sense is that which we do for its own sake, not as a means to something else. The philosopher Leo Strauss wrote of his friend Kurt Riezler that "the activity of his mind had the character of noble and serious employment of leisure, not of harried labor."[26] It is in this sense that we wish "leisure" to be understood.

Leisure in our sense has no very close connection to leisure as it is generally understood. Paid work could be leisure in our sense if undertaken not primarily as a means to money but for its own sake. (Many writers would carry on writing even if they earned nothing for it, or could earn more doing something else.) Conversely, many "leisure activities" are not leisure in our sense, either because they are undertaken instrumentally—playing squash to lose weight, for instance—or because they are too passive to count as *action* at all. (Watching television and getting drunk are actions only in the minimal sense that everything we do is an action. They lack the spontaneity and skill characteristic of action in the full sense, and are therefore best viewed as "rest" rather than leisure.) Leisure in our sense is distinguished not by lack of seriousness or strenuousness but by absence of external compulsion. It thus comes close to what Marx called non-alienated labor, which he defined as "a free manifestation of life, hence an enjoyment of life."[27]

The importance of leisure has been recognized by civilizations across the world. The three great Abrahamic religions all set aside a weekly Sabbath or day of rest, though this is not quite leisure in our sense, being primarily for the purpose of worship, not free activity.[28] Aristotle came closer in his distinction between the "liberal" and "mechanical" arts, the former being those suitable to freemen, the later to workmen and slaves ("We call those arts mechanical which tend to deform the body, and likewise all paid employments, for they absorb and degrade the mind").[29] But it was in Edo Japan that the cultivation of leisure was taken furthest. Deprived by centuries of peace of its traditional occupations, the feudal aristocracy turned instead to the arts of life, transforming everyday activities like bathing and tea drinking into exquisite ceremonies. The French philosopher Alexandre Kojève looked to Japan as the first successful "post-historical" society. We may hope, he wrote, tongue only partially in cheek, "that the recently begun interaction between Japan and the Western World will finally lead not to a rebarbarization of the Japanese but to a 'Japanization' of the Westerners."[30]

Why is leisure a basic good? The reason is clear: a life without leisure, where everything is done for the sake of something else, is vain indeed. It is a life spent always in preparation, never in actual living. Leisure is the wellspring of higher thought and culture, for it is only when emancipated from the pressure of need that we really *look* at the world, ponder it in its distinct character and outline. (The ancient Greek for leisure, *scholē*, hints at this connection.) "When we really let our minds rest contemplatively on a rose in bud, on a child at play, on a divine mystery, we are rested and quickened as though by a dreamless sleep," writes Josef Pieper. "It is in these silent and receptive moments that the soul of man is sometimes visited by an awareness of what holds the world together."[31] Without leisure, there is no genuine, but only that "mechanical," civilization spoken of by Marcel Labordère. The modern university, with its machinery of "targets" and "outputs," embodies this grim spectre.

Such a conception of leisure may seem narrowly highbrow, but that is not the intention. All recreations involving active, skilled participation—playing football in the park, making and decorating one's own furniture, strumming the guitar with friends—are leisure in our sense. What matters is not the intellectual level of the activity, but its character of "purposiveness without purpose."

What are the economic conditions of leisure? First of all, a reduction of *toil*, a category that includes not just paid work but all necessary activity, including commuting and housework, and excludes paid work undertaken primarily for its own sake, such as that of the devoted writer or artisan. Where toil occupies so great a portion of one's day as to leave time only for sleep and rest, leisure is impossible. But a mere reduction of toil is not sufficient for leisure in our sense, as the figure of Keynes's boréd housewife suggests. To live "wisely and agreeably and well" requires not just time but application and taste. It is ironic, if unsurprising, that the old arts of life—conversation, dancing, music-making—are atrophying just when we have most need of them. An economy geared to maximizing marketable output will tend to produce manufactured rather than spontaneous forms of leisure.

Realizing the Basic Goods

These, then, are the basic goods. A life that realizes all of them is a good life. "Realizes" is of course a vague term. How much respect counts as having "realized" respect? Answers to this question will no doubt encompass a good deal of legitimate variety, individual as well as cultural. Still, as mentioned above, vagueness is not necessarily a failing in an inquiry that is by nature vague.

A more serious worry concerns the possibility of conflict. What if personal self-expression requires me to abandon an old friend? What if enjoyment of leisure requires me to forgo the respect that comes from earning a living? Such dilemmas prompt the thought that there must be some "master-good" under which all others can be subsumed as aspects or means. Unless such a good exists, there seems to be no rational basis for choosing one end over another. We face the prospect of a blind, arbitrary leap—the predicament imagined by existentialists such as Jean-Paul Sartre.

Two candidates for the role of master-good dominate the literature of modern ethics. One is happiness or utility. The other is a "good will" in Kant's sense, a will obedient to the moral law. Neither strikes us as plausible. Happiness cannot be our master-good for the reasons outlined in Chapter 4: taken in the classical sense, it is simply a synonym for the good life and so cannot arbitrate between its several elements; and taken in the standard modern sense, as a pleasant state of mind, it is not necessarily good at all. Neither can Kant's moral will function as our master-good, for it is far too narrow to encompass all the things we value in life. Only a moral fanatic (as Nietzsche called Kant) could imagine that nothing is good without qualification except a good will.

Plurality, then, is irreducible. We face the possibility of "tragic" dilemmas, in which one basic good must be sacrificed to another. But this need not trouble us unduly. Deliberating over and choosing between incommensurable ends is a fact of everyday life. Should I pursue a political career at the cost of leisure and reflection? Should I persevere with tennis and ditch the piano? Individuals faced with such choices can sensibly decide on a best course of action without resort to some universal algorithm. On the civic level, debate over incommensurable ends is the bread and butter of democratic politics, at least when it is working as it should. Only the inveterate technocrat sees no middle ground between calculation and chaos.[32]

The plurality of basic goods has the important consequence that lack of one cannot be offset by abundance of another, in the way that a lack of euros might be offset by an abundance of dollars. A life without friendship or leisure lacks a specific something, for which no amount of respect can compensate. This is why moralists from Aristotle and Confucius onwards have cautioned against excess specialization. Single-minded concentration on one small branch of art or science may enrich the common stock, but only at the cost of deforming the individual artist or scientist. Of course, those in possession of the full set of basic goods may reasonably strive for additional, more specific goods. We have no wish to make mediocre generalists of everyone. But no one, however successful in a single domain, can claim to lead a good life if he lacks the rudiments of health, leisure, personality and so forth.

If the first goal of the individual is to realize the good life for himself, the first duty of the state is to realize, insofar as lies within its power, the good life for all citizens. (This principle of justice is founded on the good of mutual respect, as discussed above.) The qualification "insofar as lies within its power" is important. Health and friendship lie largely in the lap of fate. Personality, respect and leisure depend partly on individual agency. Still, the state has an important and legitimate role in creating the *material conditions* under which these and other goods can flourish. Such conditions include not just a certain overall level of national wealth but its just distribution, its wise public expenditure and much more besides. The rest lies in the hands of individuals and civil institutions. To adapt a phrase of Keynes, the state is the trustee not of civilization but of the possibility of civilization.

We have said that the state's *first* duty is to create the material conditions of a good life for all. It is perfectly entitled, once this is fulfilled, to pursue beauty, power and *grandeur*. Versailles and the pyramids have a place in the system of civilization, though not at the cost of life, health and well-being. This doctrine has acquired the ugly name of "sufficientarianism," but its root idea is the common-sense one that needs should not be sacrificed to luxuries. Finally, where a basic good admits of many possible realizations, a state should feel free to follow its own historical traditions in choosing one over another. India and China are under no obligation to follow the growing Western sentiment in favor of legalizing gay marriage and criminalizing cruelty to animals. It is only when a historical tradition destroys a basic good that justice requires its abandonment.

Where does all this leave growth? Obviously no sane policy has growth itself as a final end. Aristotle was merely repeating common sense when he wrote that "wealth is clearly not the good we are looking for, since it is useful, and for the sake of something else."[33] But even if growth is not an end in itself, it might still be desirable for other reasons. Three such reasons spring to mind.

First, growth might sensibly be pursued as a *means* to one or more of the basic goods. Health requires decent food and medicine. Leisure requires time away from toil. Personality requires a place to withdraw, a "room behind the shop." Populations too poor to afford these goods have every reason to seek to become richer. Here in the affluent world, however, the material prerequisites of health, leisure and personality have long since been achieved; our difficulty is making proper use of them. As for the other basic goods—security, respect, friendship and harmony with nature—these depend not so much on the absolute level of wealth as on the organization of economic life, as well as on other non-economic factors. They provide us with no reason to persevere with growth.

Second, growth might interest us as an *index* of something else we value. In his 2010 Robbins Lectures, Adair Turner suggests that growth "should not be considered the *objective* of economic policy, but rather the highly likely outcome ... of two things desirable in themselves—economic freedom to make choices, and a spirit of continual enquiry and desire for change."[34] Growth, in other words, might function like a cardiograph—in itself a trivial gauge of something important. But it can perform this function only if (a) it is reliably correlated with economic freedom and (b) economic freedom is itself an overriding good. This second assumption is especially dubious. Clearly some degree of economic freedom is a good thing (in our terms, it is part of the basic good of personality), but other things are good too, some of which might inhibit growth.* A society in which people were secure in their jobs and devoted long hours to leisure pursuits might well be sluggish, economically speaking. Whether a well-balanced economy favors growth or not is an empirical question; it cannot be assumed a priori that a fast-growing economy is a healthy one.

Finally, growth might be pursued for short-term pragmatic reasons. During a recession, with high unemployment and public debt, growth is rightly a priority. But we must distinguish the short term from the long term. Growth should be viewed as a kind of Prozac: useful for getting the patient back on his feet, not a permanent dope. Unfortunately, like dope, growth is addictive. Skilled political doctoring is required to prevent a temporary expedient becoming a lifelong habit.

The continued pursuit of growth is not only unnecessary to realizing the basic goods; it may actually damage them. The basic goods are essentially non-marketable: they cannot properly be bought or sold. An economy geared to maximizing market value will tend to crowd them out or to replace them with marketable surrogates. The result is

---

* Lord Turner admits this possibility. In his third lecture, he writes that the ends of change and economic freedom "need to be balanced against other potentially desirable objectives." But he should add that this undermines the utility of growth as an indicator of economic health.

a familiar kind of corruption. Personality becomes part of the jargon of advertising, with consumers of the most everyday products said to be "expressing" or "defining" themselves. Friendship is no longer the ethically serious relationship it was for Aristotle but an intrigue for the enjoyment of leisure. Meanwhile, leisure itself is subject to the same economizing logic that governs production, with sports, games and nightclubs striving to pack the maximum of excitement into the minimum of time. "The market penetrates areas of life which had stayed outside the realm of monetary exchange until recently," writes sociologist Zygmunt Bauman. "It relentlessly hammers home the message that everything is or could be a commodity, or if it is still short of becoming a commodity, that it should be handled *like* a commodity."[35]

Such shifts are hard to represent statistically. The basic goods are qualities, not quantities, objects of discernment, not measurement. What can be measured are proxies for the basic goods—quantities presumed to rise and fall in tandem with them. The results of such an exercise are dispiriting. British per capita income has more than doubled since 1974. Yet during that period, as far as we can judge, the basic goods have not grown at all, or have positively atrophied. Other wealthy nations reveal a more mixed picture.

Health. Average life expectancy in Britain rose by just over seven years from 1974 to 2009. This increase owes little to growth, however. Life expectancy has improved in almost all countries over this period, regardless of growth rates, mainly as a result of advances in medical technology and infrastructure.[36] China and Brazil now trail the West by only six or seven years, while Cuba, one of the poorer nations of the world, boasts a life expectancy equal to that of the USA. Moreover, as argued above, mere length of life is a poor index of health, since it tells us nothing about *quality*. "The good life is surely not measured by its length in years," wrote an 86-year-old James Lovelock, "but by the intensity of the joy and good consequences of existence."[37]

In certain respects, health may actually be deteriorating with affluence. Alcohol-related deaths have gone up sharply in the UK since the 1990s, though not in other wealthy nations. Obesity has risen threefold across Europe since the 1980s, even in countries with traditionally low

Chart 9. Alcohol-related Deaths in the UK

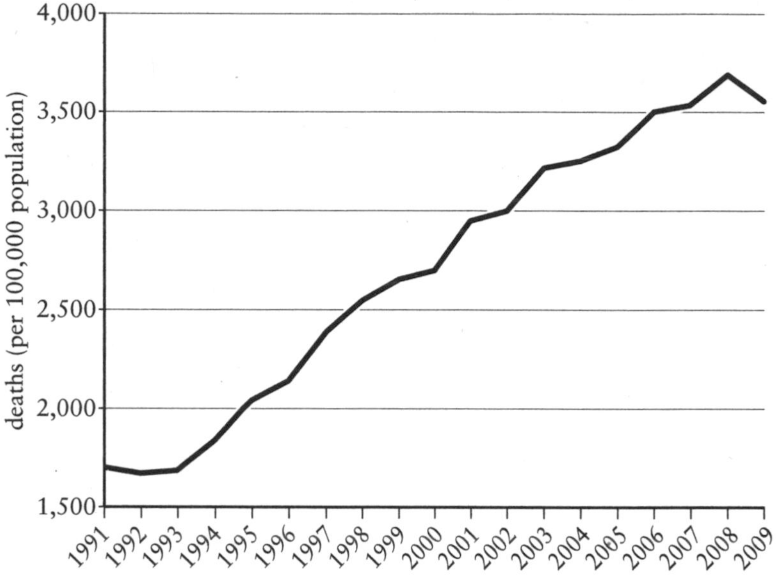

Source: WHO Global Information System on Alcohol and Health

rates.[38] UK prescriptions for depression have also increased, though that may not reflect any rise in depression itself.[39] And work-related stress has got worse since 1992, especially for women.[40] By historical standards, we remain extremely healthy, but the old assurance that this state of affairs would continue in perpetuity is fading. The maladies of affluence may yet come to outweigh those of poverty.

Security. Full employment as a goal of macroeconomic policy was abandoned during the Reagan/Thatcher era and has not been reinstated. UK unemployment exceeded the 5 percent mark in 1980 and has largely stayed there since, soaring during recessions to 10 percent or higher. A similar pattern prevails across the OECD, as Chart 11 shows. In Britain and the USA, jobs for life have increasingly been replaced by temporary or open contracts. Job tenure for British men fell 20 percent from 1975 to 1995. (The change for women was less significant, mainly because they are now less likely to quit their jobs to have children.)[41] At the same time, there has been a marked growth

Chart 10. Obesity in the UK

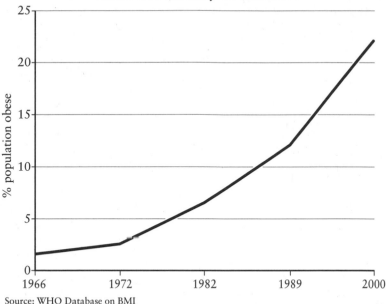

Source: WHO Database on BMI

in temporary, especially agency, workers, whose numbers have doubled since 1992.[42] These trends are partly structural, an effect of the
ongoing shift from industry to services, but they have been exacer-
bated by policy. Security has been regarded as a legitimate sacrifice to
the greater good of growth, not as a basic human need.

Respect. The greatest barrier to mutual respect in most Western
nations is the emergence, beginning in the 1970s, of a permanent
body of state dependants.* Once shielded by a residue of Christian
and social democratic sentiment, "chavs" and "scroungers" are now
treated with open contempt in the press and on television. Another
barrier to mutual respect is excessive inequality. This destroys respect
not just for those at the bottom, but also those at the top, especially if

---

* The precise dimensions of the British underclass are perennially hard to establish,
but the trebling of incapacity benefit claimants from the late 1970s to 2.7 million in
2006 is telling (Carol Black, *Working for a Healthier tomorrow* [London: Department for Work and Pensions, 2008], p. 34).

Chart 11. Unemployment in OECD Countries

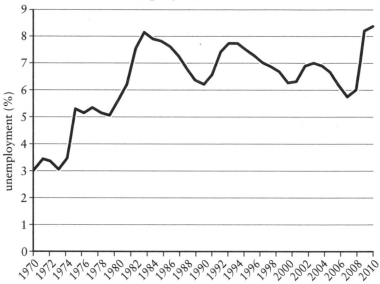

Source: OECD Employment Outlook, 2011

their advantages are perceived as unmerited. Inequality has risen in most Western countries since the 1970s, in Britain and the USA especially, as Chart 12 shows. This trend is partly a function of autonomous social forces, but the slashing of the top rate of income tax under Thatcher and Reagan undoubtedly accentuated it.

Finally, the "turbo-capitalism" enshrined in Wall Street and the City of London over the last thirty years has led to a brutalization of working relations. "His BlackBerry and security pass are taken from him by burly men, he has no further access to work email, and five minutes to clear his desk," runs an article describing the fate of an equity analyst, sacked for taking time off to see his sick wife.[43] Such scenes are all too common. Today, high salaries are no security against proletarianization and its attendant humiliations.

Personality. We have said that the main economic safeguard of personality is property. This might seem to spell good news for Britain,

Chart 12. Income Inequality since 1977

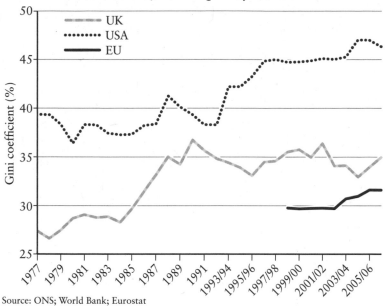

Source: ONS; World Bank; Eurostat

where home ownership rose steadily over the course of the last century and now stands at 68 percent, having fallen from an all-time high of 71 percent in 2003. However, since most property is bought on mortgage, with outright ownership coming only late in life, if at all, its effects are anything but emancipatory. Mortgaged property binds its owner to a regular job. It is specifically *wealth*—that is, an individual's total assets minus his or her liabilities—that confers freedom to pursue an autonomous plan of life. British governments have sporadically launched initiatives to distribute wealth more broadly; this was the aim of the Thatcher privatizations of the 1980s. Wider share-ownership schemes have also been promoted on a company basis, including, famously, by John Lewis, Britain's leading retail chain, which is owned and run by its 76,500 permanent employees.[44] However, such visionary enterprises have failed to counteract the overall trend towards the concentration of wealth in the hands of the few, as shown in Chart 13.

Chart 13. Distribution of Wealth in the UK

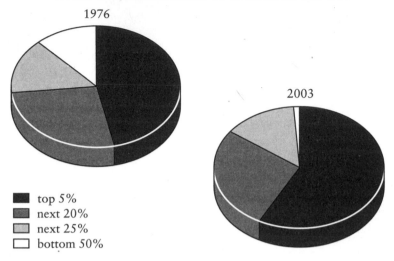

1976

2003

■ top 5%
■ next 20%
▨ next 25%
☐ bottom 50%

Source: ONS; HMRC [Note: Marketable wealth (also known as net worth) is the value of all assets that can be bought and sold—shares, property, bank savings and so on—minus liabilities. It excludes, for example, occupational pensions that cannot be transferred. Here the value of dwellings, assets that are often passed down or inherited rather than bought, are excluded.]

Harmony with nature. British agriculture has long been less variegated than its French and Italian counterparts and is growing less so still. A decreasing proportion of our food is farmed locally, an increasing proportion imported from abroad. In 1970, food imports were at £2 billion; since then they have grown twice as fast as exports, to around £20 billion. The UK self-sufficiency ratio (which approximates how much of our own food we could produce) is the lowest it has ever been, just below 60 percent; in the 1970s it was consistently between 70 and 80 percent.[45] Chain stores have expanded steadily at the expense of local shops, now accounting for over 97 percent of the food retail market.[46] In most British main streets, Keynes's "shops that are really shops" are thinly scattered amidst the "branches of the multiplication table." Some relief from the monotony is provided by farmers' markets, organic food cooperatives and the like. But these are just middle-class baubles, the modern equivalent of French courtiers playing at milkmaids. Expensive and precious, they make no dent on the overall trend, which continues relentlessly in the other direction.

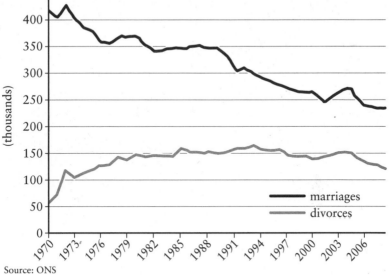

Chart 14. Marriage and Divorce in the UK

Source: ONS

Friendship. Sociologists dispute whether friendship in our sense (or "social capital," to use the current barbarism) is flourishing or fading. What is not in doubt is that many of the old institutional forms of sociability—the Churches, the trade unions, the public houses, working men's clubs—are in long-term decline in Britain.[47] Substitutes are springing up, however. New-age sects are on the rise. Single-issue pressure groups are multiplying. And then of course there is the web, with its vast networking possibilities. Overall, there has been a shift from relationships based on shared ways of life to those based on special interests and identities, these latter being better suited to the protean, post-modern self.[48] Similar trends have been observed in other OECD nations.[49]

One institution in particular calls for concern. Across the developed world, fewer marriages are taking place, and of those that do, more end in divorce.[50] It is often said that exclusive, lifelong commitments are a trap, for women in particular. However, the evidence suggests that stable relationships are good for all concerned, children especially, and that marriages are generally more stable than informal unions.[51] This, presumably, is why sex is regulated by rituals and penalties across the world. It is only in the modern West that sexual freedom is regarded as a basic right.

Leisure. As we showed in Chapter 1, time off work has not increased in the last twenty years, and may actually be shrinking, once commuting and other chores are added in. But since "leisure" in our sense is not simply time off work but free, non-purposive activity, it is relevant to ask how the vacant hours are occupied. Trends are mixed. Television remains the dominating presence in Britain and other nations, with the average Briton watching more than four hours a day.[52] Video games and online social networks are increasingly popular, especially among the young. The number of British adults playing at least one sport fell from 48 to 43 per cent between 1990 and 2002, a trend replicated in Canada and the USA.[53] Time spent reading has increased slightly in the UK and France since 1975, though the overall number of readers, particularly of newspapers and magazines, has declined. In the USA, both readers and reading hours have declined sharply.[54] Attendance at British cultural events rose slightly between 1986 and 2003, as Chart 15 shows. Such statistics are inevitably too crude to resolve the ongoing debate between cultural pessimists and optimists. What is clear is that Keynes's vision of middle-class culture spreading to the masses with the increase of leisure has not been realized.

The expansion of higher education in Britain and elsewhere over the past thirty years might naturally be thought of as an addition to leisure. However, because higher education has also been refashioned along increasingly utilitarian lines, its status as leisure is no longer self-evident. An education whose primary function is to "add value" to the student by teaching him "transferable skills" is no longer leisure in our sense, but toil—distinct in intensity, but not in character, from the toil of paid work.

The overall picture is not encouraging for the advocates of growth at all cost. Despite the doubling of UK per capita income, we possess no more of the basic goods than we did in 1974; in certain respects, we

Chart 15. Attendance at Cultural Events in the UK

	1986/87	96/97	98/99	2000/01	01/02	02/03
cinema	31%	54%	57%	55%	57%	61%
plays	23%	24%	22%	23%	24%	24%
art galleries/ exhibition	21%	22%	21%	21%	22%	24%
classic music	12%	12%	11%	12%	12%	13%
ballet	6%	7%	6%	6%	6%	7%
opera	5%	7%	6%	6%	6%	7%
contemporary dance	4%	4%	4%	4%	5%	5%

Source: Target Group Index, BM RB International; Cinema Advertising Association

possess less of them. We have chased after superfluities and neglected necessities. This, incidentally, may explain the "flat line" of happiness discussed in Chapter 4, if indeed it is anything more than a statistical artifact. It could be that people sense, correctly, that their lives are objectively no better now than they were then. Jil Matheson, head of the UK Office for National Statistics, has identified the things that matter most for happiness as "health, relationships, work and the environment"—a list that tallies closely with our basic goods.[55] Given that our lives have not noticeably improved in these respects since 1974, it is hardly surprising that we do not feel any happier.

Are we then suggesting a return to the living standards of 1974? Not necessarily, for the luxuries acquired since then may, even if they have added nothing to our real well-being, be painful to forgo. (This is an instance of the general truth that damaging social changes cannot always be rectified simply by being reversed, any more than a man flattened by a steamroller can be restored to life by being run over backwards.) What we are saying is that the long-term goal of economic policy should henceforth not be growth, but the structuring of our collective existence so as to facilitate the good life. How this might be achieved is the topic of the final chapter.

7

Exits from the Rat Race

What is the meaning of this never-ending, breathless
pursuit of a progress that always eludes one just when one
believes one has conquered it sufficiently in order to enjoy
it in peace?

—Pope Paul VI, *Octogesima Adveniens*

The Keynes generation of economists assumed that as people became more efficient at satisfying their wants, they would—and should as rational agents—work less and enjoy life more. We have identified two blockages to the fulfilment of Keynes's prophecy: those arising from power relationships and those arising from the insatiability of human wants. The two work in combination to produce an ethic of acquisitiveness, which dooms societies to continuous, objectless, wealth-creation—something that did not exist in earlier times, and that remains, in some sense, peculiar to capitalism.

International rivalries add fuel to the acquisitive fire. Despite the high degree of affluence already achieved, we are constantly being told to gear up to further challenges, particularly from the Chinese and other poor but industrious peoples. "Surviving the Asian Century" is a typical call to purposive action: "The UK needs to be operating at the top of its game, and yet we remain bedevilled by four weaknesses . . . lower business investment, a weaker skills base, less innovative and productive firms, and a smaller presence in the most vibrant emerging markets."[1] But why, if we already have enough, should we strive for a larger presence in the "most vibrant emerging markets"?

For the sake of remaining "at the top of our game" we maintain a system that continues to celebrate acquisitiveness at the expense of enjoyment. Our leaders can offer no more than a continuation of economic growth for ever and ever; and this despite the plentiful evidence that the capitalist system in our part of the world is entering its degenerative phase. The chief sign of this is the dominance of finance, in love with itself but increasingly bereft of useful things to do. The Anglo-American version of individualistic capitalism is kept going largely for the benefit of a predatory plutocracy, whose members cream off the richest prizes while justifying their predation in the language of freedom and globalization. Political leaders continue to enjoy the sound bites of power; the reality is well hidden from public scrutiny, or even understanding. At the core of our system is a moral decay that is tolerated only because the cleansing of its Augean stables is too traumatic to contemplate.

It is worth recalling that the ideal of economic growth as an end without end is of fairly recent origin. When British prime minister Harold Macmillan told the voters in 1959 that they'd "never had it so good," he was echoing the widely held view at the time that the capitalist countries of the West were rapidly approaching a consumption plateau, and the main problem of the future would be to ensure that the fruits of the new abundance were democratically distributed. Galbraith's hugely influential *The Affluent Society* (1958) with its image of "private affluence, public squalor" caught this mood. As we showed in Chapter 2, the assumption of abundance, and consequent revulsion against technology and psychological distancing from the world of work, was the imaginative backdrop of the American utopian movements of the 1960s.

The question is: why did the perception of imminent Bliss of the 1960s lead to the restoration of Darwinian capitalism in the 1980s? What brought Reagan and Thatcher to power and led to the renewal of free-market fundamentalism?

It is easy to see that, in the form in which the followers of Marcuse imagined it, Bliss was an illusion. For reasons analyzed in Chapter 1, richer societies are likely to become more, rather than less, acquisitive, as the power of relative wants grows. But this secular trend does not explain the sudden collapse of the system of political economy that had brought the rich part of the world to the dawn of universal abundance.

The question is: why did economic growth, so quickly and decisively, come to trump all other objects of economic policy? The simple, though surprising, answer is that, with the assumed achievement of permanent full employment by policy, *there were no other objects of economic policy left.* In these circumstances, economic thinking was free to concentrate once more on the efficiency with which output was produced. This was more congruent with the *maximizing* spirit of economics, getting the most use out of a given stock of resources. That growth could become an object of economic policy was in large measure due to the development of national income statistics—GDP—which enabled comparisons between countries' economic performance. And, in the aftermath of two supremely destructive wars, to make peoples richer, rather than nations more bellicose, seemed an eminently civilized object of striving.

There were two ancillary reasons. The first was that the West as a whole felt it needed to speed up its rate of growth to maintain the arms race with the Soviet bloc. Not only did the Soviet system seem to be growing faster than Western capitalism in the 1960s, but, by suppressing private consumption, it was able to devote a much higher proportion of its growing wealth to military spending. The West needed to show it could produce both guns and butter. The second reason was that faster economic growth was a way of circumventing the facts of power. It offered a way of improving the position of the poor without having to increase taxes on the rich. In this second aspect, economic growth was a left-wing policy to benefit the working class without igniting latent class conflict over the distribution of the national product. The apostles of growth of the 1960s were mainly left-wing economists and politicians who had abandoned—or in the United States never embraced—public ownership as a mechanism, but retained their socialist aspirations for a more equal society. They hankered for a democratic version of the Soviet planning system, one that would nudge private enterprise to greater energy by means of targets, subsidies and tax incentives, while allocating an increasing share of the fruits of enterprise to education, welfare and public services. This was particularly appealing in slow-growing Britain.

However, this was still some way from the crisis-prone Darwinian capitalism of our own day. The essential ingredient that Thatcher (elected in 1979) and Reagan (elected in 1980) added to the philosophy of growth was an ideological faith in the market system. The way to faster growth lay not through planning, but freeing up markets from red tape, improving incentives through lighter taxes, reducing the power of trade unions, and extending markets through privatization and deregulation. These steps in combination would make the allocation of capital more efficient. The Thatcher–Reagan dispensation also viewed the growth of income inequality as acceptable insofar as it improved the incentives of the "wealth creators": there would be a "trickle down" from rich to poor. This set of ideas became what Adair Turner calls the dominant "instrumental conventional wisdom" across the political world over the following thirty years.[2]

In retrospect, it was the shift to a market-based philosophy of growth rather than to a growth-based philosophy as such that inflamed the insatiability of wants we identified in Chapter 1. "Planning for growth" need have entailed nothing more than bringing the welfare of the poor gradually up to the standard of rich. By contrast, reliance on market-led growth marked the abandonment of any interest in the *social* outcome of the growth process. The economic system was to be geared to the maximization of individual satisfaction as expressed in markets. Individuals were no longer to be viewed as part of wholes; the wholes were simply the sum of individual parts. This reduction of economic life to a crude individualism can be dated from the 1970s. In economics, microeconomics, the study of individual economic behavior, replaced macroeconomics, the study of the economy as a whole; in political thought, the rights and duties of individuals replaced the rights and duties of groups. This kind of market order was bound, of course, by the rule of law; but there was no longer any moral, political or cultural restraint on individual pursuit of wealth; the only restraint might arise from natural limits to growth itself.

Any radical shift in consciousness requires the stimulus of crisis. For the free-marketeers it was the "crisis of Keynesian economics"— that combination of rising unemployment and rising inflation identified by Milton Friedman as an ineluctable consequence of full employment policy. Free-marketers made some telling points: the existing system had become sclerotic, the power of trade unions excessive, and rates of taxation not merely redistributive but punitive. However, more decisively destructive of Keynesian social democracy were the two big hikes in the price of oil 1973 and 1979. These represented a cumulative transfer equivalent to $1,900 billion in today's money from the rich oil importers to the oil producers, mainly Middle Eastern sheikdoms. The rise in energy costs required a fall in the real incomes of the oil consumers. In the face of widespread union-led opposition to wage reductions, the brunt of this transfer initially fell on profits rather than wages. The restoration of the rate of profit via the abandonment of the full employment commitment, the elimination of trade union control over wages, and the restructuring of the economy from manufacturing to services became the concrete project for which the ideology of the free market lent an ideal support. In effect, the governments of Reagan and Thatcher handed economies back to the businessmen. The role of the state in management, ownership, regulation, allocation, and distribution was drastically pared back. Governments gave up attempts to steer market forces to desirable social outcomes, limiting themselves to maintaining framework conditions for successful market performance. The wealth of nations would be made to grow faster by releasing acquisitiveness from its communal restraints, in a reprise of the arguments first advanced by Adam Smith and his followers.

In this kind of world there is no reason why capitalism should ever end, provided everything goes according to plan. Keynes's notion of satiety has no place: the progress of the system will create new wants and stimulate positional competition without limit. And any observed tendency for rich societies to rest on their laurels by working and consuming less can be countered by the logic of globalization and the stimulus of additional income inequality. But of course, such a system will not, cannot, work according to plan. It is both economically and morally inefficient. It survives only because we have lost a sense of what wealth is for, a language of the good life. With a few exceptions to be noted below, the main currents in economics and political theory hold that the state should be neutral as between individual choices. But in our kind of system this inevitably and inescapably hands the choice of system and instruments to those with the greatest amount of wealth and power.

So we turn finally to the main question: what intellectual, moral, and political resources still exist in Western societies to reverse the onslaught of insatiability and redirect our purposes towards the good life?

Virtue Revisited

In his book *After Virtue*, the philosopher Alasdair MacIntyre asks the reader to imagine a catastrophe that has destroyed the natural sciences. All that survives is fragments of fact and practice detached from any knowledge of their theoretical context. MacIntyre suggests that "in the actual world which we inhabit the language of morality is in the same state of grave disorder as in the imaginary world which I described." What we possess are fragments of past moralities detached from the conceptual schemes and contexts that gave them coherence. But we do not recognize that any catastrophe has occurred. The academic disciplines that study moral questions are unaware of it. They are aware only of the fragments, about which they dispute furiously. That is why moral debate is interminable, and *neutrality* between different moral beliefs is regarded as the only possible stance of a modern liberal state.[3]

The catastrophe MacIntyre has in mind is the rise of the modern state and its accompanying ideology. Thus the only possible remedy he can foresee is a complete withdrawal from the political sphere—a new monasticism. "What matters at this stage," he concludes in prophetic vein, "is the construction of local forms of community within which civility and the intellectual and moral life can be sustained through the new dark ages which are already upon us ... We are waiting not for a Godot, but for another—doubtless very different— St. Benedict."[4] MacIntyre's words bring to mind the environmentalist communes that have sprung up across the West in the last thirty years, as well as initiatives such as the voluntary simplicity movement in America and the slow food movement in Italy and elsewhere.

MacIntyre offers us a powerful diagnosis of our civilization's ills, but he is too despairing of the possibilities of political reform. The fact is that, until recently, public policy in the Western world was shaped, implicitly if not always explicitly, by ideas of the good life and the good society. These ideas were not doomed to failure; they were defeated in the political struggle outlined above. Many of them remain powerful under the surface or in the margins of our public life. It would take only a modicum of political courage to restore them to their place at the center. Private initiatives of the sort envisaged by MacIntyre are to be applauded, but they will remain precarious and marginal without public backing. St. Benedict, it should not be forgotten, was preceded by the Emperor Constantine.

Of the fragments of older social moralities still available to us, the most extensive is Catholic social teaching, conveniently summarized in the twelve papal encyclicals starting with *Rerum Novarum* in 1891 and running to *Caritas in Veritate* in 2009. This teaching is, of course, the property of a particular Church, but one does not have to be a Catholic or even a Christian to appreciate it. Unlike many of its Protestant counterparts, the Catholic Church has always been open to the best of pagan wisdom. Its defense of property, its call for just prices and wages and its condemnation of avarice and usury owe as much to Aristotle as they do to the Gospels. Where Catholic teaching is distinctively Christian, and quite un-Aristotelian, is in its emphasis on work as the necessary expiation of man's sin. ("Man is born to labour as the bird to fly," wrote Pius XI.) That said, Catholic social thought has never held up *unremitting* toil as an ideal. "The true and rational doctrine," wrote Monsignor John Ryan, an early twentieth-century American theologian, "is that when men have produced sufficient necessaries and reasonable comforts and conveniences to supply all the population, they should spend what time is left in the cultivation of their intellects and wills, in the pursuit of the higher life."[5]

One of the many strengths of Catholic teaching is that it cuts in equal measure against state socialism and unrestrained capitalism. Leo XIII's *Rerum Novarum* (subtitled "On the Condition of the Working Class") of 1891 opens with a splendid denunciation of capitalism of which Marx would have been proud:

> Hence, by degrees it has come to pass that working men have been surrendered, isolated and helpless, to the hard-heartedness of employers and the greed of unchecked competition. The mischief has been increased by rapacious usury ... To this must be added that the hiring

of labour and the conduct of trade are concentrated in the hands of comparatively few; so that a small number of very rich men have been able to lay upon the teeming masses of the labouring poor a yoke little better than that of slavery.[6]

The pontiff's remedies, however, were far from Marx's, whose doctrines he denounced as a pernicious error. The solution to the social question was "justice between classes," specifically a wide distribution of property. The Catholic ideal was that of the small family farm or workshop. It was through property that a man (women did not feature in the early encyclicals except as wives and mothers) left the "impress of his personality" on the soil and provided security for his family. Wages and conditions of work should be sufficient to enable the thrifty to save enough to acquire modest properties; holidays should be sufficiently ample to recover from the wear and tear of work and attend to the care of the soul. *Rerum Novarum* placed its faith, not in the state, but in intermediary bodies—we would now call them "civil society"—chief of which was the Church itself. The rich had a duty of charity; employers and workers were encouraged to form Catholic political parties and trade associations. The role of the state, though initially restricted to that of backstop and final guarantor of justice, gradually expanded over the history of the encyclicals as the goal of "justice between classes" became more ambitious.

These Catholic doctrines have variously been labelled "distributivism," "corporatism," "personalism." They may be seen as a defense of a non-capitalist, non-market form of private ownership as a crucial condition of personality; they stressed the duties rather than rewards of ownership, emphasized charity and demanded preferential respect for the poor.

All the popes insisted, though, that "the things of earth cannot be valued aright without taking into account the life to come . . . Exclude the idea of futurity, and forthwith the very notion of what is good and right would perish; nay, the whole scheme of the universe would become a dark and unfathomable mystery."[7] In short, religious belief, and the institutions of religion, were the only way to keep rapacity in check.

The chief secular fruit of Catholic social theory was the "social market economy."* Developed by a group of anti-Nazi intellectuals in the 1940s, its main purpose was to rebuild a heavily cartelized, shattered and compromised German economy on the basis of family businesses, thus securing the goal of dispersed ownership of assets, which was seen as an indispensable condition of freedom. Stiff inheritance taxes would ensure just initial conditions for all, "co-determination" of employers and workers in large plants and at national level was needed to achieve the trust of all strata. These ideas were endorsed first by the Christian Democrats in 1948, then by the Social Democrats in 1959. The theory of the social market economy helped shape the social model of the European Union. A relatively weak state but strong civil institutions was its hallmark. There is a strong family resemblance between Continental social Catholicism, the sociological liberalism of French thinkers like Montesquieu and Tocqueville, the Burkean conservatism espoused by pre-Thatcherite leaders of the British Conservative party, and various hybrid forms of property relations (for example, mutual societies and employee cooperatives) that hark back to the medieval guilds.[8]

In the Protestant world, the parallel contribution to social Catholicism may be loosely labelled "New Liberalism." In contrast to its Catholic counterpart, this was secular, progressivist and broadly statist, but it converged practically on many of the same conclusions. The first wave of New Liberalism, in pre-1914 Britain, was similarly inspired by the distressed position of the poor. Influenced by Hegelian Idealism, it aimed to update the "classical" liberalism of the political economists. *Homo economicus* gave way to a picture of the individual realizing himself in community with others; the state was elevated from an enforcer of rights and contracts into an embodiment of the common good. The New Liberals backed their reforming projects with two specific arguments. First, moral failure is not just, or mainly, the result of character defects, but the product of a diseased social environment. Second, unregulated capitalism provides the wealthy with an "unearned increment" (or "taxable surplus") that can be justly applied to the relief of poverty. The chief policy instruments of

---

* The Italian Fascist theory of the "corporate state" was a fraudulent application of the ideas of Leo's encyclical.

New Liberalism were thus the inheritance tax and progressive income tax, whose proceeds were to be spent on education, social protection and other improving measures. The New Liberal theory of the "enabling state"—a state that enabled human flourishing—is a forerunner of many later theories, including those of Amartya Sen and Martha Nussbaum, which have had as their aim state action to facilitate individual "capabilities."

A second wave of New Liberalism associated with Keynes, Beveridge and Roosevelt took root in the troubled 1930s and 1940s and came of age in the 1950s and 1960s. Keynes aimed to fill the most important "gap" in the classical market economy, its failure to provide for continuous full employment. In his *General Theory of Employment, Interest, and Money* (1936), he argued that it was the state's duty to maintain enough aggregate demand to ensure the continuous use of all potential resources. Continuous full employment was not only an essential condition of security, but, as we have seen, part of Keynes's ethical project for getting over the hump of "economic necessity" as quickly as possible in order to open up the possibility of a good life for all. William Beveridge, founder of the British welfare state, and one of the original New Liberals, aimed to slay the five giant evils of squalor, ignorance, want, idleness and disease. The contribution of his famous Report (1942) was to provide people with "cradle to grave" security, via compulsory social insurance, against the "hazards" of retirement, unemployment and disability. A National Health Service and school system, both financed by taxation, would complete Beveridge's grand design. The New Deal was introduced by President Franklin Delano Roosevelt to stave off the collapse of the US economy in the Great Depression. While New Deal policies were largely pragmatic responses to the problems of particular sectors of the US economy, in his inaugural speech of 1933 Roosevelt, in Aristotelian mode and biblical language, vowed to drive the "money changers from the temple." The New Deal programs were continued, and even extended, in the 1960s, to improve the life chances of ethnic minorities.

A third fragment of social theory was provided by social democracy, which began as a late-nineteenth-century breakaway from revolutionary socialism. Its chief claim was that socialism, defined as the common ownership of productive instruments, could be achieved by democratic means (i.e., by parliamentary majorities). After the Second World War, democratic socialism, by now irrevocably severed from communism, split again between those who still aimed to bring about socialism, and those who, calling themselves social democrats, abandoned the socialist goal and put their faith in a reformed capitalism to improve the condition of the poor. Social democracy thus added a strong egalitarian commitment to New Liberalism in a "mixed economy" of private and public sectors. With many variations on the basic model, it found political homes in Britain, France, Italy and Scandinavia.

Economics, too, retained fragments of older moralities. Scientific economics started off life by imposing substantial qualifications on the hegemony of the market. As well as a general obligation to maintain the conditions of competition, Adam Smith gave the state the three duties of defense, administration of justice and "erecting and maintaining" public institutions and works that, while beneficial to the whole society, would not repay private individual entrepreneurs to provide, and that might therefore be properly defrayed from taxation. Included in this third category was education.[9] These hints of non-market goods were developed into the modern theory of *public* goods and *merit* goods: goods that societies want, and should have, but that, for various technical reasons, markets will not produce. At the end of the nineteenth century, welfare economists developed utilitarian arguments for redistribution of income, based on the proposition that the last dollar or pound was worth less to the rich man than to the poor man, with the consequence that greater equality increased total utility or welfare. Typically, though, economics smuggled essentially ethical arguments into its utilitarian framework via the language of "market failure," thus robbing them of their moral bite.

Nevertheless, these overlapping fragments of social theory were sufficiently influential in the first half of the twentieth century to enable Western society to make great strides towards realizing both the moral and the material conditions of Keynes's utopia. We cannot do justice here to the many variations on the central themes of policy, but one might summarize them by saying that governments consciously aimed to secure the material requisites of well-being for all citizens. Capitalism was not abolished, but it was restricted to such an extent that thinkers like Anthony Crosland (in the *Future of Socialism*, 1956)' wondered whether it was any longer the same beast. The main achievements of the twenty-five years from 1950 to 1975 were the maintenance of continuous full employment, reduction in inequality through progressive income taxes, a big extension of social security and the preservation of peace. Increases in productivity enabled real wages to rise and working hours to fall, with only very moderate inflation. Degrading poverty of the nineteenth-century kind was abolished. There were advances in health, education, women's rights. For most of the period, economic growth was taken to be a by-product of the whole mix of policies, not an independent, much less the overriding, policy objective. There was strong social cohesion based on real improvements in the living standards of all classes.

In many ways the political economy of the period was admirably tailored to realizing our basic goods. The problem was that it lost the language for describing itself in these terms. This is the main reason why it failed to survive the economic and social troubles that beset Western societies in the 1970s. The historian Peter Clarke has usefully distinguished between "moral" and "mechanical" reformism. Moral reformism saw improvements in material conditions as ways of elevating the moral condition of the people; mechanical reformism simply aimed to increase their prosperity.[10] Deprived of their ethical language by the collapse of religion and the strongly individualist fashion in economics and political philosophy, "moral" liberals were forced back on purely "mechanical" arguments. They stressed the positive effect on productivity of a better fed, better housed, better clothed, healthier and better educated workforce. This was almost certainly true. However, once the commonly accepted language became one of efficiency, the moral reformers were vulnerable to the charge that their reforms had created inefficiency by lessening the incentives to work and save, and by stealing resources from the productive sector. The social liberalism of the 1950s and 1960s had nothing left to put in place of the profit motive, only qualifications that applied to particular examples of "market failure." So when the social liberal states ran into fiscal crisis in the 1970s, they had no intellectually cogent defenses to offer against the restatement of the philosophy of untrammelled self-interest. Tax rates tumbled, the welfare state was reined in, state industries were privatized, the financial sector was set free.

The *coup de grâce* was delivered by the fall of communism. In the Cold War era, the West had to proclaim its own concept of the good life to counter the appeal of communism. This necessity was now gone; there was no ideological challenger left; in post-communist Russia, the acquisitive instinct, after long suppression, was ferociously unleashed. The recent crisis of capitalism has produced spontaneous outbursts of anti-capitalism but not yet given rise to any alternative ideology. Market individualism remains the only game in town.

However, the irony of our situation is that we no longer have to sacrifice the good life, as we have defined it, to efficiency. If, indeed, we have reached the point where, as Keynes put it, the "accumulation of wealth is no longer of high social importance," we become free to discard "all kinds of pseudo-moral principles . . . social customs and economic practices, affecting the distribution of wealth and economic rewards and penalties, which we now maintain at all costs . . . because they are tremendously useful in promoting the accumulation of wealth." What will this mean in practice?

Social Policy to Realize the Basic Goods

We are not in the business of writing a party manifesto, and can therefore only give broad indications. Nor are we suggesting that our goals can be immediately achieved. Like Keynes, we want to take "flight into the future," though from a position at once more and less favorable than his: more favorable, because we are now four or five times as wealthy; less favorable, because we have lost a great deal of the moral language that came naturally to him and his readers; and because new sources of scarcity, resulting from population growth and depletion of natural resources, imperil our future.

What would an economic organization geared to realizing the basic goods look like? It would have to produce enough goods and services to satisfy everyone's basic needs *and* reasonable standards of comfort. It would furthermore have to do so with a big reduction in the amount of necessary work, so as to free up time for leisure, understood as self-directed activity. It would have to ensure a less unequal distribution of wealth and income, not just to diminish the incentive to work, but to improve the social bases of health, personality, respect and friendship. Finally a society that aims to realize the basic goods of friendship and harmony with nature would put more emphasis on localism, less on centralization and globalization. These material requisites hang together, and the failure of one jeopardizes the others, though to an unequal degree. If people have to work too hard to achieve their standards of material sufficiency, basic goods like leisure are sacrificed. Great inequality may be compatible with everyone having enough material goods, but the fact that a minority would in such circumstances have much more than is enough would stimulate insatiability and render wealth insecure. Finally, localism, whether in production or political life, seems inseparable from personality, respect, and harmony with nature.

How far should policy be pushed to realize these aims? The crux of the matter is the extent to which a liberal state is justified in interfering with individual decisions about how much to work and what to consume. Liberal economists and philosophers are strongly committed to non-paternalism, that is, to the view that individuals are the best judge of their own interests; or even if they are not, that they should be free to make their own mistakes. Economists believe that people should be allowed to work as long as they want, and that what consumers want to buy ought to determine what is produced, because only that allocation of goods that satisfies the wants of individual consumers maximizes the welfare of the community. More generally, most modern liberals believe that any departure from "neutrality" in these matters on the part of the state constitutes a violation of individual freedom.

Our position may be described as non-coercive paternalism. We believe that state powers may be used to promote the basic goods, but only insofar as this does not damage the central good of personality. Our preference is therefore always for non-coercive over coercive measures. So what we propose below involves encouraging or discouraging certain kinds of behavior, without introducing any new limitations on the individual's freedom of choice; indeed, our proposals are designed to increase the average individual's freedom of choice.

In Chapter 1, we identified the main drivers of the work treadmill as the superior power of capital vis-à-vis labor, and our insatiable desire for consumption goods, inflamed by advertising. The first determines the amount of real income that people have to set against the disutility or pain of work; the second, the amount of income they feel they need to give up work. In both aspects our present system works to increase the domain of toil at the expense of leisure, in the first by preventing a rise of median income in line with productivity, in the second, by inflaming the psychological urge to consume at any level of income. Our task, then, is twofold: to ensure that the fruits of productivity, are shared more evenly; and to reduce the pressure to consume.

A key aspect of the first problem is that the current distribution of income does not reflect the average rise in productivity. Had the productivity gains in manufacturing and some specialized services accrued to the whole population, average hours of work would probably have continued to fall after 1980. As it turned out, capital has absorbed an increasing share of productivity growth; and in the public services, where productivity growth is hard to measure, and is often irrelevant, the machinery for raising pay in line with average productivity has broken down. This has left public sector pay at the mercy of the exigencies of public finance.

Thus the problem which Keynes identified in 1930—"our discovery of means of economising the use of labour outrunning the pace at which we can find new uses for labour"[11] has not been solved in the way he envisaged. Automation in manufacturing has led not to a massive increase in leisure but to a massive transfer of labor to the lower-paid service sector where people have to work longer hours to make ends meet; while those not reabsorbed in the service economy have become unemployed, under-employed or casualized. It is true that this last method does reduce the total of hours worked, but it adds greatly to the uncertainty of employment, thus contradicting our basic good of security. The stagnation of incomes, in turn, produces growing indebtedness, as the unappeased desire for consumption can no longer be satisfied by income from work.

An increase in the share of services in the economy is a natural development for a rich society. But the service sector should not be as skewed as it is today to the servicing of the needs of "oligarchic wealth." (See above, pp. 34–35.) Indeed, we are slowly reverting to the conditions of earlier times, when societies were divided into a small class of *rentiers* and a large class of servants, without, however, the hierarchical structure that made such inequality of status more palatable. All those possessing substantial assets will be able to afford the services of all those compelled to work long hours for lack of them—chauffeurs, gardeners, domestic servants, cleaners, nannies, tutors, trainers, beauticians, groomers, shop assistants, waiters and so on. In this kind of society, superior privately financed services for the rich will be paralleled by inferior collectively financed services for the rest.

This would be a dreadful outcome for an age of abundance. How can we avoid it? We need to reduce inequality of income, because average hours of work will continue to fall only if the real incomes of the majority are raised relatively to those now enjoyed by a minority. In the UK and USA, the gap between top and median incomes has become a chasm. A sustained effort should be made to raise the share of income received by teachers, doctors, nurses and other public service professionals. This will require a higher rate of taxation, and for that reason will encounter more political resistance than in countries that start with a more equal income distribution.

But this is not enough. There is also the issue of inequality of power in the workplace, emphasised by Juliet Schor (see above, pp. 32–33). This enables employers to dictate the terms and conditions of work, apart from the remuneration of their employees. It is more profitable for employers to work a smaller number of workers longer hours than to spread the work over a larger number. The result is that the labor market is divided into those who are compelled to work longer than they want, and those who cannot get enough work.

Tackling the power of the boss over terms and conditions of employment will require a number of different approaches. The simplest step would be to legislate for a progressive reduction in the hours of work, by limiting weekly hours and/or increasing statutory vacation times. There is nothing new in this: hours of work have been controlled ever since the Factory Acts of the early nineteenth century. Today, they are limited to forty-eight hours a week by the European

Working Time Directive (though in the UK individual workers can opt out of this restriction), and to thirty-five hours a week by French legislation of 2000. It would be better to set maximum hours of work in most occupations, and allow exemptions for all those outside the ring-fence: self-employment, partnerships, family employment and small businesses.

Within such a framework it would be open to employers and employees to negotiate flexible retirement and work-sharing arrangements. Work-sharing has always been shunned by economists as smacking of the "lump of labor" fallacy: the idea that there is only a certain amount of work to go round, which should be shared among all those wanting to work. This objection is decisive if the object of economic policy is to maximize growth. But if growth is abandoned as the main policy objective, work-sharing is the civilized way of bringing about a balance between the demand for, and supply of, labor, in a world in which automation is shrinking the demand for manufacturing jobs. Work-sharing can also be implemented in lower-paid jobs in the service sector, but will require the support of additional measures.

There is no reason why a general reduction in working hours should bring about a fall in most people's wages. The Dutch, for example (see p. 22), work shorter hours than the British but enjoy a higher average income per head ($42,000 as against $36,000), with a more equal distribution of wealth and income. Productivity may even go up as workers pack more punch into the shorter hours worked, or employers improve work organization. This seems to have happened in places where the experiment has been tried. Hardly any production was lost in the two months Edward Heath put Britain on a three-day week in 1974. In the 1980s, Volkswagen reduced its working week from 36 to 28.8 hours to avoid having to lay off 30,000 workers: its plant reorganizations have in fact increased productivity. Shorter working hours mean that the factories can run more shifts, increasing operating hours even as they reduce employee working hours, thus reducing unit costs.[12] Similar schemes were introduced in other parts of Europe in the 1980s and 1990s to offset the great "downsizing" of industry. They are still very much in operation and the evidence suggests they have proved effective, not just at reducing working time but equalizing pay inequalities between full- and part-time employees (such as exist in the USA), and even increasing productivity.[13]

Moreover, there is plenty of evidence that people are willing to trade income for leisure if they are allowed to and if the fall in income is not too great. A Danish law of 1993 recognizes people's right to work discontinuously, while guaranteeing their right to a continuous income. This allows an inventive form of work-sharing. Employees can choose a "sabbatical" year every four or seven years, which can be divided into shorter periods. During the period of leave, unemployed people take the place of those on leave who, for their part, receive 60 percent of their salaries. Trade unions have managed to use such individual rights, enshrined in law, to reduce the working hours of entire company workforces, and thus increase the number of permanent jobs. One company has increased its permanent staff by 10 percent by ensuring that 10 percent are always on leave. Evidently workers who choose to work less get paid less, but this is their choice. The success of the Danish scheme is evidence that many workers, unlike economists, do not equate living standards with per capita income. Income enhances the value of leisure, but it does not comprise it.

Despite their attractions, these work-sharing schemes are not affordable to many lower-paid workers, who need their income from full-time work. These workers would have to be put in a position in which they could afford to work less. It is in this context that the idea of a basic income, independent of any obligation to work, becomes appealing.

Basic Income

"Basic income is an income paid by the state to each full member or accredited resident of a society, regardless of whether he or she wishes to engage in paid employment, or is rich or poor, or, in other words, independently of any other sources of income that person might have, and irrespective of cohabitation arrangements in the domestic sphere."[14]

Basic income must be distinguished from "minimum income," whose purpose is to prevent incomes from falling below what is called the "poverty line." Minimum income is means-tested and is linked to the job market, either through its requirement that the recipient must be actively seeking work (in the UK, unemployment benefit has been relabelled "job seeker's allowance") or by its being used to top up exceptionally low wages. By contrast, basic income is an unconditional payment to all citizens, ideally at a level high enough to give them a genuine choice of how much to work.

Basic income schemes—or citizen income schemes, as they are sometimes called—have a very long history. We can trace them from Hobbes in the seventeenth century, through Tom Paine in the eighteenth, to the nineteenth-century followers of Charles Fourier (favorably mentioned by John Stuart Mill) and American writers in the Jeffersonian tradition. In more recent times, they have been advocated by Quakers and socialists, and by James Meade, Samuel Brittan, André Gorz among others.[15] In 1943, the Liberal politician Lady Rhys Williams proposed a "social dividend," payable to all families, regardless of income, to be financed by income taxes, with the dividend increasing in line with national income. More recent proposals, such as Milton Friedman's "negative income tax"—a single cash payment to all those whose incomes fell below a certain threshold—have been seen as cheaper way of providing social security.[16] Something called "basic income" has also been promoted as a way of topping up wages when the market-clearing wage fell below subsistence, and in this form has been widely adopted in the form of tax credits.

Most of the earlier arguments were rights-, or entitlement-, based, a typical one being that each citizen had a right to a share of the nation's patrimony—its stock of assets, natural or inherited—in compensation for the original act of property despoilation. There was also an appreciation of the value of independence and leisure.

In its pure form of an unconditional income guarantee for all, basic income has always fallen foul of two objections, the first that it would be a disincentive to work, the second that society was too poor to afford it. As a result of such objections the only basic income schemes in existence are those found in a few regions like Alaska and (partially) the United Arab Emirates, whose wealth consists in natural resources that take little labor to extract, and that therefore offer few employment opportunities to their citizens.*

However, these two objections fail when the problem is not one of scarcity but abundance, and the goal of policy is not to maximize growth but secure the basic goods. In this situation the aim is precisely to *reduce* the incentive to work, by making leisure more attractive; furthermore, a rich society can increasingly *afford* to pay its citizens a basic income. An unconditional basic income would make part-time work a possibility for many who now have to work full-time; it would also start to give all workers the same choice as to how much to work, and under what conditions, as is possessed now by owners of substantial capital. Samuel Brittan in 2005 stated the rationale for a basic income in terms that most appeal to us:

> The object of a basic income is to make every citizen into a renter in a small way. Private property and unearned income, so denounced by the Marxists, are not inherently evil. The trouble is that so few people have them (apart from their own homes) with all the benefits they provide of personal independence. Surely in the better society to which some of us aspire, these advantages should be more widespread.[17]

Confusingly, what is called basic income can come in two alternative forms: a capital endowment or a guaranteed annual income. One can argue that analytically they come to the same, the capital endowment

---

* The Alaska Permanent Fund was established in 1976, financed by revenues from Alaskan oilfields. Anyone not convicted of a felony, who legally resides in the State of Alaska for more than six months, receives an annual Basic Income, based on a five-year average of the Fund's performance. In 2010, the dividend was $1,281, but in 2008 it was as large as $3,269, including a one-off rebate. The Fund has made Alaska the most equal of all the American states. In the 1990s, the dividend represented 6 percent of Alaska's GDP. The result was that, in a decade where the average income of the poorest families in the US grew by 12 percent, and the richest by 26 percent, in Alaska the trend was reversed: the poorest gained 28 percent while the incomes of the richest only grew by 7 percent. The dividend is popular, but politically contentious, as its finance derives from a finite pool of natural resources. Although Alaska is the only example of a basic income in operation, in Brazil a law enacted in 2004 mandates the establishment of a basic income, to be implemented gradually from 2005, starting with the neediest categories. Oil-revenue-related dividends are also paid to the minority of citizens of the United Arab Emirates, but not to the majority of non-citizens who do most of the work.

being merely the discounted value of its expected future yield. But the possession of capital provides its owner with a choice: he can either "live off the income" or spend the capital: buy a house, start a business, save it or blow it. A guaranteed income gives greater security over a lifetime; a capital endowment gives greater freedom of choice. On balance, we prefer the capital endowment because it would achieve the aim of bringing about a wider distribution of disposable assets—and thus the bases of respect and personality. However, since no single basic good should exclude others, a basic income scheme might consist of both a capital and an income part; or, with experience, offer a choice between the two.[18]

The argument that a basic income—one that lifts all citizens above the poverty line—is unaffordable is ceasing to be true in rich societies. In his *Agathotopia* (1989), Nobel Laureate James Meade reckoned that a subsistence income, equal to unemployment benefit, for all citizens could be financed through a combination of capital taxes and profits from state-owned but privately managed investment trusts. It would be set to grow in line with national income.[19] Others suggest that the sale of pollution permits, like carbon credits, based on environmental impact, would be enough to finance a basic income of €1,500 in the EU.[20] Taxes on capital transactions—known as Tobin taxes—are another potential source of income. In 2001, two American professors, Bruce Ackerman and Anne Alstott, put forward a costed plan for capital endowment based on a tax on private wealth.[21] A small step towards a capital endowment for all was Gordon Brown's "baby bond" scheme, the Child Trust Fund, which he set up as Chancellor of the Exchequer in 2001. This was to have provided a tax-free bond worth up to £800 for every newborn child.* It could

---

* Under the plan, the state would open an account for the 700,000 children born each year, at an estimated cost of £480 million. The money would be invested by the financial industry until the child reached 18, when it could be drawn on for approved purposes such as education, training, buying a home or starting a business. The value of the bond provided by the Government ranged from £400 for children from better-off families to between £750 and £800 for the poorest. To encourage poor families to save, the state would provide mean-tested "matching funds" if they contributed to the accounts. They would receive an annual statement showing how their funds had grown. Figures compiled by the Institute for Public Policy Research (IPPR), a think tank that persuaded the Government to adopt the scheme, suggested that a £750 "baby bond" invested in 1981 would have grown to £2,625 by 1999.

have become part of a much larger scheme pooling revenues from social security taxes, capital and transaction taxes, and profits from state investment trusts. The Coalition government abolished it in 2010 as part of its cuts.

It is often said that basic income schemes, of either type, would merely encourage idleness and debauchery. A guaranteed annual income would turn a large part of the adult population into state dependants, lethargic and demoralized. A capital endowment, given to irresponsible 18-year-olds, would quickly evaporate in drugs and designer clothes, leaving its recipients exactly where they were before, if not worse off.

These risks are not negligible. However, there are two more hopeful possibilities. The first applies to a capital endowment. There is no reason why the lump-sum recipients should be any worse at preserving their capital than any inheritor, especially as the endowment will not be an isolated windfall (such as winning the lottery) but part of a social contract. Of course, many children of rich parents have squandered or gambled away their inheritances. But over the generations the wealthy have been remarkably successful at keeping their wealth. They have not done so entirely unaided. Inheritances have been tied down in various ways, for example in trusts, which limit the ability of heirs to alienate them. The same principles of restriction can be applied to the much more modest citizen endowments. The risk of them being "blown" in riotous living can be reduced by limiting their spending to approved objects (such as education) and pushing out the age of receipt to 30 or older, as is now the case with normal inheritance.

Second, we would rely on educating people for leisure. At present, education aims to fit pupils for the job market by providing them with merely useful knowledge and skills. In the future we envisage that education will be informed by the understanding that the "job-bing" part of a person's life will be a decreasing fraction of his waking hours, and that one of its main tasks will be to prepare people for a life of fulfilment outside the job market. Most independent schools, which educate the better-off, understand the importance of education for leisure by offering their pupils a well-rounded curriculum, but state schools have become increasingly utilitarian. A drastic change in the ethos (and increase in the funding) of state education is needed if rich societies are to avoid preparing the minority for the good life, and the majority for a life of drudgery. In the past, economists were part of a wider group of thinkers who argued that rising incomes required education in order for people to lead the good life. It was only subsequently that economics abandoned this ambition and came to think of schools solely as conveyor belts of human capital.[22]

Basic-income schemes would not stop people working—in the sense now understood—as long and hard as they want to in jobs exempt from regulation of hours. No doubt many would use their basic income merely to top up earnings from existing hours of paid work. But those who wanted to spend more time in unpaid activities—and, as we saw in Chapter 1, many do—would have the option of doing so. And those who wanted to move from boring but remunerative to more fulfilling but less remunerative work—from estate agent to craftsman, say—would also have the choice. (Basic income, in Frithjof Bergmann's phrase, would "liberate work from the tyranny of the job."[23]) In our terms, both these options constitute a gain in leisure—in spontaneous, self-directed activity—and are thus to be welcomed. But they are only part of a larger set of policies to direct people towards the good life.

Reducing the Pressure to Consume

Reducing the pressure to consume is an important way of reducing the pressure to work, because we work mainly to consume, so the less we want to consume, the less we will want to work. Yet our society promotes conspicuous and extravagant consumption, even by those who cannot afford it. This is an important reason why the newly rich are no longer "idle."

On September 5, 2011, a London newspaper reported that squatters had occupied the house of a Harley Street neurologist. The neurologist said that he started with no advantages in life, and was working a sixty-hour week to afford the 90 percent mortgage on his £1 million "dream house." This is a perfect vignette of modern capitalist civilization. The wealthy mortgage their future for dreams—and the poor take their revenge. How much will our neurologist need to be earning pre-tax to pay interest and principal on his £900,000 mortgage? Depending on the terms and length of borrowing it could be something like £200,000 a year. And the overwork will continue. Such a house, and the family it will contain—the neurologist's wife was expecting a baby—are very costly to run. There will be a servant or two, a nanny, a trainer (to keep fit for the sixty hours!), expensive gadgets, holidays and clothes, and looming over all the expenses of private education for probably two children. Why are they needed? Surely, because they are the kinds of expenses that professionals in the neurologist's income bracket expect to have. But there is a snag. A £1 million house puts our neurologist into the ranks of the successful young, not the successful old. More senior friends or acquaintances will have £2 or £3 million houses—houses in more exclusive areas, which, perhaps, can boast underground swimming pools. Sixty hours of work a week may well not be enough. Thus our way of life feeds our insatiability, and our insatiability feeds our way of life.

The neurologist is a conspicuous consumer. But the urge to consume is not confined to luxuries. Modern capitalism inflames through every pore the hunger for consumption. Consumption has become the great placebo of modern society, our counterfeit reward for working irrational hours. Parents pass "compulsive consumerism" on to their children by showering them with toys and gadgets instead of spending time with them.[24] True enough, many of the innovations that are forced onto the market improve the quality of people's lives. But most do so only marginally, while setting up a competition in consumption that prevents hours of work falling. One of the great complaints about modern capitalism is that it overproduces work and underproduces leisure and the things that go with it—friendship, hobbies, volunteer work.

So what can the state do to reduce the pressure to consume?

The state already influences the direction of consumption through tax and other policies. It forces people to pay taxes for services they do not want, or which they would rather provide from their own (non-taxed) incomes, and deprives them of services they do want, such as better schools, hospitals and railways. The state's influence over consumption is even more obvious in the case of *merit* goods,

goods judged to be good for society whether or not people want to buy them. Examples include free school lunches, subsidies for low-priced housing and free medical treatment for the poor.[25] Other examples of state subsidy are art galleries, museums, concert halls, theaters, opera houses. There is also the category of so-called demerit goods, like smoking and drinking, whose consumption, it is judged, ought to be discouraged. On these governments imposes "sin taxes." In both cases, the economist, by sinuous argument, can claim that government is acting on behalf of the consumer, or at least of his "better" self. So, though people do not want taxes on tobacco, they do value their health. In fact, the state is making an ethical judgement that a certain level of provision of these goods is desirable or undesirable. It is only our impoverished public language that denies that the state *has* to make ethical judgements on a wide variety of matters.

In Chapter 1, we identified an insatiable desire to consume more and more, a desire stemming in large part from consumption's role as a marker of status. Above a certain economic level, the bulk of income is spent on items that are not needed in any absolute sense but rather serve to mark out their possessors as superior, or at least not inferior, to others. Such items must always be expensive relative to the average level, else they cannot serve their differentiating function; thus incomes are forced up competitively in order to acquire them. The same is true of some desired goods whose supply is fixed: that is why the price of Old Masters rises to ever more stratospheric heights. This spiral of competitive consumption keeps working hours long and thus frustrates the basic good of leisure; by forcing people into competitive relations with others, it also damages the basic goods of friendship, personality and security.

The traditional method of reducing competitive spending was sumptuary laws, which forbade various forms of conspicuous consumption. The Athenian "laws of Solon," dating from the sixth century BC, limited the size of funeral processions, and the value of food that could be served at them. There were also rules restricting the value of dowries and presents and regulating bridal dresses. Early Roman sumptuary law had a similar focus on extravagance and ostentation at family events, restricting, for example, the size of mausoleums and of funeral meals. In later periods, the focus shifted from weddings and funerals to the conspicuous consumption of food. In concentrating their restrictions on luxurious items of consumption, the sumptuary laws were well adapted to prevent the competitive escalation of wants, though this was not their main intention.

Sumptuary laws had behind them both moral and economic arguments. They drew support from the pervasive view that luxury was a moral evil. The vice of luxury contrasted with the virtues of frugality and hardiness. Rousseau put it bluntly: "luxury is diametrically opposed to good morals." Luxury was not only socially divisive, but because it debilitated the aristocracy, it weakened military virtue. In economic discourse, "extravagance" implied that economic resources were being diverted from productive uses; in societies where scarcity was a constant reality, squandering was linked to dearth, famine and ruin. In the seventeenth and eighteenth centuries, sumptuary laws, directed against the importation of luxuries, were part of the mercantilist state's regulation of the balance of trade.[26] In later periods, outright prohibition gave way to taxes, similar to the sin taxes described above, but covering more items.

The decay of sumptuary legislation closely follows luxury's path towards acceptability, as described in the Faustian bargain of Chapter 2. It was Mandeville who first argued that luxury fuelled economic prosperity, describing luxury as "the engine room of inventiveness and innovation."[27] But even he allowed that it was still a private vice, if also a public benefit. The abolition of sumptuary laws was also a consequence of the conviction that consumption could safely be left to individual choice. Adam Smith thought that "frugality" was part of self-interest, and that laws restraining luxury spending were therefore unnecessary.[28] What he failed to foresee was that, in affluent societies, the competitive spending on luxuries previously confined to the very rich would become universal, resulting in the endless postponement of plenty. This state of affairs suggests a new rationale for sumptuary legislation.

In a dynamic economy, the prohibition or taxation of particular goods is ineffectual as well as arbitrary, since individuals determined to show off their wealth can always find alternative ways of doing so. However, this objection does not apply to a *general* consumption tax. Consumption (or more accurately expenditure) taxes were proposed by Nicholas Kaldor in 1955 and James Meade in 1978, chiefly as a macroeconomic device for reducing private consumption and increasing private saving and investment at full employment. The aim of a consumption tax, wrote Kaldor, "is to limit consumption demand to that fraction of the national resources the community, acting through the agency of government, desired to devote to that purpose."[29] Kaldor used an argument that goes back to Hobbes: consumption is at the expense of long term growth, whereas working and saving promote it.[30] Thus people should be taxed on their expenditure, not on their income. That the tax should be progressive stemmed from a political judgment in favor of greater economic and social equality,[31] and from its economic purpose to "forc[e] wealthy rentiers to save and invest rather than engage in conspicuous consumption."[32] (In India, where the Kaldor tax was partially applied in the 1950s, it was called a "tax on maharajahs.")[33]

The expenditure tax had distinguished supporters before Kaldor, including John Stuart Mill, but it had always been dismissed as impracticable, as it seemed to require that people keep a record of everything they spent. In 1937, the American economist Irving Fisher pointed out that this was not so; expenditure could be computed as the difference between money incomings and outgoings. All the tax authority needed to know was a person's yearly income, the amount he saved/invested and tax the difference.[34] There would be an exemption threshold to protect the poor.

The economist Robert Frank has revived the Kaldor proposal, not to promote growth, which was Kaldor's aim, but to restrain "consumerism."[35] "The runaway spending at the top," writes Frank, "has . . . spawned a luxury fever that . . . has all of us in its grip."[36] The more conspicuous is the consumption of the rich, the longer becomes the escalator of emulative spending. Conspicuous consumption also diverts resources from "inconspicuous consumption": "freedom from traffic congestion, time with family and friends, vacation time, a variety of favourable job characteristics . . . higher air quality, more urban parkland . . . cleaner drinking water . . . reduction in violent crime . . . medical research."[37] Frank's list of "inconspicuous goods" is not identical to our list of basic goods, but the thought is the same: capitalism as now practised biases consumption in favor of the insatiable. The prices of goods bought by the rich force up all prices through the operation of the snob, bandwagon and Veblen effects, and therefore induce people at all levels to work harder than they otherwise would to keep up with their particular "Joneses."

In Frank's proposal, all spending above $7,500 per individual would be subjected to an escalating rate of tax. The larger the value of a person's consumption, the higher his rate of tax would be, culminating in a top marginal rate of 70 percent. The heaviest taxes would fall on the luxury spending of the rich, who alone would have incomes large enough to indulge it.[38] Even if the full replacement of income tax by consumption tax turns out to be impracticable,* a consumption tax could be a way of increasing the marginal rate of taxation if political resistance prevents governments from increasing income tax. This would have much the same effect as a full expenditure tax in restraining conspicuous consumption, reducing the income (and thus work) required to feed insatiability. As Keynes remarked in another context, "the game can be played for lower stakes."[39]

Kaldor wanted a tax that exempted saving in order to encourage faster growth. This is not something that carries so much weight in today's conditions of affluence. But an added inducement to save might also be necessary to finance the lengthening period of retirement. One could set the consumption tax at levels necessary to produce enough private and public saving to fund a comfortable retirement for all, thus fulfilling the two basic goods of respect and security. Thus a progressive consumption tax would have two advantages over a progressive income tax: it would reduce positional competition in consumption and increase saving for retirement. It could also be used as a source of finance for basic income.

It would not, on its own, reduce the love of money for its own sake. This is most clearly exhibited in the ever expanding financial

---

* The main problems are the tax treatment of durable goods and gifts. Should the purchase price of costly durable goods be regarded as an investment exempt from tax or treated as taxable expenditure? Should gifts be exempted from tax and treated as the liabilities (if spent) of the beneficiaries? In the second case, there is scope for the rich to take advantage of a progressive expenditure tax to use gifts to get lower taxed beneficiaries as a means to do their spending for them. Despite the notional simplicity of the expenditure tax, its enforcement would almost certainly require a more intrusive IRS investigation of personal circumstances than the income tax.

services industry, the real driver of contemporary capitalism, and the most egregious source of personal and corporate enrichment. Adair Turner, former chairman of the UK Financial Services Authority, has called much financial innovation "socially useless."[40] From our point of view it is worse than that. It is a cause of the insatiability we seek to control. One way to rein in the financial sector would be to tax trades in financial instruments like derivatives. Such "Tobin taxes" would both serve to reduce the power of finance to dictate economic activity and provide revenue for socially desirable objects of public spending.

Reducing Advertising

The pressure to consume is inflamed by advertising. It is often claimed that the only effect of advertising is to make it easier for people to get what they want. Even if this were true, it would not meet our objective, which is that people should first of all get what they need, not what they want. But in any case, it is not true that advertising merely helps people get what they want.

As always, the economist throws a sharp, but misleading, light on a complex issue. His account of the role of advertising is based on the doctrine of consumer sovereignty. Decisions on what to buy are made by rational consumers maximizing their utilities in competitive markets. In this model, there is no scope for advertising to alter preferences, because the consumer already has a well-defined "utility function." The only role of advertising is informational: to enlighten the customer about a product, its quality and its price, so as to allow him to make more informed choices. The law is needed only to protect children and guard against fraud. All benign views of advertising—and there are many complicated versions—are essentially variations on this theme. In one way or another, advertisements simply help the consumer get what he wants. There can be no "overconsumption" of goods of any kind, since by definition a good is simply something a consumer wants to buy.[41]

This "informational" view of advertising once had some plausibility— early twentieth-century advertisements tended to be fact-heavy—but is increasingly at odds with reality. Today most advertising contains hardly any information at all; its aim is rather to create an atmosphere around the product, to enhance its glamour and allure, in short, to make us want something we would otherwise not have thought of wanting. Take the highly successful iPod campaign of 2003, which featured nothing but silhouetted figures dancing ecstatically against a brightly colored background. Can we doubt that its goal was to evoke feelings rather than to impart information?

Faced with these facts, economists maintain their rosy view of advertising only with the aid of various subterfuges. It is said, for instance, that all advertisements, even non-informative ones, inform the consumer of at least one thing: that the commissioning company cares about its brand reputation enough to spend money on it. Another theory holds that advertising enhances a product's value by bolstering its image. (Not only do you buy a Renault; you also buy the "va va voom.") Most ingenious of all is the argument of Gary Becker and Kevin Murphy to the effect that even if consumers' preferences are altered by advertising, this is only because they have a prior preference—a meta-preference, if you like—for having their preferences altered. There is nothing sinister about this, any more than there is in the fact that buying a pencil increases your desire for pencil sharpeners. Of course, unlike pencils, advertisements are not usually sought after; they may even—Becker and Murphy concede disarmingly—"produce anxiety and depression, stir up envious feelings towards the success and happiness of others, and arouse guilt towards parents or children."[42] That is why advertisements are generally embedded in enjoyable articles or television programs: to compensate their audience for the disutility of reading or watching them. Nevertheless, the fact that people voluntarily watch advertisements suggests that that they should be considered as "complements" to other goods, not as causing a shift of tastes. The Internet has taken the theory of "complements" to heart, enticing its users with a whole lot of products similar to the ones they have already ordered.

All these neoclassical theories of advertising reflect a view of a world in which people come to market with fixed preferences, which they strive to satisfy to the utmost. They overlook the way in which the market shapes the very preferences it claims to satisfy. The Marxist tradition, with its Hegelian roots, has a sharper sense for the dynamic, relational character of human wants—or "needs," as they are usually called. "A need," wrote Hegel, "is ... created not so much by those who experience it directly as by those who seek to profit from its emergence."[43] This thought became the basis of Marcuse's critique of consumerism, examined in Chapter 2, and also of J. K. Galbraith's *The New Industrial State* (1967), which argued that producers, not consumers, initiate the production process, conditioning the needs of consumers to what they produce. Stanley Resor, president of the largest advertising agency in the United States in the 1950s, agreed. Consumers, he wrote,

> don't feel the need for a second car unless you remind them forcefully of the fact. This need has to be created in their minds and you have to make them realize the advantages a second car will bring them. At times they are even hostile to the idea. I see advertising as the educative, activating force capable of bringing about the changes in demand that we need. By teaching many people a higher standard of living, it increases consumption to a level commensurate with our productivity and resources.[44]

If advertising inflames our tendency to insatiability, there is a strong case for restricting it. Various controls on advertising are already in place, in connection with "sin goods" and children in particular. For example, Sweden and Norway prohibit advertising of any kind during children's television, as well as any advertisements specifically targeted at children under 12. Many European countries reduce television's attractiveness for advertisers by insisting that advertisements be "bunched" in magazine formats at the beginning and end of programs, so that the viewer can avoid them altogether. In Britain, unfortunately, the general tendency of the last few decades has been to ease rather than increase restrictions on advertising. The ban on advertising by solicitors was lifted in 1984, leading to a growth of US-style compensation claims. The ban on product placement on television shows—showing the guy or girl using the branded product of the program's sponsor—was removed in 2011; its effects have yet to be felt.

Restrictions on advertising can also be justified in the name of consumer protection. A lot of consumption is wasteful in the sense that people buy products about whose qualities they are ignorant or misinformed: the products do not work or do not do the work they were bought for. They either have to be discarded, or consumers have to seek compensation, which often involves expensive litigation. (This applies to financial products as well as consumption goods.) It would be better to try to prevent this kind of waste by requiring all advertisements to carry prominent health warnings, as is now mandatory for cigarettes. Caveat emptor—buyer beware!

One tax reform would cut at the root of the advertising culture: disallowing firms to write off advertising as a business expense.* Firms would have to weigh up whether the expected benefit from advertising their product exceeded the cost of paying the tax. Firms that advertise might have to put up the prices of their goods and services, but this would have the desirable result of reducing their sales. Necessities need little advertising, so the goods most affected would be those with the weakest link to needs. Such a tax would damage the financing of commercial television, which currently gets 49 percent of its revenue worldwide from advertising. This means that more money would have to come from viewer subscription (currently 42 percent), or from television licence fees and public funding, which now finance the (shrinking) share of public service broadcasting. Internet advertising could be taxed in the same way.

The policies suggested above to reduce the pressure to work, consume and accumulate wealth are not free of problems. They are indications of direction, not blueprints for legislation. They are paternalist, but non-coercive. They are designed to edge societies towards the good life, not force it down their throats.

International Implications

We need to return to Keynes's "Economic Possibilities" for a last time. He wrote: "It will be reasonable to be economically purposive for others after it has ceased to be reasonable for oneself." The "others"

---

* There is nothing new in the idea of taxing costs. For example, payroll taxes are taxes on the cost of employing labor.

here refers, he explains, to "classes and groups of people." The former can be interpreted quite naturally to mean the poor in one's own country, but "groups of people" implies no geographic limit.[45] It is our duty to help the poor wherever they might be.

In his essay, Keynes paid no specific attention to the developing world. Indeed, the idea of development hardly existed. Some parts of the world were richer than others, just as some groups were richer than others in Britain. Keynes believed that the poorer parts of the world would quite soon catch up with the richer, converging with them on a point of satiety. He no more thought that the rich countries would pull away from the poor ones than he thought that the rich would pull away from the poor in his own country.

This turned out to be a huge mistake. Although some Asian economies have caught up or are catching up with the West, a quarter of the world's population remains mired in poverty. Keynes failed to anticipate the global population explosion. He also assumed that capital and technological progress would be rapidly diffused round the world through the twin agencies of colonialism and liberal economics. Most of the poor countries of the world were colonial dependencies of the rich countries, and the exploitative idea of imperialism was giving way to one of "trusteeship," according to which the colonial masters took in hand the political and economic development of their colonies. The concrete economic form of this project—at least for Britain—was to maintain a free market for imports of goods and a free market for export of capital. Both made a great deal of sense in a world in which one part had much more wealth than the other. Capital flowed from regions where it was abundant to regions where it was scarce, to earn a higher return; and the policy of free—that is, untaxed—imports provided the borrowers with the means to service and repay their loans. There were already those in rich countries who complained that capital exports were at the expense of their own development; that free imports were destroying jobs. But on the whole the exchange between rich and poor countries was complementary, not competitive. The rich countries exported industrial goods, the poor countries exported food and commodities.

Thinking in these terms, and with no apprehension of the population time bomb in store, Keynes in 1930 not unreasonably imagined that a hundred years hence much of the poor world would have "caught up" with the rich world. At this point, the logic of free trade and capital exports, which is the logic of scarcity, would become redundant, because the world would already have as many goods as it wanted. People would be in a position to choose how much to trade with each other. Trade would revert to what Adam Smith had seen it as: a matter of "natural" advantage.* Global redistribution, in the form of aid policies, would mitigate the remaining geographical inequalities.

Our starting point is different: the rich countries have reached the threshold of their own "Bliss," as Keynes predicted they would, but much of the rest of the world is still trapped in poverty, largely because the growth of population outstripped the accumulation of capital. Further, and in conjunction with uncontrolled population growth, the world faces the threat of an absolute scarcity of resources. How, in these circumstances, should rich countries conduct their economic relations with poor countries?

Many people fear immigration because they believe it will take away jobs from current job holders. Insofar as the policy of work-sharing and basic income reduces the pressure for citizens or residents to work, it should help to lessen the fear of immigrants taking our jobs. On the other hand, the basic good of mutual respect is harder to achieve in a society where citizens receive a basic income and immigrants do not. This is in fact what does happen in the United Arab Emirates, which restricts basic income to citizens, and gets most of its work done by a helot class of non-Emirati immigrants, without rights of citizenship or settlement. A common approach to maximum hours, work-sharing and basic income would help prevent the emergence of

---

* The "natural" form of trade is between areas of the world with different resource and climatic endowments. This makes it impossible or extremely costly to produce all desired goods in the same place. If the Scots want to drink wine they will have to import it from wine-growing areas, exchanging in return, say, tartan kilts. However, the most *efficient* form of trade takes place according to *comparative* advantage: that is, it will pay country A to specialize in that good, or goods, which it can produce relatively more cheaply than B, even if it can produce all goods more cheaply than in B. This is the basis of the modern doctrine of free trade. Evidently, its persuasive power declines in conditions of abundance, when cheapness is no longer the main consideration.

a two-tier economy in the European Union, while leaving labor free to move.

Trade in Keynes's day was largely complementary; now it is largely competitive. Rich country capitalists have been offshoring manufacturing and some services to poor countries where labor is much cheaper. These cheaper goods and services are then imported to rich countries. Under these conditions, free trade can be at the expense of rich country jobs, since wages cannot be sufficiently flexible to maintain continuous full employment in the face of low wage competition. And even if jobs destroyed can always be replaced, the question remains whether the new jobs are as good as the old ones. The offshoring of jobs to China and India has caused the real incomes of many Western workers to fall or stagnate, despite the gains of trade.[46] As Nobel Laureate Paul Samuelson put it in an interview, "being able to purchase groceries 20 percent cheaper at Walmart does not necessarily make up for the wage losses" suffered as a result of these goods being made in China.[47] Even when trade does produce a surplus of winners over losers so that winners could in principle compensate losers, there is no guarantee that they will.

Free trade is not necessarily beneficial for poor countries either. The biggest problem is that it prevents them from protecting their infant industries. The economist Erik Reinert argues that "it may be better to have an inefficient manufacturing sector than not to have a manufacturing sector at all," and proposes a deal whereby the rich countries are allowed to protect their own agriculture (but prevented from dumping their surpluses on the world markets) while poor countries are allowed to protect their manufacturing and advanced service sectors. This replicates the actual conditions under which development occurred over hundreds of years, till it was swept away by free-trade dogma.[48] No country has become rich under a free-trade regime. They have entered the global market from a starting point of initial wealth, not one of initial poverty. In Ha-Joon Chang's words: "With only a few exceptions, all of today's rich countries, including Britain and the US—the supposed homes of free trade and free market—have become rich through the combinations of protectionism, subsidies and other policies that today they advise the developing countries not to adopt."[49]

This leaves capital exports as the main way of meshing the interests of rich and poor countries. Mainstream economic theory tells us that for the rich, the export of capital to poor countries offers a higher return than is available at home, and should also lower the cost of borrowing for the poor. In actual fact, a great deal of capital flows "uphill"—from poor to rich—because of the risk of investing in poor countries that are politically unstable, a risk much less significant in the nineteenth century with its colonial or quasi-colonial arrangements. Today's strongmen and their cronies, with their Swiss bank accounts, are only the most egregious example of "capital flight" from poor to rich countries. To make free capital movements mutually beneficial, a major reform of the world's currency system, as well as a restriction on flows of "hot money," would be needed. Further, if trade were to decline as a proportion of world GDP, part of the capital exports from rich to poor would need to be in the form of grants, rather than loans, because means of repayment in goods would be restricted and returns would be low.

The conclusion we draw is that in order to satisfy the requirements of the good life we will have to retreat from the further shores of economic integration, at least until "catch-up" has become a fact, not an aspiration. Developed countries will have to rely more on domestic sources of production to satisfy their needs; developing market economies will need to abandon export-growth models that rely on ever-increasing consumption demand in developed countries. If rich countries integrated less with poor countries, the poor countries might well be all the better for it. At any rate, our active involvement in their domestic economies could cease without necessarily hurting them in the long run. We would, however, still need to keep our markets open to the very poor countries of Africa. This can be done at pretty much no cost to us. The whole of sub-Saharan Africa has an economy smaller than Belgium.

Let us step back a moment. In the world of enoughness that Keynes envisaged, the returns to new investment fall towards zero. Saving would be mainly for old age and to replace existing equipment. There might be some returns for developing new products. However, in these conditions, the main incentive to be "economically purposive for others after it has ceased to be reasonable for oneself" would be to help the very poor of the world climb to our already achieved level of sufficiency.

"Working for the poor" need not take the form of traditional paid work. As the satisfactions of the "old Adam" decline, one might expect them be replaced by many kinds of ambition that come into our domain of "leisure." A voluntary sacrifice of one's own comforts for the sake of helping the less fortunate is universally recognized as morally admirable. Even today more and more people find a natural outlet for their generous (and adventurous) instincts in voluntary service at home and abroad. In expending effort, experience, expertise and love helping others such people are sacrificing income for leisure in our sense. They are leading the good life, and pointing others to it.

Our aim in this chapter has been to outline a social and economic organization that reflects the reduction in the amount of work necessary to achieve the material requisites of well-being. This has meant abandoning the scarcity perspective built into economics that makes an idol of efficiency. Rather we ask: how might a society that already has "enough" think about the organization of its collective life? As a consequence, we have advocated arrangements for living that contravene some the best-established economic nostrums, devised for conditions of poverty.

The material basis for our updated version of Keynes's "Economic Possibilities" is rooted in the logic that gave rise to his possibilities in the first place: the long-term decrease in the demand for labor resulting from continuous improvements in labor productivity. We can either turn this to our advantage by greatly expanding the domain of shared work and leisure—a solution that at least some European countries have adopted—or continue with the Anglo-American system of want-creation powered by insatiability, maintained at the cost of growing job insecurity and income inequality, and heedless of humanity's future.

What about the political possibility of realizing the good life? Marxists, always alert to the material bases of political change, argue that the "exit from capitalism has already begun." Capitalism has created the instrument of its destruction in the form of digital technology. The sociologist André Gorz sees the digital hacker as the "emblematic figure" of the revolt against private ownership of knowledge, leader of a new "anarcho-communist ethic." The stage is set for the coming struggle between the digital elites and the digital proletariat.[50]

We doubt whether it will come to this. If it does, the digital elites are bound to win, since they will find ways to privatize knowledge. And even if the digital proletariat win, what have they to put in place of what they destroy? Without a robust idea of the good life, their efforts will come to nought, win or lose.

This book is offered as a contribution to rethinking what we want out of life: what money is for and what is meant by "the good life." This has involved reanimating philosophical and ethical ideas that have long been out of favor but that are by no means extinct. People are actually quite torn about their ethics. Most City of London bankers admit that they are overpaid, and that doctors and teachers are underpaid.[51] But they are so institutionalized by their occupations, as prisoners are by their incarceration, that they can no longer imagine life outside their accustomed habitats. People who strive to do the best they can within the prevailing system may nevertheless aspire to live in a better system. This book is an attempt to help them discover one.

Our commitment to personality and respect rules out coercion. Rather we aim to bias social arrangements in favor of the good life— to make it easier for people to organize their own exits from the rat race, for instance by discovering for themselves ways of life in which money-making is not central. No political or legal system can avoid bias, however much it proclaims its neutrality. In fact, our present system is full of biases, as we have shown. Some of them we approve; others seem to us to point in the wrong direction. What we ask is that the state makes its ethical choices explicit, so we can have a proper moral debate, rather than pretending that it acts solely as the agent of the isolated consumer. If we are to be paternalists, let us be honest rather than backdoor paternalists.

Would such a reorientation of policy require the support of religion? Possibly. The basic goods, as we present them in Chapter 6, are not logically dependent on any single religious doctrine, but their realization is probably impossible without the authority and inspiration that only religion can provide. Most of the liberal reformers of the nineteenth and early twentieth centuries were Christians; others were among those who, as Keynes said of himself, "destroyed Christianity and yet had its benefits."[52] Could a society entirely devoid of the religious impulse stir itself to pursuit of the common good? We doubt it.

Whatever readers may think of our particular proposals, not to try to develop a collective vision of the good life, simply to blunder on without having a view about what wealth is *for*, is an indulgence rich societies can no longer afford. The greatest waste now confronting us is not one of money but of human possibilities. "Once we allow ourselves to be disobedient to the test of an accountant's profit," declared Keynes in 1933, "we have begun to change our civilisation." The time for such a change is overdue.

Afterword

The central message of our book, that rich societies should ease off trying to get even richer and start thinking about how to lead a good life, has resonated much more on the Continent of Europe than in the United States. American sales have been respectable, but the book got only two major reviews, in the *New York Times* and *Wall Street Journal*, both disobliging; it provoked little further discussion. As we said in the book, Americans, exiles from the Old World, have always had a much sunnier attitude to money-making than Europeans, for whom it is shadowed by a contrary morality buried deep in classical and Catholic thought. The German tradition of *Bildung*, or education as self-development rather than the acquisition of skills, perhaps also explains our book's success in that country.

The irony is that in the 1950s and 1960s Americans were much more open to thinking about what life "beyond money" might be like than they are today. J. K. Galbraith's best seller *The Affluent Society*, published in 1958, was the iconic statement of a "post-economic" view of the future. Its basic premise was that Americans, on average, already had "enough" and that the real problem was how to distribute that "enough" between private and public, rich and poor, work and leisure. Much American writing, political activism, and utopian experimentation over the following decade was caught up in its slipstream. The idea that no society, however wealthy, would ever have "enough" is a product of Reaganism: the ideology of an economic organization whose dominant aim is to perpetuate scarcity by promoting income inequality while constantly inflaming the desire for more through advertising.

There was some division of opinion along party lines. Democrats, while sympathetic to the thrust of our argument, dismissed our proposals as utopian. For the Republican right, the fact that we looked to government to redress the balance of private power in the marketplace was enough to condemn us as crypto-communists.

One common form of the first critique was that our proposals for reform lacked "political agency." How were steps to limit working hours, start a basic income scheme, institute a progressive consumption tax and place curbs on advertising to be brought about? The answer is: by having enough political momentum behind them. For this two conditions need to exist: (a) dissatisfaction with the existing order of things, and (b) a set of ideas capable of challenging it persuasively. Otherwise the dissatisfaction will get nowhere. Our book aims to provide a set of ethical ideas that we believe capable of reining in greed and growing inequality. If they resonate they will become part of politics, but it is a bit unfair to blame us for not starting a political movement!

Richard A. Posner in the *New York Times* (August 17, 2012) voiced one familiar type of conservative criticism. Posner argued that if, as we suggest, people in rich societies needed to work on average only twenty hours a week, they would find nothing better to do with their leisure than "brawl, steal, overeat, drink and sleep late." The devil makes work for idle hands. This goes back to the pessimistic view of human nature hardwired into early classical economics. Posner's version of this old Puritan saw is a bit more subtle than others. His claim is not that leisure is bad in and of itself, but that it is liable to become boring unless enhanced with consumption goods. This limits the degree to which it can expand, since consumption goods are available only to those who work hard enough to afford them. The argument here draws on an insight of the Swedish economist Staffan Linder. In his 1970 book, *The Harried Leisure Class*, Linder observed that leisure is not only a benefit but also a cost—the cost of not working. And this cost rises together with the productivity of work. To hold its own against work, leisure must become more "productive" too—which means more filled with expensive gadget-packed activity. Thus the increase in productivity that Keynes thought would liberate us for leisure has had the paradoxical effect of chaining us ever more tightly to the work/spend treadmill.

There are two responses to Posner. First, he takes the distribution of income as given. He ignores the fact that fifty million Americans live below the official poverty line. No doubt these, and many more millions of Americans, are too poor to enjoy a leisure packed with gadgets. In addition, he seems to think that the only way of "enhancing the value" of leisure is by spending money on it. He takes for granted that a leisure packed with gadgets is the kind of leisure most Americans really want, ignoring the huge power of advertising to shape preferences: something that Galbraith emphasized, but that has been almost willfully denied by economists of neoclassical persuasion.

Posner forgets that many of the most enjoyable leisure activities— reading, conversation, making music, making love—cost very little or nothing at all. They do require skill, however, and this skill has been eroded as leisure has been commercialized. Our book calls for a revival of the older conception of leisure as disciplined, spontaneous activity. It is only in this sense that leisure might become a real counterweight to the work ethic.

Jamie Whyte, writing in the *Wall Street Journal* on September 21, 2012, produced a libertarian argument. What right do we have to impose our tastes on those who do not share them? As Whyte puts it:

> The Skidelskys have no account of what makes any level of health enough, or enough security enough, or enough of anything enough. They rely instead on their own ineffable but consistently conservative judgments, and on their repeated assertion that their judgments are "objective"—unlike yours, which are subjective and the result of capitalist manipulation.

This is witty, and potentially devastating. Were it true that our concepts of health and the other basic goods—security, personality, respect, friendship, harmony with nature, and leisure—expressed nothing more than local cultural expectations, our project would collapse. But is it true? We think it possible to outline an objective account of health (to take just one example) by reflecting on the activities central to the human way of life, such as talking, walking, hearing, seeing and eating. Health is that state of the body that allows us to engage in these activities unimpeded; sickness or disability is what hinders us from engaging in them. Someone too fat to walk is *objectively* unhealthy, and remains so even if he belongs to a society in which this condition is normal. Health is relative to the human way of life, not to the expectations of particular social groups.

Such an account of health leaves, as it should, considerable space for historical and cultural variety. Expectations about teeth, height and life expectancy will of course vary hugely with technology and affluence, and it would be absurd to single out any one as uniquely correct or "natural." The point is that this variety is not limitless. Death at the age of twenty is premature by any standard. To have no teeth at all is a privation by any standard. Jamie Whyte's error here is a common one. He gives up too soon. He moves too swiftly from the observation that cultures and epochs differ in what they consider healthy or moral to the conclusion that it makes no sense to talk about what is healthy or moral as such. This is a non sequitur. It is rather like saying that because some people rate Tolstoy above Dostoevsky, others Dostoevsky above Tolstoy, neither Tolstoy nor Dostoevsky is objectively any better than Ayn Rand.

Other criticisms result more from our own failure to make our ideas clear enough. Some arguments could have been more sharply put, or linked up with more familiar lines of thought.

Critics have pointed out the apparent contradiction between our Keynesian urge to stimulate economic growth by expanding demand and our aim of dampening the urge to accumulate money and the things it can buy.

The distinction here is between the short run and the long run. If an earthquake has destroyed your city, you don't advocate living the "good life" amidst its ruins. Your first priority is to rebuild the city. Similarly the first priority for very poor countries must be to eliminate poverty. When we say that rich societies already have the "material prerequisites" for a good life, we are talking of societies producing and consuming normally, not societies that have suffered the equivalent of an earthquake.

However, we should aim to rebuild the city on improved lines, avoiding the faults that caused it to collapse in the first place. This is where short-run recovery merges with medium- and long-run preparations for the good life: for example, in reforms to the banking system to prevent predatory lending, or in channelling demand towards energy-efficient infrastructure and public services.

Others have asked: doesn't our assertion that we already have "enough" logically entail the end of economic growth? Not necessarily. We want more of some things (health, security, personality, friendship, respect, leisure, harmony with nature), less of others (pollution, despoliation of nature). It is the great defect of measured GDP that it includes "bads" such as pollution and excludes "goods" such as friendship. In our conception, measured GDP will be a residual, or by-product, of our striving for the basic goods; it could be positive or negative, but it would not be the overriding objective of economic policy.

We have been accused of taking as our model of the good life the old aristocratic ideal of leisure and applying this, without further argument, to possibilities for the majority. It is true that we are taking a bet on human nature not so heavily disciplined by the work ethic. But it seems to us that the onus is on our critics to show why the leisured way of life hitherto enjoyed by a wealthy minority should not in principle be available to the majority once their struggle for existence has been eased by technological progress. This was the premise of John Maynard Keynes's futuristic essay "Economic Possibilities for our Grandchildren," published in 1931.

It is, nevertheless, a sensible criticism of our book that we spend far too little time discussing the crucial question of how the cultural capital which has, in the past, been inherited by an aristocratic or bourgeois minority can be diffused to the newly affluent majority. Education must play a central role in the preparation for the good life. In the nineteenth century, John Stuart Mill suggested that cultivation of the feelings through poetry and art was the only way to debarbarize the masses in a commercial society. In a somewhat different vein, John Ruskin championed education as a training in craftsmanship. But modern education is overwhelmingly utilitarian: state-funded schools are being driven by their political paymasters to teach only the skills useful for jobs and money-making. This large subject of "education for leisure" deserves much more attention than we gave it.

Critics fear that a society deprived of the spur of money-making would become stagnant, devoid of achievement. This is like saying people invent things only to become rich. Undoubtedly some people become rich because of their inventions, and some people are only made inventive by the thought becoming rich. But it seems to us that, historically, inventiveness has not been at all closely tied to the money motive, but is an aspect of an inherent human curiosity. The society we advocate would not, therefore, be devoid of excellence or extraordinary achievement, either in the arts or sciences.

Critics wonder how a society with the values we advocate could hope to remain "competitive" with the still-poor and more "dynamic" parts of the world. Current growthmanship rhetoric sees economic activity as a competitive race, in which there must be no slacking off. This is a bad metaphor, because it makes no sense to go on racing forever and ever. To our way of thinking, globalization is a device for the perpetuation of scarcity. It is also highly disruptive of security. We share the view of the economist Dani Rodrik that globalization should be slowed down. No more than economic growth itself, should it be made an overriding aim of policy. The question should be, how much globalization is consistent with the good life?

One theme is common to all our critics: that we rate human beings too highly. They say that, with the collapse of traditional morality, work is the only discipline left. Certainly, it was not our intention to minimize the force of "original sin"; we argue that insatiability is inherent in human nature. All systems of morality, after all, ancient and modern, were designed to check and limit the evil propensities in human nature. Our argument is that the specific moral checks against "love of money," embedded in the teaching and social arrangements of all pre-modern societies, have broken down. The final breakdown was in fact quite recent.

To single out love of money as the chief vice of contemporary society is not to deny that there are other, and possibly more dangerous, insatiabilities (lust, cruelty, love of power, fanaticism, etc.) and that a successful check on love of money might inflame the others. This is a very important consideration.

However, it seems to us that the insatiabilities come together—they are all aspects of the tendency to excess—and that a philosophy, or more exactly an ethic, of moderation will simultaneously curb all of them. Ultimately, our book is a plea for a return to ethics as the standard to which economic activity should conform, and by which it should be judged. Whether such an ethical standard requires the support of religion is a question we leave open.

Robert and Edward Skidelsky
May 16, 2013

Notes

INTRODUCTION

1. John Maynard Keynes, *Essays in Persuasion*, The Collected Writings of John Maynard Keynes, vol. 9 (Cambridge: Cambridge University Press, 1978), p. 293.
2. George Orwell, *The Road to Wigan Pier* (London: Penguin, 1989), p. 182.
3. W. Stanley Jevons, *The Theory of Political Economy* (London: Macmillan, 1911), p. 37.
4. Bertrand Russell, *In Praise of Idleness and Other Essays* (London: Routledge, 2004), p. 11.
5. Charles Baudelaire, *Journaux intimes* (Paris: Mercure de France, 1938), p. 61.
6. John Maynard Keynes, *The General Theory of Employment, Interest, and Money*, The Collected Writings of John Maynard Keynes, vol. 7 (Cambridge: Cambridge University Press, 1973), p. 374.
7. IMSciences.net, accessed 09/09/11.
8. H. J. Johnson, "The Political Economy of Opulence," *Canadian Journal of Economics and Political Science*, vol. 26, pt. 4 (1960), p. 554.
9. Adam Smith, *The Wealth of Nations* (Lawrence, Kan.: Digireads.com, 2009; first publ. 1759), p. 40; Alfred Marshall, *Principles of Economics* (London: Prometheus Books, 1920), p. 1; Lionel Robbins, *An Essay on the Nature and Significance of Economic Science* (London: Macmillan, 1932), p. 16.
10. Keynes, *Essays in Persuasion*, p. 332.

CHAPTER 1. KEYNES'S MISTAKE

1. Quoted in Robert Skidelsky, *John Maynard Keynes: The Economist as Saviour 1920–1937* (London: Macmillan, 1992), pp. 72, 235.

2. For the essay as a whole see John Maynard Keynes, *Essays in Persuasion*, The Collected Writings of John Maynard Keynes, vol. 9 (Cambridge: Cambridge University Press, 1978), pp. 321–32. It is reprinted from Keynes's 1931 *Essays in Persuasion*. For the earlier outings, see Skidelsky, *Keynes: The Economist as Saviour*, p. 634, n. 53.

3. G. E. Moore, *Principia Ethica* (Cambridge: Cambridge University Press, 1903), pp. 188–9.

4. A.W. Plumptre, quoted in Skidelsky, *Keynes: The Economist as Saviour*, p. 237.

5. For a discussion of growth rates in the USA, Europe and the rest of the world, see Fabrizio Zilibotti, "Economic Possibilities for our Grandchildren 75 Years After: A Global Perspective," in Lorenzo Pecchi and Gustavo Piga (eds.) *Revisiting Keynes: Economic Possibilities for Our Grandchildren* (Cambridge, Mass.: MIT Press, 2008), pp. 27–39.

6. Keynes, *Essays in Persuasion*, p. 325.

7. Wenchao Jin *et al.*, *Poverty and Inequality in the UK* (London: Institute for Fiscal Studies, 2011).

8. *The Week*, July 16, 2011.

9. Jonathan Gershuny, "Busyness as the Badge of Honour for the New Superordinate Working Class," *Institute for Social and Economic Research Working Paper* 2005–09 (2005).

10. US Bureau of Labor Statistics.

11. See Axel Leijonhufvud in Pecchi and Piga (eds.), *Revisiting Keynes*, pp. 117–24.

12. Henry Phelps-Brown, *The Inequality of Pay* (Oxford: Oxford University Press, 1977), pp. 84–6.

13. V. I. Lenin, *The State and Revolution* (London: Penguin Classics, 2010), ch. 5, section 3; Adam Smith, *The Wealth of Nations* (Lawrence, Kan.: Digireads.com, 2009), Book 1, ch. 5; Jeremy Bentham, *A Table of the Springs of Action* (1817), p. 20.

14. This criticism of Keynes runs through the essays collected in Pecchi and Piga (eds.), *Revisiting Keynes*. See the essays by Stiglitz, p. 46, Freeman, pp. 140–41, and Fitoussi, p. 157.

15. Tom Rachman, *The Imperfectionists* (London: Querais Publishing, 2010).

16. Aditya Chakrabortty, "Why our Jobs are Getting Worse," *Guardian*, August 31, 2010. See also Irina Grugulis *et al.*, "'No Place to Hide': The Reality of Leadership in UK Supermarkets," *SKOPE Research Paper* 91, on the McDonald's-ization of work. On digital Taylorism, see Philip Brown *et al.*, *The Global Auction: The Broken Promises of Education,*

Jobs and Incomes (New York: Oxford University Press, 2010), pp. 65–82. For the grisly world of call centers, see Simon Head, *The New Ruthless Economy: Work and Power in the Digital Age* (New York: Oxford University Press, 2003), pp. 100–16.

17. St Paul's Institute, *Value and Values: Perceptions of Ethics in the City Today* (London: St Paul's Institute, 2011).

18. H. Bielenski, G. Bosch and A. Wagner, *Employment and Working Time in Europe* (Dublin: European Foundation for the Improvement of Living and Working Conditions [EFILWC], 2002). The exact question in the survey was: "Provided that you (and your partner) could make a free choice so far as working hours are concerned, and taking account of the need to earn a living, how many hours a week would you prefer to work at present?" This does make reference to the trade-off with income, even if not explicitly.

19. Jeremy Reynolds, "When Too Much is Not Enough: Actual and Preferred Work Hours in the United States and Abroad," *Sociological Forum*, vol. 19, no. 1 (2004), pp. 89–120. A note of caution: participants in this survey, in contrast to the EFILWC survey, were asked only whether they would like to work more, less or the same amount of time than at present. No mention was made of wages. Reynolds thinks it likely that "when respondents indicated their preferences for more or fewer hours of work, they considered how such changes could affect job rewards." But even if the respondents did not take account of wages, the results suggest that most of them view work as a disutility.

20. Sarah Andersen *et al.*, *Executive Excess 2010: CEO Pay and the Great Recession*, (London: Institute for Policy Studies, 2010).

21. UK Office of National Statistics; US Bureau of Labor Statistics.

22. *Guardian*, August 15, 2011.

23. Juliet Schor, *The Overworked American: The Unexpected Decline of Leisure* (New York: Basic Books, 1991), p. 66.

24. Juliet Schor, "Towards a New Politics of Consumption," in Schor and Douglas B. Holt (eds.), *The Consumer Society Reader* (New York: New Press, 2000), p. 459. Schor argues that if policy-makers want individuals to develop more sustainable lifestyles, they should not rely on asking people to reduce their current levels of income and consumption: "approaches that structurally stem the flow of increased income into consumer's hands are more promising." See also several papal encyclicals to the same effect: e.g. Pope Paul VI, *Octogesima Adveniens* (1971; http://www.vatican.va/holy_father/paul_vi/apost_letters/documents/hf_p-vi_apl_19710514_octogesima-adveniens_en.html; accessed January 12,

2012): "While very large areas of the population are unable to satisfy their primary needs, superfluous needs are ingeniously created."

25. André Gorz, *Ecologica* (Chicago: University of Chicago Press, 2010), p. 4.

26. *The Week*, July 16, 2011. *The Week* runs a regular column "For those who have everything."

27. Roy Harrod, "The Possibility of Economic Satiety—Use of Economic Growth for Improving the Quality of Education and Leisure," In *Problems of US Economic Development* (Washington: Committee for Economic Development, 1958), pp. 207–13.

28. Fred Hirsch, *Social Limits to Growth* (London: Routledge, 1977), pp. 16–23.

29. Gary Becker, "A Theory of the Allocation of Time," *Economic Journal*, vol. 75, no. 299 (1965), pp. 493–517.

30. Staffan Linder, *The Harried Leisure Class* (New York: Columbia University Press, 1970), p. 79.

31. Keynes, *Essays in Persuasion*, p. 365.

32. The pioneering discussion of these concepts is Harvey Leibenstein, "Bandwagon, Snob, and Veblen Effects in the Theory of Consumers' Demand," *Quarterly Journal of Economics*, vol. 64, pt. 2 (1950), pp. 183–207.

33. Craufurd D. Goodwin (ed.), *Art and the Market: Roger Fry on Commerce and Art* (Ann Arbor: University of Michigan Press, 1998).

34. Schor, *The Overworked American*, p. 120.

35. Alexis de Tocqueville, *Democracy in America* (1835, 1840), ch. 28.

36. Richard B. Freeman, "Why Do We Work More than Keynes Expected?" in Pecchi and Piga (eds.), *Revisiting Keynes*, pp. 133–42.

37. Smith, *The Wealth of Nations*, Book 2, ch. 3.

38. Karl Marx, "Grundrisse," in Marx, *Selected Works*, ed. David McLellan, 2nd. edn. (Oxford: Oxford University Press, 2000), p. 414 (tr. altered).

CHAPTER 2. THE FAUSTIAN BARGAIN

1. John Maynard Keynes, *Essays in Persuasion*, The Collected Writings of John Maynard Keynes, vol. 9 (Cambridge: Cambridge University Press, 1978), p. 372.

2. See Krishan Kumar, *Utopia and Anti-Utopia in Modern Times* (Oxford: Wiley-Blackwell), pp. 3–9.

3. Thomas More, *Utopia*, ed. Ralph Robinson (1869), editor's introduction.

4. Kumar, *Utopia and Anti-Utopia*, p. 35.

5. More, *Utopia*, pp. 13, 84.
6. Niccolò Machiavelli, *The Florentine History* (Charleston, SC: Forgotten Books, 2010), vol. 2, p. 1.
7. Pope Leo XIII, *Rerum Novarum* (1891), par. 59.
8. Karl Löwith, *Meaning in History: The Theological Implications of the Philosophy of History* (Chicago: University of Chicago Press, 1957), p. 149.
9. William Blake, *The Marriage of Heaven and Hell* (1790), p. 3.
10. Bernard Mandeville, *The Fable of the Bees: or Private Vices, Publick Benefits*, ed. Phillip Harth (Harmondsworth: Penguin, 1989), pp. 49, 51.
11. See ibid., editor's introduction; also N. T. Phillipson, *Adam Smith: An Enlightened Life* (London: Allen Lane, 2010), p. 48.
12. Mandeville, *The Fable of the Bees*, p. 25.
13. David Hume, "Of Refinement in the Arts," in Hume, *Essays Moral Political and Literary* (London: Grant Richards, 1903), p. 287.
14. The genealogy of "interest" and "*le doux commerce*" is traced by Albert O. Hirschman in *The Passions and the Interests: Political Arguments for Capitalism before its Triumph* (Princeton: Princeton University Press, 1997), pp. 31–66. "Self-love" began its life as an Augustinian term of opprobrium, but was transformed by Rousseau, and Adam Smith following him, into a neutral term designating a natural regard for one's own welfare. For details, see Pierre Force, *Self-Interest before Adam Smith* (Cambridge: Cambridge University Press, 2003), pp. 57–67.
15. Alexander Pope, *Essay on Man*, ed. Henny Morley, Project Gutenberg (http://www.gutenberg.org/ebooks/2428; accessed January 12, 2012).
16. Edward Burke, *Reflections on the Revolution in France* (1790).
17. Adam Smith, *The Theory of Moral Sentiments* (Oxford: Oxford University Press, 1979; first pub. 1759), pp. 308–13.
18. Ibid., pp. 184–5.
19. Ibid., p. 461.
20. John Stuart Mill, *Principles of Political Economy* (1886), "Of the Stationary State," book iv, ch. vi, p. 748; for a critique of Mill's "moralism," see Michael Montgomery, "John Stuart Mill and the Utopian Tradition," in Jürgen Georg Backhaus (ed.), *The State as Utopia: Continental Approaches* (Berlin: Springer, 2011), pp. 19–34.
21. Theodor Ziolkowski, *The Sin of Knowledge: Ancient Themes and Modern Variations* (Princeton: Princeton University Press, 2000), p. 68.
22. Goethe, *Faust,* tr. Barker Fairley (Toronto: University of Toronto Press, 1970), pp. 25, 26.
23. Ibid., pp. 196–7.

24. Johann Peter Eckerman, *Conversations of Goethe* (New York: M. Walter Dunne, 1901), p. 85.

25. Karl Jaspers, *Unsere Zukunft und Goethe* (Bremen: Storm, 1948), p. 18.

26. See John Gray, *Black Mass: Apocalyptic Religion and the Death of Utopia* (London: Allen Lane, 2007).

27. Quoted in Leszek Kołakowski, *Main Currents of Marxism*, vol. 1: *The Founders* (Oxford: Clarendon Press, 1978), p. 285.

28. Ibid., p. 285.

29. See Eric Hobsbawm, *How to Change the World: Tales of Marx and Marxism* (Boston: Little, Brown, 2011), p. 147: "No mechanism for the breakdown [of slave society] is outlined . . . ."

30. Karl Marx and Friedrich Engels, *The Communist Manifesto*, Project Gutenberg (http://gutenberg.org/ebooks/61; accessed January 12, 2012), p. 9.

31. Ibid., p. 9.

32. Ibid., p. 8.

33. Ibid., p. 13.

34. Ibid., p. 9.

35. Karl Marx, "Capital," in *Marx: Collected Writings* (London: Lawrence and Wishart, 1974), pp. 714–15.

36. Marx and Engels, *The Communist Manifesto*, p. 10.

37. Quoted in Meghnad Desai, *Marx's Revenge: The Resurgence of Capitalism and the Death of Statist Socialism* (London: Verso, 2004), p. 95.

38. Ibid., p. 79.

39. Quoted ibid., p. 44.

40. Karl Marx, "The German Ideology," in *Karl Marx: Selected Writings* ed. David McLellan (Oxford: Oxford University Press, 1977; first pub. 1846), p. 169.

41. Leon Trotsky, *Literature and Revolution*, ed. William Keach (New York: International Publishers, 2005), p. 207.

42. Jung Chang and John Holliday, *Mao: The Unknown Story* (London: Jonathan Cape, 2005), p. 457.

43. See, for example, John Strachey, *Contemporary Capitalism* (London: Gollancz, 1956), and Anthony Crosland, *The Future of Socialism* (London: Jonathan Cope, 1956).

44. Charles Reich, *The Greening of America* (New York: Random House, 1970), p. 259; quotation from R. N. Berki, "Marcuse and the Crisis of the New Radicalism: From Politics to Religion?," *Journal of Politics*, vol. 34, pt. 1 (1972), p. 151.

45. Theodore Roszak, *The Making of a Counter-Culture: Reflections on the Technocratic Society and its Youthful Opposition* (Berkeley: University of California Press, 1969), pp. 17–18.

46. For the capitalist "golden age," see Robert Skidelsky, *Keynes: The Return of the Master*, 2nd edn. (London: Penguin, 2010), ch. 5.

47. In the Preface to *The Making of a Counter-Culture*, a theme he subsequently developed in *Where the Wasteland Ends*. J. K. Galbraith coined the phrase "the technostructure" in his *The New Industrial State* (Princeton: Princeton University Press, 2007).

48. Reich, *The Greening of America*, pp. 381–2.

49. Quoted in Alain Martineau, *Herbert Marcuse's Utopia* (Montreal: Harvest House, 1984), p. 7.

50. Quoted ibid., p. 20.

51. Herbert Marcuse, *One-Dimensional Man: Studies in the Ideology of Advanced Industrial Society*, ed. Douglas Kellner (Boston: Beacon Press, 1991), pp. xlii, xxx.

52. Ibid., p. 246.

53. Herbert Marcuse, *Eros and Civilization* (New York: Random House, 1961), p. 48.

54. Ibid., p. 260.

CHAPTER 3. THE USES OF WEALTH

1. Joseph Schumpeter, *History of Economic Analysis* (New York: Oxford University Press, 1954), p. 57.

2. Aristotle, *Nicomachean Ethics*, tr. Christopher Rowe and Sarah Broadie (Oxford: Oxford University Press, 2002), p. 251. In Aristotle's other major ethical work, the *Eudemian Ethics*, he is more even-handed between the active and the philosophical life.

3. Aristotle, *Politics* in *The Complete Works of Aristotle*, ed. Jonathan Barnes, vol. 2 (Princeton: Princeton University Press, 1984), p. 1989.

4. Georg Simmel, *The Philosophy of Money*, tr. Tom Bottomore and David Frisby (Boston, Mass.: Routledge, 1978), p. 255.

5. Quoted in Robert Skidelsky, *John Maynard Keynes: The Economist as Saviour 1920–1937* (London: Macmillan, 1992), p. 476.

6. Aristotle, *Politics*, p. 1997.

7. Ibid., p. 1996.

8. Aristophanes, "Wealth," in *The Knights/Peace/The Birds/The Assembly-women/Wealth*, tr. Alan H. Sommerstein (London: Penguin, 1978), pp. 277–8.

9. Horace, *Satire* 1, lines 39-40, in *Satires, Epistles and Ars Poetica*, tr. H. Rushton Fairclough (London: Heinemann, 1961), p. 7.

10. See Peter Brown, *Poverty and Leadership in the Later Roman Empire* (Hanover, NH: Brandeis University Press, 2002).

11. Thomas Aquinas, *Summa Theologiae*, tr. T. C. O'Brien, vol. 41 (London: Blackfriars, 1972), p. 243.

12. Quoted in Anne Derbes and Mark Sandona, "Barren Metal and the Fruitful Womb: The Program of Giotto's Arena Chapel in Padua," *Art Bulletin*, vol. 80 (1998), p. 227.

13. Max Weber, *The Protestant Ethic and the Spirit of Capitalism*, tr. Talcott Parsons (London: Routledge, 1992), p. 73.

14. Patrick Olivelle, tr., *The Dharmasūtras* (Oxford: Oxford University Press, 1999), pp. 35, 31.

15. For further discussion, see Max Weber, *The Religion of India: The Sociology of Hinduism and Buddhism*, tr. Hans H. Gerth and Don Martindale (Glencoe, Ill.: Free Press, 1958), pp. 84–5.

16. Olivelle, *The Dharmasūtras*, p. 326.

17. Robert Ernest Hume, tr., *The Thirteen Principal Upanishads* (Oxford: Oxford University Press, 1921), p. 141.

18. See Chakravarthi Ram-Prasad, *Eastern Philosophy* (London: Weidenfeld and Nicolson, 2005), p. 212: "It is undeniable that logical theory is somewhat marginal in Chinese philosophy, playing only a small part during the short Buddhist ascendancy."

19. Confucius, *The Analects*, tr. Arthur Waley (Ware: Wordsworth, 1996).

20. Li Bai, "On a Banquet with my Cousins on a Spring Night in the Peach Flower Garden," in Burton Watson (tr.), *Chinese Lyricism: Shih Poetry from the Second to the Twelfth Century* (New York: Columbia University Press, 1971).

21. Quoted in Lin Yutang, *The Importance of Living* (New York: Harper, 1998), pp. 132–6.

22. Burton Watson, *Records of the Grand Historian of China*, vol. 2, tr. from the *Shih chi* of Ssu-ma Ch'ien (New York: Columbia University Press, 1961), pp. 491–2.

23. This point has been made with great force by Michael Sandel in his *Justice: What's the Right Thing to Do?* (London: Allen Lane, 2009), pp. 244–69.

24. Taraq Modood, for instance, has defended religious establishment in Britain, but argued that it might now be extended to other religious groups. See Tariq Modood, *Multicultural Politics: Racism, Ethnicity,*

Muslims in Britain (Minneapolis: University of Minnesota Press, 2005), pp. 146–50.

25. John Kenneth Galbraith, *The Affluent Society* (London: Hamish Hamilton, 1958), p. 115.

26. John Locke, *An Essay Concerning Human Understanding*, vol. 1 (Oxford: Clarendon, 1894), p. 351.

27. For a classic modern discussion of the needs/wants distinction, see David Wiggins, "Claims of Need," in Wiggins, *Needs, Values, Truth: Essays in the Philosophy of Value* (Oxford: Oxford University Press, 1998), pp. 1–49.

28. Aristotle, *Politics*, p. 1989.

29. Carl Menger, *Principles of Economics*, tr. James Dingwall and Bert F. Hoselitz (Glencoe, Ill.: Free Press, 1950), pp. 120–21.

30. Ibid., p. 229.

31. Virgil, *Aeneid*, Bk. 3, line 56; John Maynard Keynes, *Essays in Persuasion*, The Collected Writings of John Maynard Keynes, vol. 9 (Cambridge: Cambridge University Press, 1978), p. 369.

32. Robert H. Frank, *Luxury Fever: Money and Happiness in an Eva of Excess* (Princeton: Princeton University Press, 2000), p. 66.

33. Friedrich Nietzsche, "Thus Spoke Zarathustra," in Walter Kaufmann (ed.), *The Portable Nietzsche* (Harmondsworth: Penguin, 1959), p. 129.

CHAPTER 4. THE MIRAGE OF HAPPINESS

1. Jean-Jacques Rousseau, *The Discourses and Other Political Writings*, ed. Victor Gourevitch (Cambridge: Cambridge University Press, 1997), p. 26

2. Herodotus, *The Histories*, tr. Robin Waterfield (Oxford: Oxford University Press, 1998), p. 14.

3. Aristotle, *Nicomachean Ethics*, tr. Christopher Rowe and Sarah Broadie (Oxford: Oxford University Press, 2002), p. 206.

4. John Locke, *An Essay Concerning Human Understanding*, vol. 1 (Oxford: Clarendon, 1894), p. 351.

5. Quoted in G. E. Moore, *Principia Ethica* (Cambridge: Cambridge University Press, 1903), pp. 77–8.

6. W. Stanley Jevons, *The Theory of Political Economy* (London: Macmillan, 1911), p. 37.

7. F. Y. Edgeworth, *Mathematical Psychics: An Essay on the Application of Mathematics to the Moral Sciences* (1881), pp. 101–2.

8. S. Solnick and D. Hemenway, "Is More Always Better? A Survey on Positional Concerns," *Journal of Economics Behaviour and Organisation*, vol. 37 (1998), pp. 373–83.

9. Whether happiness continues to rise with income above the $15,000 threshold is debated. According to more recent surveys, it does. For details, see Angus Deaton, "Income, Health and Well-Being around the World: Evidence from the Gallup World Poll," *Journal of Economic Perspectives*, vol. 22, pt. 2 (2008), pp. 53–72.

10. See Richard Layard, *Happiness: Lessons from a New Science* (London: Penguin, 2005), p. 45.

11. See Robert H. Frank, *Luxury Fever: Money and Happiness in an Era of Excess* (Princeton: Princeton University Press, 2000), pp. 207–26.

12. Will Wilkinson, "In Pursuit of Happiness Research: Is It Reliable? What Does It Imply for Policy?," *Policy Analysis*, no. 590 (2007).

13. The argument of the last two paragraphs is indebted to Helen Johns and Paul Ormerod, *Happiness, Economics and Public Policy* (London: Institute of Economic Affairs, 2007), pp. 28–34.

14. Richard Layard and Diener and Suh both cite a certain Shao 1993 to the effect that Hong Kong students report almost identical levels of happiness in both Chinese and English. Footnotes reveal Shao 1993 to be an unpublished master's thesis written for the University of Illinois. In any case, the study tells us nothing, since the respondents had presumably learnt the meaning of "happy" by comparison with *xingfu* or some other Chinese term. The same problem infects all such studies. See Layard, *Happiness*, p. 34, and Ed Diener and Eunkook Mark Suh, "National Differences in Subjective Well-Being," in Daniel Kahneman *et al.*, *Well-Being: The Foundations of Hedonic Psychology* (New York: Russell Sage, 1999), p. 437.

15. Anna Wierzbicka, "'Happiness' in Cross-Linguistic & Cross-Cultural Perspective," *Dædalus*, vol. 133, pt. 2 (2004), p. 36.

16. For details, see Layard, *Happiness*, pp. 17–20.

17. Diener and Suh, "National Differences in Subjective Well-Being," p. 437.

18. Andrew J. Oswald and Stephen Wu, "Objective Confirmation of Subjective Measures of Human Well-Being: Evidence from the U.S.A.," *Science*, no. 327 (2010), pp. 576–9. The happiness data was adjusted to control for income and age, so New Yorkers may not be unhappiest all things considered, but only in respect to their living conditions.

19. Ibid., p. 578.

20. See Johns and Ormerod, *Happiness, Economics and Public Policy*, p. 81.

21. Julia A. Eriksen and Sally A. Steffen, *Kiss and Tell: Surveying Sex in the Twentieth Century* (Cambridge, Mass.: Harvard University Press, 1999), p. 34.

22. See Layard, *Happiness*, pp. 62–5.

23. Derek Bok, *The Politics of Happiness: What Government Can Learn from the New Research on Well-Being* (Princeton: Princeton University Press, 2010), p. 36.

24. See Juliet Michaelson *et al.*, *National Accounts of Well-Being: Bringing Real Wealth onto the Balance Sheet* (London: New Economic Foundation, 2009).

25. Henry Sidgwick, *The Method of Ethics* (Indianapolis: Hackett, 1981), pp. 120–21.

26. See Daniel Kahneman and Alan B. Krueger, "Developments in the Measurement of Subjective Well-Being," *Journal of Economic Perspectives*, vol. 20, pt. 1 (2006), pp. 3–24.

27. See Julia Annas, "Happiness as Achievement," *Dædalus*, vol. 33, pt. 2 (2006).

28. *Daily Telegraph*, October 18, 2011.

29. Fred Feldman, *What Is This Thing Called Happiness?* (Oxford: Oxford University Press, 2010), p. 176.

30. For details, see Yew-Kwang Ng, "Happiness Surveys: Some Comparability Issues and an Exploratory Survey Based on Just Perceivable Increments," *Social Indicators Research*, vol. 38, pt. 1, pp. 1–27.

31. Layard, *Happiness*, p. 13.

32. Aristotle, *Nichomachean Ethics*, p. 247.

33. Ludwig Wittgenstein, *Tractatus Logico-Philosophicus* (London: Routledge and Kegan Paul, 1922), 6.43.

34. Philippa Foot, *Natural Goodness* (Oxford: Oxford University Press, 2001), p. 85.

35. Ibid., p. 88.

36. Samuel Brittan, "Commentary: A Deceptive Eureka Moment," in Johns and Ormerod, *Happiness, Economics and Public Policy*, p. 93.

37. Layard, *Happiness*, p. 23.

38. Metropolitan Anthony of Sourozh, *God and Man* (London: Darton, Longman and Todd, 1983), p. 16.

39. Friedrich Nietzsche, "Maxims and Arrows," in *Twilight of the Idols* (1888), no. 12.

40. Yew-Kwang Ng, "A Case for Happiness, Cardinalism, and Interpersonal Comparability," *Economic Journal*, vol. 107, no. 445 (1997), p. 1849.

41. Layard, *Happiness*, p. 221.

CHAPTER 5. LIMITS TO GROWTH:
NATURAL OR MORAL?

1. Thomas Malthus, *An Essay on the Principle of Population*, Electronic Scholarly Publishing Project (http://www.esp.org/books/malthus/population/malthus.pdf; accessed January 12, 2012), p. 44.
2. Donella H. Meadows *et al.*, *The Limits to Growth* (London: Pan, 1974), pp. 45–87.
3. For a thorough rebuttal of Malthusian fears of resource scarcity, see Bjørn Lomborg, *The Sceptical Environmentalist: Measuring the Real State of the World* (Cambridge: Cambridge University Press, 2001), pp. 118–48.
4. Paul Ehrlich, *The Population Bomb* (New York: Ballantine Books, 1968).
5. George Monbiot, "Bring on the Recession," *Guardian*, October 9, 2007.
6. Tim Jackson, *Prosperity without Growth: Economics for a Finite Planet* (London: Earthscan, 2009).
7. House of Lords Select Committee on Economic Affairs, *The Economics of Climate Change* (London: MMSO, 2005), p. 58.
8. Intergovernmental Panel on Climate Change, *Third Assessment Report* (Cambridge: Cambridge University Press, 2001), Working Panel 1, Technical Summary, p. 79.
9. K. R. Popper, *The Poverty of Historicism* (London: Routledge, 1961), pp. v–vi.
10. Intergovernmental Panel on Climate Change, *Third Assessment Report*, Working Panel 2, ch. 3, p. 154.
11. Quoted in Mike Hulme, "Chaotic world of climate truth," 2006, BBC News website, 2006, news.bbc.co.uk/1/hi/6115644.stm (accessed November 9, 2011). news.bbc.co.uk/1/hi/6115644.stm (accessed September 9, 2011).
12. Ibid. See also Ellen Raphael and Paul Hardaker, *Making Sense of the Weather and Climate* (London: Sense about Science, 2007), p. 3: "The idea of a point of no return, or 'tipping point,' is a misleading way to think about climate and can be unnecessarily alarmist."
13. James Lovelock, *The Revenge of Gaia* (London: Penguin, 2006), p. 189.
14. Sir Partha Dasgupta, *Comments on the Stern Review's Economics of Climate Change* (www.econ.com.ac.uk/faculty/dasgupta/STERN.pdf; accessed January 12, 2012), p. 5. Sir Partha is summarizing the views of William Nordhaus, the most influential modern climate economist. He does not necessarily endorse these views.

15. Nicholas Stern, *Stern Review on the Economics of Climate Change* (London: UK Treasury, 2006), p. xii.
16. Jackson, *Prosperity without Growth*.
17. Nigel Lawson, *An Appeal to Reason: A Cool Look at Global Warming* (London: Duckworth, 2009), p. 87.
18. George Monbiot, *Heat: How We Can Stop the Planet Burning* (London: Penguin, 2007), p. 215.
19. Quoted in John Passmore, *Man's Responsibility for Nature: Ecological Problems and Western Traditions* (London: Duckworth, 1974), p. 21.
20. Ludwig Klages, *Mensch und Erde* (Jena: Eugen Diederichs, 1929), p. 25.
21. Martin Heidegger, "The Question Concerning Technology," in Heidegger, *Basic Writings* (London: Routledge, 1993), p. 321.
22. Quoted in Passmore, *Man's Responsibility for Nature*, pp. 60-61.
23. J. E. Lovelock, *Gaia: A New Look at Life on Earth* (Oxford: Oxford University Press, 1979), p. 10.
24. Ibid., pp. ix–x.
25. James Lovelock, *The Ages of Gaia* (London: Penguin, 1988), p. 206.
26. Lovelock, *The Revenge of Gaia*, p. 188.
27. Quoted in Passmore, *Man's Responsibility for Nature*, pp. 23–4.
28. Mary Midgley, "Duties Concerning Islands," in Robert Elliot (ed.), *Environmental Ethics* (Oxford: Oxford University Press, 1995), pp. 89–103.
29. The first principle of deep ecology, according to Arne Naess, is: "The flourishing of human and nonhuman life on earth has inherent value. The value of nonhuman life-forms is independent of the usefulness of the nonhuman world for human purposes." Arne Naess, "The Basics of the Deep Ecology Movement," in Alan Drengson and Bill Devall (eds.), *The Ecology of Wisdom: Writings by Arne Naess* (Berkeley: Counterpoint, 2008), p. 111.
30. Arne Naess, "The Shallow and the Deep, Long-Range Ecological Movement: A Summary," in Andrew Dobson (ed.), *The Green Reader* (London: Deutsch, 1991), p. 243.
31. The term speciesism was popularized by Peter Singer, *Animal Liberation* (Avon, 1977).
32. Aldo Leopold, "A Sand County Almanac," in Dobson (ed.), *The Green Reader*, pp. 240–41.
33. For a persuasive defense of this claim, see Michael Thompson, *Life and Action* (Cambridge, Mass.: Harvard University Press, 2008).
34. Bernard Williams, *Ethics and the Limits of Philosophy* (London: Routledge, 2006), p. 118.

35. Oswald Spengler, *The Decline of the West*, tr. Charles Francis Atkinson, vol. 1 (London: George Allen, 1932), p. 168.
36. See David E. Cooper, *A Philosophy of Gardens* (Oxford: Oxford University Press, 2006), for an interesting defense of the importance of gardens and gardening to the good life.
37. Lovelock, *The Revenge of Gaia*, pp. 169–70.
38. J. Baird Callicott, "Animal Liberation: A Triangular Affair," in Robert Elliot (ed.), *Environmental Ethics* (Oxford: Oxford University Press, 1995), p. 50.
39. Quoted in Passmore, *Man's Responsibility for Nature*, p. 105.

CHAPTER 6. ELEMENTS OF THE GOOD LIFE

1. Milton Friedman, "The Methodology of Positive Economics," in Friedman, *Essays in Positive Economics* (Chicago: University of Chicago Press, 1953), p. 5.
2. Evidence for the universality of these and other practices can be found in Alexander MacBeath, *Experiments in Living* (London: Macmillan, 1952) and Morris Ginsberg, *On the Diversity of Morals* (London: Heinemann, 1956).
3. See Martha Nussbaum, *Women and Human Development: The Capabilities Approach* (Cambridge: Cambridge University Press, 2000), p. 73: "Insofar as we are able to respond to tragic tales from other cultures, we show that this idea of human worth and agency crosses cultural boundaries."
4. Ernst Cassirer, *The Logic of the Cultural Sciences*, tr. S.G. Lofts (New Haven: Yale University Press, 2000), p. 76.
5. John Rawls, *A Theory of Justice* (Oxford: Clarendon Press, 1971), p. 433.
6. Nussbaum, *Women and Human Development*, pp. 78–80.
7. Ibid., p. 69.
8. Ibid., p. 87. Amartya Sen has a more relaxed attitude to the relevance of functionings; he allows for "the possibility of simply relying on the valuation of achieved functionings (should we wish to go that way) …" Amartya Sen, *The Idea of Justice* (London: Allen Lane, 2009), p. 236.
9. Nussbaum, *Women and Human Development*, p. 87.
10. Ibid., p. 79. Nussbaum adds in a footnote that this list is based on the Indian Constitution, Article 15, with the exception of non-discrimination on the basis of sexual orientation, which is not guaranteed by the Con-

stitution. But this in itself is hardly a guarantee of universality, since the Indian Constitution was heavily modelled on British and American prototypes. And in any case, what authority does a political document have in a discussion of "central human functional capabilities"?

11. John Finnis, *Natural Law and Natural Rights* (Oxford: Oxford University Press, 2011), pp. 87–90.

12. Quoted in Georges Canguilhem, *The Normal and the Pathological* (New York: Zone Books, 1991), p. 91.

13. Aristotle, *Politics* in *The Complete Works of Aristotle*, ed. Jonathan Barnes, vol. 2 (Princeton: Princeton University Press, 1984), p. 2101.

14. Josef Pieper, *Leisure: The Basis of Culture*, tr. Alexander Dru (San Francisco: Ignatius, 1963), p. 105.

15. Primo Levi, *If This Is a Man* (London: Abacus, 1987), p. 111.

16. The damage done by inequality to respect is explored in Richard Sennett, *Respect in a World of Inequality* (London: Allen Lane, 2002).

17. Quoted in Robert Skidelsky, *John Maynard Keynes: The Economist as Saviour 1920–1937* (London: Macmillan, 1992).

18. Pope Leo XIII, *Rerun Novarum* (1891), par. 46.

19. Nussbaum, *Women and Human Development*, p. 157.

20. Aristotle, *Nicomachean Ethics*, tr. Christopher Rowe and Sarah Broadie (Oxford: Oxford University Press, 2002), p. 208.

21. Aristotle, *Politics*, p. 2003.

22. Ibid., p. 2032.

23. Confucius, *The Analects*, tr. Arthur Waley (Ware: Wordsworth, 1996), p. 3.

24. Ibid., p. 3.

25. See http://moneywatch.bnet.com/career-advice/blog/other-8-hours/addition-by-subtraction-dont-let-bad-friends-drag-you-down/2080/ (accessed November 9, 2011).

26. Leo Strauss, "Kurt Riezler," in Strauss, *What is Political Philosophy?* (Chicago: University of Chicago Press, 1988), p. 234.

27. Karl Marx, "On James Mill" in *Karl Marx: Selected Writings*, ed. David McLellan, 2nd edn. (Oxford: Oxford University Press, 2000), p. 132.

28. For an interesting discussion of this point, see Sarah Broadie, "Taking Stock of Leisure," in Broadie, *Aristotle and Beyond: Essays on Metaphysics and Ethics* (Cambridge: Cambridge University Press, 2007), p. 194.

29. Aristotle, *Politics*, p. 2122.

30. Alexandre Kojève, *Introduction to the Reading of Hegel* (New York: Basic Books, 1969), p. 162.

31. Pieper, *Leisure*, pp. 47–8.
32. See Sen, *The Idea of Justice*, pp. 239–41.
33. Aristotle, *Nicomachean Ethics*, p. 98.
34. Adair Turner, *Economics after the Crisis: Objectives and Means*, Lecture 1: "Economic Growth, Human Welfare and Inequality" (http://www2.lse.ac.uk/publicEvents/pdf/20101011%20Adair%20Turner%20transcript.pdf; accessed January 12, 2012), p. 35.
35. Zygmunt Bauman, *Liquid Life* (Cambridge: Polity, 2005), p. 88.
36. For a persuasive defense of this claim, see Anthony and Charles Kenny, *Life, Liberty and the Pursuit of Utility* (Exeter: Imprint Academic, 2006), pp. 65–93.
37. James Lovelock, *The Revenge of Gaia* (London: Penguin, 2006), p. 126.
38. Francesco Branca *et al.*, *The Challenge of Obesity in the WHO European Region and the Strategies for Response* (Copenhagen, World Health Organization, 2007),
39. Michael Moore *et al.*, "Explaining the Rise in Antidepressant Prescribing: A Descriptive Study Using the General Practice Research Database," *British Medical Journal* (2009), bmj.com.
40. Francis Green, *Praxis: Job Quality in Britain* (London: UK Commission for Employment and Skills, 2009).
41. Stephen Nickell *et al.*, "A Picture of Job Insecurity Facing British Men," *Economic Journal*, no. 112 (2002), pp. 1–27.
42. Mark Beatson, "Job 'Quality' and Job Security," *Labour Market Trends* (2000), pp. 441–9.
43. Simon English, "The Poisonous City Work Ethic That Is in Urgent Need of Reform," *Evening Standard*, July 5, 2011.
44. For examples of European employee-ownership schemes, see http://www.efesonline.org/PRESS%20REVIEW/2011/October.htm (accessed November 20, 2011).
45. Department for Environment, Food and Rural Affairs, *Agriculture in the United Kingdom* (London: MMSO, 2007).
46. TNS Global till data for the three months to November 2009 shows independent stores have a 2.2 percent market share, the rest being taken up by so-called multiple stores, from Tesco down to Lidl, Netto and other smaller chains. See http://www.tnsglobal.com/news/news-56F59E8A99C8428989E9BE66187D5792.aspx (accessed November 21, 2011).
47. Pefer A. Hall, "Social Capital in Britain," *British Journal of Politics*, vol. 29 (1999, pp. 417–61), reports that while the number of pubs fell substantially—from 102,000 in 1900 to 66,000 in 1978 (and 57,500 in 2007—Market and Business Development, *Pub Companies—7th*

Report of Session 2008–9 [London: MMSO, 2008], p. 9) the number of people visiting pubs and the amount of time spent there actually increased from the 1960s to the 1980s. This probably reflects the fact that pubs became increasingly women-friendly during this period. More recent data is unavailable.

48. This theme has been eloquently explored by Bauman in *Liquid Life* and other works.

49. See Organization for Economic Cooperation and Development, *The Well-being of Nations: The Role of Human and Social Capital* (Paris: OECD, 2001), for evidence of changing patterns of association across OECD nations.

50. See the OECD Family Database, www.oecd.org/els/social/family/data base (accessed November 21, 2011).

51. See Patricia Morgan, *Marriage-Lite* (London: Civitas, 2000). However, the conclusion that marriage improves relationship stability has recently been questioned on the grounds that the kind of people who get married tend to have more stable relationships anyway. See Claire Crawford *et al.*, *Cohabitation, Marriage, Relationship Stability and Child Outcomes: An Update* (London: Institute for Fiscal Studies, 2011).

52. See Broadcasters' Audience Research Board, *Trends in Television Viewing*, http://www.barb.co.uk/facts/tv-trends/download/2011-yy-TVTrends.pdf (accessed January 23, 2012).

53. Sport England, *Trends in Sport Participation 1987–2002* (London: Sport England, 2002); Fidelis Ifedi, *Sport Participation in Canada* (Ottawa: Statistics Canada, 2005); Robert Putnam, *Bowling Alone: The Collapse and Revival of American Community* (London: Simon X Schuster, 2000), p. 113.

54. Dale Southerton *et al.*, *Trajectories of Time Spent Reading as a Primary Activity: A Comparison of the Netherlands, Norway, France, UK and USA since the 1970s*, CRESC Working Paper 39 (www.cresc.ac.uk/ sites/default/files/wp39.pdf; accessed January 12, 2012).

55. See Randeep Ramesh, "Happiness index planned to influence government policy," *Guardian*, July 25, 2011.

CHAPTER 7. EXITS FROM THE RAT RACE

1. Adam Lent and Mathew Lockwood, *Creative Destruction: Placing Innovation at the Heart of Progressive Economics* (London: Institute for Public Policy Research, 2010).

2. Adair Turner, *Economics after the Crisis: Objectives and Means*, Lecture 3: Economic Freedom and Public Policy: Economics as a Moral Discipline, Lionel Robbins Memorial Lecture (http://www2.lse.ac.uk/publicEvents/pdf/20101013%20Adair%20Turner%20transcript.pdf; accessed January 12, 2012).

3. Alastair MacIntyre, *After Virtue: A Study in Moral Theory* (Notre Dame, Ind.: University of Notre Dame Press, 1981), pp. 1–3.

4. Ibid., p. 263.

5. Quoted in Juliet Schor, *The Overworked American: The Unexpected Decline of Leisure* (New York: Basic Books, 1991), p. 121.

6. Pope Leo XIII, *Rerum Novarum* (1891), par. 3.

7. Ibid., par. 21.

8. See David Marquand, in *New Statesman*, August 22, 2011. Marquand convincingly argues that the achievement of the founders of the European Union was to effect a "historic reconciliation between the Roman Catholic Church and the ideals of the French Revolution," making possible the collaborative capitalism of Germany and Italy.

9. Adam Smith, *The Wealth of Nations* (Lawrence, Kan.: Digireads.com, 2009), p. 407.

10. Peter Clarke, *Liberals and Social Democrats* (Cambridge: Cambridge University Press, 1979).

11. John Maynard, Keynes, "Economic Possibilities for our Grand Children," in *Essays in Persuasion*, The Collected Writings of John Maynard Keyres, vol. 9 (Cambridge: Cambridge University Press, 1978), pp. 354–5.

12. André Gorz, *Reclaiming Work: Beyond the Wage-Based Society* (Cambridge: Cambridge University Press, 1999), p. 94

13. Robert LaJeunesse, *Work Time Regulation as a Sustainable Full Employment Strategy* (London: Routledge, 2009).

14. Daniel Raventós, *Basic Income: The Material Conditions of Freedom* (London: Pluto Press, 2007), p. 8.

15. See John Cunliffe and Guido Erreygers (eds.) *The Origins of Universal Grants: An Anthology of Historical Writings on Basic Capital and Basic Income* (London: Palgrave Macmillan, 2004); Samuel Brittan, *Capitalism with a Human Face* (Cheltenham: Edward Elgar, 1995); James Meade, *Agathotopia: The Economics of Partnership* (Aberdeen: Aberdeen University Press, 1989); André Gorz, *Farewell to the Working Class: An Essay on Post-Industrial Socialism* (Cambridge, Mass.: Southerd Press, 1982).

16. Milton Friedman, *Capitalism and Freedom: Fortieth Anniversary Edition* (Chicago: University of Chicago Press, 2002).

17. Samuel Brittan, review of Gay Standing, *Promoting Income Security as a Right: Europe and North America* (Anthen Press), *Citizens Income Newsletter*, no. 2 (2005).

18. Chandra Pasma, "Working through the Work Disincentive," *Basic Income Studies*, vol. 5, pt. 2 (2010), pp. 1–20. For a discussion of pros and cons of capital endowment and basic income, see Stuart White, "Basic Income Versus Basic Capital: Can We Resolve the Disagreement," *Policy and Politics*, vol. 39, pt. 1 (2011), pp. 67–81. On basic income more generally, see Stuart White, "Reconsidering the Exploitation Objection to Basic Income," *Basic Income Studies*, vol. 1, pt. 2 (2006), pp. 1–17.

19. Meade *Liberty, Equality and Efficiency*; Karl Widerquist *et al.* (eds.), *The Ethics and Economics of the Basic Income Guarantee* (Aldershot: Ashgate, 2005).

20. Yannick Vanderborght and Philippe van Parijs, *L'Allocation universelle* (Paris: La Découverte, 2005).

21. Bruce A. Ackerman and Anne Alstott, *The Stakeholder Society* (New Haven: Yale University Press, 1999).

22. This point was forcefully made by Axel Leijonhufvud at the Luxemburg seminar (see our Preface).

23. Quoted in André Gorz, *Ecologica* (Chicago: University of Chicago Press, 2010), p. 170.

24. UNICEF, *Child Well-Being in the UK, Spain and Sweden: The Role of Inequality and Materialism* (York: UNICEF UK, 2011).

25. Richard A. Musgrave, "A Multiple Theory of Budget Determination," *Finanzarchiv* vol. 17, pt. 3 (1956), p. 341.

26. See Alan Hunt, *Governance of the Consuming Passions: A History of Sumptuary Law* (New York: St Martins, 1996).

27. Bernard Mandeville, *The Fable of the Bees: or Private Vices, Publick Benefits*, ed. Phillip Harth (Harmondsworth: Penguin, 1989), p. 96.

28. See Christopher Berry, *The Idea of Luxury*, (Cambridge: Cambridge University Press, 1994), p. 115.

29. Nicholas Kaldor, *An Expenditure Tax* (London: Allen and Unwin, 1955), p. 176. See also Institute of Fiscal Studies, *The Structure and Reform of Direct Taxation: Report of a Committee Chained by Professor J. E. Meade* (London: Institute of Fiscal Studies, 1978).

30. Ibid., p. 53.

31. Ibid., pp. 26–7.
32. Steven Pressman, "The Feasibility of an Expenditure Tax," *International Journal of Social Economics*, vol. 22, pt. 8 (1995), p. 6.
33. Kaldor, *An Expenditure Tax*; John Kay, *The Meade Report after Two Years* (London: Institute of Fiscal Studies, 1980). For a critique see Pressman, "The Feasibility of an Expenditure Tax."
34. "Chargeable" expenditure was defined by Kaldor, *An Expenditure Tax*, pp. 191–3, as the money a person has available for spending in a year (his wage, salary, dividend income, cash in bank) minus money spent on buying capital assets, his bank balance at the end of the year, and certain allowances and exemptions.
35. For details of his scheme, see Robert H. Frank, *Luxury Fever: Money and Happiness in an Era of Excess* (Princeton: Princeton University Press, 2000), pp. 211–16.
36. Ibid., p. 3.
37. Ibid., pp. 90-91.
38. See Ibid., pp. 211–16.
39. John Maynard Keynes, *The General Theory of Employment, Interest and Money*, The Collected Writings of John Maynard Keynes, vol. 7 (Cambridge: Cambridge University Press, 1973), p. 374
40. "How to Tame Global Finance," *Prospect*, August 27, 2009.
41. For this definition of a good, see Gary Becker and Kevin Murphy, "A Simple Theory of Advertising as Good or Bad," *Quarterly Journal of Economics*, vol. 108, pt. 4 (1993), p. 941. Conversely a "bad" is something the consumer pays to get rid of, or must be compensated to accept. In the strong version of the rational consumer model there are no public or merit goods.
42. Ibid., p. 962.
43. G.W.F. Hegel, *Elements of the Philosophy of Right* (Cambridge: Cambridge University Press, 1991), p. 229.
44. Quoted in Gorz, *Ecologica*, p. 104.
45. Keynes, *Essays in Persuasion*, p. 331.
46. An alternative hypothesis for the observed wage stagnation is the growing premium on skills in rich societies. The empirical data on which effect dominates is inconclusive—see Paul Krugman, "Trade and Wages, Reconsidered," unpubl. paper for the 2008 Brookings Institute Panel on Economic Activity.
47. Interview with Steve Lohr, "An Elder Challenging Outsourcing Orthodoxy," *New York Times*, September 9, 2004.

48. Erik S. Reinert, *How Rich Countries Got Rich ... and Why Poor Countries Stay Poor* (London: Constable, 2008), pp. xxv–xxvi.
49. Ha-Joon Chang, *23 Things They Don't Tell You About Capitalism* (London: Penguin, 2010), p. 63.
50. Gorz, *Ecologica*, pp. 15 f.
51. St. Paul's Institute, *Value and Values: Perceptions of Ethics in the City Today* (London: St. Paul's Institute, 2011).
52. Robert Skidelsky, *John Maynard Keynes: Economist, Philosopher, Statesman* (London: Pan, 2004), p. 515.

Index